The Jack Cade Rebellion of 1450

The Jack Cade Rebellion of 1450

A Sourcebook

Edited by Alexander L. Kaufman

LEXINGTON BOOKS
Lanham • Boulder • New York • London

Published by Lexington Books
An imprint of The Rowman & Littlefield Publishing Group, Inc.
4501 Forbes Boulevard, Suite 200, Lanham, Maryland 20706
www.rowman.com

6 Tinworth Street, London SE11 5AL, United Kingdom

Copyright © 2020 The Rowman & Littlefield Publishing Group, Inc.

All rights reserved. No part of this book may be reproduced in any form or by any electronic or mechanical means, including information storage and retrieval systems, without written permission from the publisher, except by a reviewer who may quote passages in a review.

British Library Cataloguing in Publication Information Available

Library of Congress Cataloging-in-Publication Data

Names: Kaufman, Alexander L., editor.
Title: The Jack Cade Rebellion of 1450: a sourcebook / edited by Alexander L. Kaufman.
Description: Lanham: Lexington Books, [2019] | Includes bibliographical references and index. | Summary: "This book collects, for the first time, primary documents associated with the Jack Cade Rebellion that have been translated into Present-Day English. It includes the rebels' petitions, entries from medieval and early modern chronicles, letters and formal correspondences, official government documents, and political poems of the fifteenth century."—Provided by publisher.
Identifiers: LCCN 2019039989 (print) | LCCN 2019039990 (ebook) |
ISBN 9781498550291 (cloth) | ISBN 9781498550314 (pbk) | ISBN 9781498550307 (epub)
Subjects: LCSH: Cade's Rebellion, 1450. | Cade's Rebellion, 1450—Historiography. | Cade's Rebellion, 1450—Sources. | Social conflict—England—History. | Great Britain—History—Henry VI, 1422-1461.
Classification: LCC DA257 J33 2019(print) | LCC DA257(ebook) | DDC 942.04/3—dc23
LC record available at https://lccn.loc.gov/2019039989
LC ebook record available at https://lccn.loc.gov/2019039990

Contents

List of Abbreviations		ix
Acknowledgments		xi
Introduction		1

PART I: MEDIEVAL AND EARLY MODERN CHRONICLES — 9

1	From *Robert Bale's Chronicle*	11
2	From *John Benet's Chronicle*: Translated from Latin into English by Molly A. Martin	17
3	From *An English Chronicle, 1377–1461*	27
4	From *A Short English Chronicle*	33
5	From *A Chronicle of London* in Oxford, Bodleian Library MS Gough London 10	37
6	From *Gregory's Chronicle*	41
7	From *Ingulph's Chronicle of the Abbey of Croyland*	47
8	From *John Stone's Chronicle*	49
9	From the Middle English Prose *Brut*	53
10	From *A Chronicle of London* in London, British Library MS Cotton Vitellius A XVI	59
11	From *The Great Chronicle of London*	65

12	From Robert Fabyan's *The New Chronicles of England and France*	71
13	From John Mair's *Historia Maioris Britanniae tam Angliae quam Scotiae (History of Greater Britain)*	77
14	From *Hall's Chronicle*	81
15	From Polydore Vergil's *Anglica Historia*	89
16	From George North's *A Brief Discourse of Rebellion and Rebels*	93
17	From *Holinshed's Chronicle*	99
18	From William Martyn's *The Historie, and Lives, of the Kings of England*	107

PART II: DOCUMENTS OF THE GOVERNMENT AND REBELS, PERSONAL CORRESPONDENCES — 111

19	The Rebels' Bills of Complaint of 1450	113
20	The Proclamation by King Henry VI Authorizing the Taking of John Cade: With Latin Translations by Evan Golightly	123
21	Letters from Jack Cade to Sir Thomas Cook	127
22	The Pardon Roll of July 1450	131
23	From *The Antient Kalendars and Inventories of the Treasury of His Majesty's Exchequer*	181
24	From the Parliament Rolls of England	185
25	From the Paston Letters	193

PART III: POLITICAL POEMS OF THE FIFTEENTH CENTURY — 201

26	"On the Arrest of the Duke of Suffolk"	203
27	"A Warning to King Henry"	207
28	"Verses Against the Duke of Suffolk"	211
29	"For Jake Napes Sowle, Placebo and Dirige": Latin Translations by Molly A. Martin	213

30	"On the Corruption of the Times I"	223
31	"On the Corruptions of the Times II"	227
32	*Robin Hood and the Monk*	233

Bibliography	245
Index	253
About the Editor	257

List of Abbreviations

Barron: Barron, Caroline M. "The Government of London and Its Relations with the Crown, 1400–1450." Ph.D. Thesis, University of London, 1970.
d.: pence
Davis: Davis, Norman, ed. *Paston Letters and Papers of the Fifteenth Century*, Part II. EETS, ss 21. Oxford: Oxford University Press, 2004.
EETS: Early English Text Society
EMC: Dunphy, R. Graeme, gen. ed. *The Encyclopedia of the Medieval Chronicle*. 2 vols. Leiden and Boston: Brill, 2010.
Gransden: Gransden, Antonia. *Historical Writing in England II: c. 1307 to the Early Sixteenth Century*. Ithaca, NY: Cornell University Press, 1982.
Griffiths: Griffiths, R. A. *The Reign of King Henry VI*. Phoenix Mill: Sutton, 1998.
Harvey: Harvey, I. M. W. *Jack Cade's Rebellion of 1450*. Oxford: Clarendon Press, 1991.
Kaufman: Kaufman, Alexander L. *The Historical Literature of the Jack Cade Rebellion*. Farnham: Ashgate, 2009.
Kekewich: Kekewich, Margaret Lucille, et al., ed. *The Politics of Fifteenth-Century England: John Vale's Book*. Phoenix Mill: Alan Sutton for Richard III and Yorkist Historical Trust, 1995.
Kennedy: Kennedy, Edward Donald. "Chronicles and Other Historical Writing." *A Manual of the Writings in Middle English, 1050–1500*, edited by Albert E. Hartung.

	Vol. 8. Hamden, CT: Archon Books for the Connecticut Academy of Arts and Sciences, 1989.
Kingsford:	Kingsford, Charles Lethbridge. *English Historical Literature in the Fifteenth Century*. Oxford: Clarendon Press, 1913.
Matheson:	Matheson, Lister M. *The Prose Brut: The Development of a Middle English Chronicle*. Medieval and Renaissance Texts and Studies 180. Tempe, AZ: Medieval and Renaissance Texts and Studies, 1998.
McLaren:	McLaren, Mary-Rose. *The London Chronicles of the Fifteenth Century: A Revolution in English Writing*. Cambridge: D. S. Brewer, 2002.
MED:	Middle English Dictionary. Ed. Robert E. Lewis, et al. Ann Arbor: University of Michigan Press, 1952–2001. Online edition in Middle English Compendium. Ed. Frances McSparran, et al. Ann Arbor: University of Michigan Library, 2000–2018. http://quod.lib.umich.edu/m/middle-english-dictionary/. Accessed 21 June 2019.
ODNB:	Oxford Dictionary of National Biography. Oxford University Press, 2019. https://www.oxforddnb.com/. Accessed 21 June 2019.
Robbins:	Robbins, Rossell Hope, ed. *Historical Poems of the XIVth and XVth Centuries*. New York: Columbia University Press, 1959.
s.:	shillings
STC:	Pollard, A. W., and G. R. Redgrave. *A Short-Title Catalogue of Books Printed in England, Scotland, and Ireland and of English Books Printed Abroad, 1475–1640*. 2nd ed., rev. and enlarged by W. A. Jackson, F. S. Ferguson, and K. F. Pantzer. London: Bibliographical Society, 1976–1991.
Wright:	Wright, Thomas, ed. *Political Poems and Songs Relating to English History, Composed During the Period from the Accession of Edward III to that of Richard III*. Vol. 2. Rolls Series 14. London: Longman, et al., 1861.

Acknowledgments

A project such as this is very much a collaborative one, and there are many people to whom I owe much gratitude. Firstly, Molly A. Martin has been an invaluable friend and colleague over the years, and she contributed greatly to this book. Molly provided Latin transitions for a number of entries in this volume: the entirety of *John Benet's Chronicle* in chapter 2, the Latin phrases that are present in the poem "For Jake Napes Sowle, Placebo and Dirige," and the Latin phrase that is found in the poem "On the Arrest of the Duke of Suffolk." Mitchell Kissick helped to transcribe a number of the chronicle entries, and Evan Golightly translated two Latin paragraphs that are found in the prose piece "Proclamation by King Henry VI Authorizing the Taking of John Cade," and I am very grateful for their help. Jan K. Bulman, Lesley Coote, Michael Evans, Lister M. Matheson, and Thomas H. Ohlgren over the years aided me with questions related to translation. Their generous advice is much appreciated. At Ball State University's Honors College, I am fortunate to be surrounded by engaging students and colleagues, and I would especially like to thank Dean John Emert for his continued support of scholarship and research.

Lexington Books has been a pleasure to work with. Brian Hill was an early supporter of this volume, and our conversations were instrumental in helping to shape the book. Eric Kuntzman and Ellen McDaniel have both been extremely helpful in shepherding the manuscript along through the production process.

I would like to thank a number of authors and publishers for allowing me to reproduce their work for inclusion in this book.

Chapter 8 is an excerpt from *John Stone's Chronicle: Christ Church Priory, Canterbury, 1417–1472*. Selected, Translated, and Introduced by Meriel Connor. TEAMS Documents of Practice Series. Kalamazoo, MI: Medieval

Institute Publications, 2010. Pp. 87–89. Used with permission. I would especially like to thank the author and Theresa M. Whitaker at MIP for allowing me to reproduce this section.

Chapter 13 is from Major, John. *A History of Greater Britain As Well England and Scotland.* Translated and edited by Archibald Constable. Scottish History Society. Vol. 10. Edinburgh: Edinburgh University Press, 1892. Pp. 374–77. Reprinted by permission of The Scottish Historical Society. Many thanks to Annie Tindley for allowing me to use this portion of Constable's translation of Mair's work.

And chapter 16 is an excerpt from Dennis McCarthy and June Schlueter. *"A Brief Discourse of Rebellion and Rebels" By George North: A Newly Uncovered Manuscript Source for Shakespeare's Plays.* Cambridge: D. S. Brewer in association with the British Library, 2018. Pp.134, 136–39, and 142–43. I would like to thank the authors, D. S. Brewer, the British Library, and Rachel Reeder for granting permission to reproduce the pages from their volume.

The author apologizes for any errors or omissions in the above list for any inadvertent infringement upon copyrighted materials, and the publishers welcome notification of corrections that ought to be incorporated in future editions or reprints of this volume.

Lastly, as always, the encouragement and love of my wife Mandy and our two rebels, Abraham and Lucinda, is measureless in this and any project.

Introduction

THE EVENTS OF THE JACK CADE REBELLION

The Jack Cade Rebellion of 1450 was a popular uprising of the commons of the counties of Kent, Norfolk, and Essex, England. The rebels, whose numbers are said to have reached at least 10,000, were led by a charismatic man who is now referred to as Jack Cade. The insurgents were frustrated and angry with King Henry VI's ineffectiveness as a leader, the over-taxation of the working classes, the crown's failed attempts to secure French territories and their subsequent losses on the continent, and corrupt and abusive officials. Henry, fearing for his life, escaped from London. The riot culminated in a night battle on London Bridge. Many were killed, and the leaders of the insurrection were executed. It remains one of the most significant popular rebellions of the Middle Ages. For a brief period, England was on the verge of a hostile take-over of the monarchy; it was a political crisis, one of many in England's fifteenth century.

The event that sets in motion the uprising is the death in March 1450 of William de la Pole, the Duke of Suffolk. John Watts comments that the death of Suffolk is really the "fall of the king himself."[1] Suffolk was a long serving soldier and commander during the Hundred Years' War, fighting in all of Henry V's campaigns (save the Battle of Agincourt). Suffolk became an important member of Henry VI's court, a person more interested in international diplomacy than warfare. However, the continued losses of English territory in France by the closing of 1449 created problems for Suffolk, and as David Grummitt comments he "had emerged as the scapegoat for the regime's various failings of the previous decade. The principal charges against him related to the impending defeat in France and his part in the diplomatic and military bungling that had given Charles VII his *casus belli*."[2] It was not just Suffolk who was held responsible for these political mishaps: Adam Moleyns, the Bishop of Chichester and ambassador, was forced to resign in November 1449, and he was murdered on 9 January 1450 in Portsmouth by a group of decommissioned sailors. On 29 January 1450, Suffolk was placed in the Tower of London on suspicion of treason, and on 7 February the House of Commons introduces a bill of impeachment. On 9 March 1450 the House of Commons introduced another bill against him, one which repeats accusations of treason and conspiring with France but which now also included additional offences related to embezzling funds from the treasury as well as "appointing his own servants and sheriffs in various counties throughout the realm" which, the Commons argued, "contributed to the general lawlessness of the realm."[3] To save his ally from imprisonment and possible execution the king decided to exile Suffolk to France for five years, beginning 1 May 1450. This sentence does not sit well with the general populace.

Suffolk, with three or four ships, leaves on 30 March 1450 for the Duke of Burgundy's the Low Countries. One of Suffolk's ships is sent ahead to Calais to verify his welcome, but the crew betrays the Duke's whereabouts and sends word to another vessel, the *Nicholas of the Tower*. The *Nicholas* and their crew stop Suffolk's ship, bring him onboard the *Nicholas*, and begin an impromptu trial. A person beheads Suffolk on a small boat, and his body is found on Dover Beach, his head is mounted on a stake. Even before Suffolk's death, small uprisings are taking place in Kent and Surrey, but the Duke's death galvanizes the commons in the Southeast of England. In the first version of the rebels' bills of complaint, included in this volume, the first item that the insurgents note is how the royal officials, presumably the sheriff of Kent, William Crowmer, authorized turning all of Kent into a wild forest as a consequence for the murder of Suffolk.

By the first week in June, rebels are organizing themselves, and at Calehill, a leader is chosen or one gravitates toward that role. The leader, in the records, goes by a number of names: John Cade, John Mortimer, John Amendal (as one who will mend all problems), a physician named John Aylmere, and Jack Cade. Some of the records also assign him the military rank of "captain," and the "captain of Kent" though there is no evidence that Cade served in any military force. Indeed, very little is known of Cade the person, and what we do know from the records is a mixture of truth, political propaganda, and legend. The surname of Mortimer suggested to some that he was Irish as well as a cousin to Richard Duke of York (1411–1460), who was one of Henry VI's political adversaries and who was instrumental in steering the nation toward civil war and the Wars of the Roses with the First Battle of Saint Albans on 22 May 1455. The link between Cade and the Duke of York is suspect, with no evidence to prove that Cade was a true political operative who was working with York to try and overthrow the king.[4]

King Henry soon becomes aware of the gathering of oppositional forces gathering around Blackheath on 11 June. On 13 June, Henry and his counselors stay at Saint John's hospital in Clerkenwell. On 15 June, messengers, including Archbishop Stafford; Archbishop Kemp; the Duke of Buckingham; William Waynflete, the Bishop of Winchester; and Viscount Beaumont, the Constable of England are sent to listen to the rebels' demands and report back to the king, but Henry decides not to accept the rebels' demands and the rebels depart from Blackheath. A small force of the king's men venture into Kent and are ambushed. Sir Humphrey Stafford and his brother William, along with several of their men, are killed near Sevenoaks.

Beginning on 18 June, the king amasses a force of around 2,000 men, including Lords Dudley and Rivers, Sir Thomas Stanley, and Thomas Daniel, to go after the retreating rebels, but the king decides not to pursue them. It is an important moment in this rebellion, where Grummitt observes that the king's "nerve failed him," and instead of advancing on the enemy Henry decides to arrest James Fiennes, Lord Saye and Sele, the Constable and Treasurer of England, and place him in the Tower of London for his own protection. Some of the king's own soldiers are growing uneasy, and there are reports of desertion among Henry's men, some threatening to join Cade unless the king arrests several of his unpopular retainers. The exact size of Cade's host is not known, though in studying the records Griffiths believes that, conservatively, at this point it could be around 20,000 men, smaller now than at the start of June, though the number will grow by an estimated 6,000 additional persons from Essex by the start of July as the group moves toward Mile End.[5] Around 20 June, Robert Poynings, an esquire from Sussex, is commanded to gather the recently demobilized English troops who had fought in France, some of whom were now robbing and pillaging at Edenbridge. Instead of obeying his charge, Poynings deserts the king and joins Cade, becoming a high-ranking officer and the leader's sword-bearer.

On 25 June, the king made another important move: he left London to go to Kenilworth Castle, leaving the city to defend itself, which they successfully do, though at a significant cost. Barron notes how the city officials encouraged Philip Malpas, the unpopular alderman of the city, to vacate, as a gesture of good will, which he did.[6] On 29 June, the rebels returned to Blackheath, and it is perhaps on this date that the city sent Thomas Cook to meet with them. At Blackheath, Cade executed Parys, a captain of his, reportedly for excessive rioting, and encounters John Payn, a servant of Sir John Fastolf. Payn was sent by his employer to visit the rebel camp to see if the host is a threat to his property. Cade's men, seeing Payn as a possible spy, declared him a traitor and almost execute him. On 1 July, the city officials, led by the mayor, Thomas Chalton, sent word to Henry that they have successfully denied Cade and his host entry into the city. But on Friday, 3 July, Cade and his army, now increased in size by a force from Essex, entered London. On 4 July, commissions under Cade's authority were held at the Guildhall, where some of the unpopular ministers and retainers of the king are tried. Cade proclaimed that anyone who robs within the city will be executed, though looting and pillaging had already began and continued, including the house of Philip Malpas.

On Saturday, 4 July, a number of officials are indicted at the Guildhall, Saye is removed from the Tower, and William Crowmer, the sheriff of Kent and Saye's son-in-law, is taken out of prison and both are beheaded, their heads placed on poles and are made to kiss one another.[7] More looting occurred in London, and on the evening of Sunday, 5 July, Londoners prevented the rebel host from entering the city after a fierce battle on London Bridge, which lasted from around 10 p.m. until 8 or 9 a.m. the following morning. All told, around 40 Londoners and 200 Kenishmen died in this battle, including the alderman and goldsmith John Sutton and the war hero Matthew Gough.[8]

Soon after, pardons are issued, the first to Cade in the name of "Mortimer" by Queen Margaret and then general pardons were issued to the rebels on 6 and 7 July. While many persons took advantage of the pardon, Cade did not. He left Southwark on 9 July with a small band and attacked Queensborough Castle, but the attack failed thanks to the efforts of Sir Roger Chamberlain. On 10 July, Cade's booty, which he had put on a boat to Rochester, was taken by authorities, and on the same day he was proclaimed a traitor: 1,000 marks were issued as a reward for his head, 500 marks as reward for a head of one of Cade's chief officers, and 5 marks as reward for any of his followers.

Cade did not make it far. On 12 July, Alexander Iden, the new sheriff of Kent after Crowmer's death, seized Cade in Heathfield, Sussex, injuring the leader.[9] While being transported to London, Cade died of his injuries. The wife of the innkeeper of the White Hart positively identifies Cade's body. He is beheaded at Newgate, his head is placed on top of London Bridge, and his body is dragged through London to Newgate, where it is quartered and sent to Norwich, Blackheath, Salisbury, and Gloucester. Alexander Iden collected his reward, which was funded from the sale of the goods retrieved from Cade. Londoners who had goods stolen were able to buy back their property from the treasury at a reduced cost.

It could have ended much worse for the citizens of London had they not managed to beat back Cade and his force. They were essentially abandoned by the king, whose "failure of leadership," Grummitt comments, "provided the circumstances for others to emerge as true defenders of the Lancastrian legacy."[10] This was not the end of uprisings in England, for more would continue throughout the 1450s in Kent and Sussex, such as Hasilden's Rising in 1451, Wilkyns' Rising in 1452, and Percy's Rising in 1456.[11] Richard, the Duke of York, however, remained Henry's chief political rival and leader of the opposition for the next few years.

Introduction 5

AIM, AUDIENCE, AND SCOPE OF THIS VOLUME

There is yet to be a volume that focuses solely on primary documents that elate to the Jack Cade Rebellion. The uprising is often included as one of the major incidents during the Wars of the Roses, it forms a major plot strand within William Shakespeare's *Henry VI, Part 2*, and it was an inspiration for many of the Americans during the Revolutionary War and even well after the War of 1812.[12] It is from Shakespeare's play that most readers (or viewers) first encountered the rebel and his uprising, and audiences often are divided on Cade's motives and Shakespeare's portrayal of the leader and his aims. Is the Bard's Cade and his army a pejorative portrayal of the commons, and thus a judgment on their base intellect and morals? Or is Shakespeare tapping into legitimate concerns on the working class, who feel as if they have value in England's economy and society, but who are ignored and ill treated?[13] This volume aims to illuminate questions such as those and to bring the writings of the Middle Ages and Early Modern period closer to readers of today, especially to those interested in urban history, popular rebellions, legal studies, criminal justice, and artistic expressions of protest.

Middle English, Latin, and Early Modern English are languages that are being taught less in high schools and undergraduate programs, if they are even taught (or encountered) at all. The majority of the original documents that form this volume are translated into Present Day English (PDE) so that students unfamiliar with the languages will be able to comprehend and appreciate the writings of the past. As such, this sourcebook is designed as a first step into the world of primary documents of the Cade rebellion for those readers unaccustomed to working with a language other than PDE. My hope is that readers who want to explore further the subject of the rebellion will search out the sources in their original language, explore the subtleties and nuances of the writers' rhetoric, and engage in original research.

This volume is organized into three sections. Part I collects entries from medieval and Early Modern chroniclers. Many of these chronicles are London chronicles of the fifteenth century, a family of historical accounts written in London in Latin, Middle English, and Anglo-Norman. The London chronicles that are complete always begin in the year 1189, when Richard I ascends the throne and the year in which, traditionally, London's civic government is first organized. The chronicle entries are organized chronologically, and I have included a number of post-medieval excerpts as these afterlives of the Cade Rebellion that were instrumental in shaping the popular opinion and historical record of the event and its players. Part II comprises official documents of the crown and of the rebels as well as personal correspondences.

The records of England's, such as the pardons issued to the rebels, Henry VI's proclamation for the taking of Cade, and the versions of the rebels' bills of complaint, presents some of the most direct evidence of the policies and beliefs of those involved. This section also includes some of the letters from individuals in the fifteenth century that are relevant to the rebellion. Lastly, Part III presents a number of popular poems of the fifteenth century that focus on events surrounding the Cade Rebellion. These verses satirize and condemn historical personages, call for a reevaluation of values, and lament the current state of political and social affairs. For each entry, I provide a brief introduction to its historical or literary context and include some bibliographic information for readers who would like to examine further the subject. The primary documents that I have included in this book are those that I think first time readers would want access to. As such, this book is not designed to be a fully comprehensive collection of all primary documents that relate to Cade's uprising; both R. A. Griffith in his monumental study *The Reign of Henry VI* and I. M. W. Harvey in her standard scholarly source on the uprising *Jack Cade's Rebellion of 1450* cite additional primary documents that have not been published and which could serve as the basis for future scholarship.

A NOTE ON THE TRANSLATIONS

Translation is interpretation and as such personal and not always precise. The prose texts have been translated from their Middle English and Latin into PDE with the aim to make the renderings both faithful and also readable. At times, the meaning of original language is vague, and I have supplied words and phrases and enclosed them in brackets to make the sentence more comprehendible. At times, I have had to alter the syntax of the original text for the translation. Certain Middle English words, such as those that relate to arms and armaments, are obsolete but have no PDE equivalent; in these and other instances, I have maintained the original word and included a definition from the *Middle English Dictionary*. To maintain the meter and rhyme of the poetry, I have chosen to transcribe all of the selections in Part III in Middle English and include marginal glosses of difficult words and phrases in PDE. The lone exception for this choice was the translation of *Robin Hood and the Monk*, a late fifteenth-century narrative poem whose meter, rhyme, and content were more easily maintained in translation without losing, I hope, any of the poem's spirit. I have included additional editorial comments related to the translation and/or transcription of documents in the introductory comments to each selection.

NOTES

1. John Watts, *Henry VI and the Politics of Kingship* (Cambridge: Cambridge University Press, 1996), 254.
2. David Grummitt, *Henry VI* (London: Routledge: 2015), 151.
3. Ibid., 153.
4. For a good overview of Cade the person, see Griffiths, 617–19. For a study of the characterization of Cade in historical literature, see Kaufman, 149–73.
5. Ibid., 619. See also Montgomery Bonha, "Armed Force and Civic Legitimacy in Jack Cade's Revolt, 1450," *English Historical Review 118* (2003): 563–82.
6. Barron, 494–99.
7. Kellie Robertson argues that this kiss, recorded in several chronicles, "should be seen as a symptom of social unease about theatrical spectacles of incorporation and the reanimation of dead bodies in public rituals," in "The Rebel Kiss: Jack Cade, Shakespeare, and the Chroniclers," in *Renaissance Retrospections: Tudor Views of the Middle Ages*, edited by Sarah A. Kelen, 127–40. Studies in Medieval Culture LII (Kalamazoo, MI: Medieval Institute Publications, 2013),138.
8. Griffiths, 619.
9. There is still some debate as to where Cade was apprehended by Iden, see, for example, the entries for John Stone and George North in this volume.
10. Grummitt, *Henry VI*,161.
11. See Harvey, 131–75.
12. Robert T. Conrad's melodrama *Jack Cade* was first performed in Philadelphia in 1835 and subsequently published in the author's collection *Alymere, or The Bondman of Kent; and Other Stories* (Philadelphia: E. H. Butler, 1852). Edwin Forrest played Cade and garnered positive reviews. See Karl Kippola, "'The Battle-Shout of Free Men.' Edwin Forrest's Passive Patriotism and Robert T. Conrad's *Jack Cade*," *Journal of American Drama and Theater* 13, no. 3 (2001): 37–86.
13. See, for example, Annabel Patterson, *Shakespeare and the Popular Voice* (Durham, NC: Duke University Press, 1989).

Part I

MEDIEVAL AND EARLY MODERN CHRONICLES

Chapter 1

From *Robert Bale's Chronicle*

OVERVIEW

The London chronicle known as *Robert Bale's Chronicle* spans the years 1189–1461. From 1189 to 1440, the entries are very brief and have been taken from other sources, but after 1440, the entries become more detailed and reveal the writings of a person witnessing events, such as Cade's Rebellion, seemingly first hand. The chronicle itself is split between two manuscripts: Dublin, Trinity College MS 509 and 604; 509 is a commonplace book and contains all but the final year of the chronicle, which is found in 604. The final page of the chronicle in MS 604 presents what is perhaps the earliest account of the Battle of Saint Albans, which took place in late February 1461. The chronicle has been attributed to the scrivener Robert Bale (d. 1473) by John Bale, Bishop of Ossory (21 November 1495–November 1563), who owned the manuscript and took it with him to Ireland when he became bishop. Both Sutton and McLaren argue convincingly, though not definitively, that Robert Bale not only owned the manuscript but also wrote the chronicle that now bears his name. Between the years 1459 and 1461, Bale served time in prison, once for an unpaid debt to a fellow scrivener.

MANUSCRIPT

Dublin, Trinity College MSS 509 and 604

SOURCE FOR TRANSLATION

Flenley, Ralph, ed. *Six Town Chronicles of England*. Oxford: Clarendon Press, 1911. Pp. 129–34.

FURTHER READING

Kennedy, 2651.
Kleineke, Hannes. "*Robert Bale's Chronicle* and the Second Battle of Saint Albans." *Historical Research* 87, no. 238 (2014): 744–50.
McLaren, 33–34; 106–8.
Radulescu, Raluca. "London Chronicles." In *EMC* 2: 1042–43.
Sutton, Anne F. "Robert Bale, Scrivener and Chronicler of London." In *Regional Manuscripts, 1200–1700*, edited by A. S. G. Edwards, 180–206. English Manuscript Studies, 1100–1400 14. London: British Library, 2008.

TRANSLATION

Moreover, on the 12th day of June [1450], a large [amount] of people, one hundred men of Kent, well arrayed, assembled at Blackheath beside London.

Moreover, the same day came the Duke of Buckingham and Lord Rivers into the city with a large army of people in liveries with swiftness and arrayed for war.

Moreover, on 15 June, the king, staying at Saint John's beside Smithfield with many people, sent heralds and knights to the said Blackheath and to bid the captain of Kent with his people there gathered to withdraw them. They sent an answer again that they were there for the king's right and the land. They had marvelously staked the entire field about them so that no army of horsemen should come and override them.

Moreover, the same day toward the evening rode the Earl of Northumberland,[1] the Lord Scales, and the Lord Lisle[2] toward the same field by the king's commandment with a great fellowship of spears and bows, and there was numbered by a herald of people in the said captain's fellowship 40,000 and more.

And in the morning, the king, along with Duke of Exeter[3] and the Duke of Buckingham,[4] and many earls, lords, and knights in substance of all this land with a mighty army of people were proposed to have met with the said captain toward the said heath. But by the advice of the king's council, they were sent to entreat with the captain the lords whose names follow, that is to say, the Cardinal Archbishop of York,[5] the Archbishop of Canterbury,[6] the Duke of Buckingham, the Bishop of Winchester,[7] and the Lord Beaumont.[8] The captain demeaned himself to the lords in such a manner and called himself and his people petitioners, answering to them that his coming to the heath was not to do any harm but to have the desires of the commons in that parliament fulfilled. The lords agreed with him that all things should be redressed, and so the lords came again to the king and promise to bring or send to the same captain by a certain hour assigned from the king a conclusion of the same agreement. Nevertheless, because the lords neither came nor sent word from the king to the captain again of the king's will to his intent and desire; therefore, the said captain refused the king's agreement sent to him and ordained and disposed himself to keep the field against the king. And then the king, with a mighty army, went toward the said heath. The said captain, having knowledge thereof, withdrew him and all his people in the night and fled and took with them their stakes and ordinance.

Moreover, on Thursday morning, Sir Thomas Stanley and one Daniel,[9] who had much control over the king, rode in order to pursue the said captain, and led with them many people, well arrayed for defense, and, as the vanguard, were the Earl of Northumberland, the Lord Rivers,[10] the Lord Scales, the Lord Grey,[11] Sir Edmond[12] and William Stafford and many other knights and nobles rode toward the heath with much power to take the said captain. However, the said captain, laying in an ambush, met and fought with these lords and slew the said Sir Edmund Stafford and William Stafford and hurt much of their people.

Moreover, the same day at nine before noon, the king rode armed through Cheap with his said dukes, earls, lords, and knights with a very notable and royal army toward the said heath, and in the afternoon came word of the discomfiture and death of the said Staffords. And all that night and in the morning came many people to strengthen the king at Greenwich, from Lancaster, Cheshire, and other shires.

Moreover, the Friday, which was the eve Translation of Saint Edward,[13] the king commanded all his host to muster upon the said heath, and there was then a mighty army, and that army was assigned by the king's council to have ridden into Kent to pursue the said captain and his people and so to have destroyed Kent and taken them. But the captain and his fellowship disposed of them in such a manner and departed his people in several ambushes to have encountered with the lords and their army. As such, king's host made then a sudden shout and noise upon the said heath, seeing destruction, woe these traitors about the king, which the said captain had intended to do or woe forever will do it. Whereupon, the king granted their desire and commanded the Lord Saye, Chamberlain of England, to be taken, and so he was arrested in the king's presence, and the said Daniel should have been arrested also. But he was inside Kent, as is above said, with a great fellowship, in order to destroy and hurt the people in Kent. But when he heard of this ruling, he left his people and fled. And the said Lord Saye was committed to the Tower.

Moreover, on the Saturday following, the king and the lords, with their great army, came again through the city from Greenwich and went to Westminster.

Moreover, the Tuesday following, the said captain came again to the said heath with his fellowship, which he did against his allegiance, although his desires were good and for the well of the land, as he submitted to have proclaimed, through which he got the hearts of the great part of the commons of the land.

Moreover, on the Thursday, the second day of July, the said captain with his people, which were a very rude people, came suddenly at four in the afternoon into Southwark, and all took up the inns and places.

Moreover, on the morning came a great fellowship out of Essex ordained by the said captain. And they encamped at Mile End outside Aldgate, and so they besieged the city, and then was London Bridge drawn and the gates of the city kept with men of arms. And one Robert Horne, alderman, Philip Malpas, alderman, and John Gest were in the serious thoughts of the captain, and he and his people called them traitors and extortioners and wished that the governors of the city should have put and sent them out of the city to the intent that they might have from them their favor, but they escaped and could not be found, as God intended.

Moreover, the same day in the afternoon, the said captain with his people entered over London Bridge into the city. And the king and his lords were then to Kenilworth. And when Cade entered, he robbed the said Philip Malpas' place and bore with him from there many goods and returned into Southwark again with his people and made his cries in the king's name that none of his people should do any harm but keep the peace.

Moreover, on the Saturday morning the judges came at nine o'clock into the Guildhall, and there were diverse and many inquests charged for the king to question extortionists and other evil doers. And in the meantime, before eleven o'clock, the said captain came riding with his people on foot from Southwark through the city to [Saint] Paul's in a blue gown of velvet, with fur sables and a straw hat upon his head and a sword drawn in his hand and returned again to London Bridge and into Southwark. And at four in the afternoon, he and his people came again into Cheap and drank there at a tavern called the Crown and returned to Mile End where, as the people of Essex encamped, beheaded there one Crowmer and another called William Bailey[14] and came again in haste into Cheap and thereupon two heads [were] carried before him on high polls. And at the Standard in Cheap he took heed, and the Lord Saye was brought there from the Guildhall, where he was indicted of treason by diverse inquests, and at the same Standard the captain ordered the Lord Saye beheaded and robbed him of his array, bound his legs with a rope to a horse, and dragged his body on the pavement through a large part of the city.

Moreover, the same night, and on the following Sunday, the said captain and his people decided to pillage diverse worthy men of the city and their goods, and the same Sunday the captain beheaded in Southwark a gentleman, called Thomas Mayn of Colchester, whom the men of Essex delivered to him. And then the mayor and the council of the city labored that Sunday all during worship hours to make and set a rule and ordinance that the said captain should no more enter into the city. And that same night, which was the eve of Saint Thomas the Martyr, all the commons of the city took to arms. And the same night and in the morning until four o'clock, the people of the city and the captain and his army fought and met together on London Bridge and in Southwark, and many people were slain and hurt on either side. And then the said captain fled and his men departed, and so his power ceased, and soon after he was slain in his defense and then beheaded and his head set on London Bridge and his body brought to the king's bench and then there dragged dead through the city on the pavement into Tyburn and quartered, and his quarters sent to diverse places of the land, and there were diverse *oyers and terminers*[15] held in diverse places, and especially in Kent, and many people [were] hanged and beheaded for the same rising and stirring done by the captain. And in the said battle and skirmish were slain John Sutton, alderman, and Matthew Gough, who was a noble warrior.

Moreover, on 21 July, diverse and many of the soldiers that came and were driven out of Normandy, took for themselves the church of the Grey Friars within Newgate, where the said Lord Saye was worthily buried, and his head laid by him, and his arms set on furs drawn about and pulled down the same arms and then reversed.

NOTES

1. Henry Percy (3 February 1393–22 May 1455), 2nd Earl of Northumberland.
2. John Talbot (ca. 1423–17 July 1453), First Baron of Lisle. He was killed along with his father John Talbot, First Earl of Shrewsbury, at the Battle of Castillon, the final pitched battle of the Hundred Years' War. He is featured in the poem "On the Arrest of the Duke of Suffolk," which appears in this volume.
3. Henry Holand (27 June 1430–September 1475), 3rd Duke of Exeter.
4. Humphrey Stafford (1402–10 July 1460), 1st Duke of Buckingham and 6th Earl of Stafford.
5. John Kemp (ca. 1380–22 March 1454), Archbishop of York.
6. John Stafford (d. 25 May 1452), Archbishop of Canterbury.

7. William Waynflete, (ca. 1398–11 August 1486). He served as Bishop of Winchester from 1447 to 1486 and Lord Chancellor of England from 1456 to 1460. He founded Magdalen College in 1458 and Magdalen College School ca. 1480.

8. John Beaumont (ca. 1409–1460), 1st Viscount Beaumont. He is featured in the poem "On the Arrest of the Duke of Suffolk," which appears in this volume.

9. Thomas Daniel.

10. Richard Woodville (1405–12 August 1469), 1st Lord Rivers.

11. Edmund Grey of Ruthin, Lord.

12. Bale is mistaken here and below regarding an "Edmund" Stafford. Sir Humphrey Stafford was slain along with his brother William.

13. Edward the Martyr (ca. 962–18 March 978), king of England from 975 until his death by murder. In medieval England, his translation took place on 20 June.

14. *Gregory's Chronicle* records the name as John Bailey. Most chronicles refer to him simply as "Bailey."

15. *MED* "oyer" n. 1.*Law*. (a) A criminal hearing under a commission of oyer and terminer. (b) ~ and terminer (determiner), a judicial procedure, regulated by commissioners appointed by the king, for determining guilt and assessing punishment or damages for various crimes under special circumstances.

Chapter 2

From *John Benet's Chronicle*

Translated from Latin into English by Molly A. Martin

OVERVIEW

This Latin chronicle is attributed to John Benet (d. 1474), vicar of Harlington in Bedforshire (1443–1471) and later rector of Broughton in Bedfordshire (1471–1474) is found within a commonplace book ascribed to him. As Harriss and Harriss demonstrate in their partial edition of the chronicle (for the years 1440–1462), Benet should not be considered the author of this work (or any other text in the manuscript) but rather the person who compiled it from a now lost source. It is difficult to assign a date of composition to the chronicle; however, Harriss and Harriss suggest 1462–1468, as the section of the manuscript that comes before the chronicle contains a written date of 1468, and nothing in the manuscript after the chronicle contains a date (157). This is a valuable, late medieval chronicle, one that provides unique information not found in other medieval works of historical writing on such figures and events as Edward IV; Margaret of Anjou; John, Duke of Suffolk; the 1452–1453 dispute of the possession of Ampthill; the riots in Oxford in 1441, and the Jack Cade Rebellion. The unknown chronicler is sympathetic toward the commoners, who are suffering under the power of the government, and Yorkist in his political leanings.

MANUSCRIPT

Dublin, Trinity College MS 516

SOURCE FOR TRANSLATION

Harriss, G. L., and M. A. Harris, ed. *John Benet's Chronicle for the Years 1400–1462*. In *Camden Miscellany*, Vol. XXIX, 151–233. Camden Fourth Series, Vol. 9. London: Royal Historical Society, 1972.

FURTHER READING

Gransden, 254–57.
Hanham, Alison, trans. *John Benet's Chronicle, 1399–1462: An English Translation with New Introduction*. New York: Palgrave Macmillan, 2016.
Harris, G. L. "Benet, John." In *ODNB*.
Kennedy, Edward Donald. "Benet, John." In *EMC* 1: 167.
Matheson, 21.

TRANSLATION

And in the year of the Lord 1449, an earthquake occurred through all of England, namely on the tenth calends of May,[1] at that time a Tuesday, around the third hour in the morning.

And on the 7th day of May was the resumption of the Parliament, and it continued until Pentecost in London, and after Pentecost the Parliament moved to Winchester, beginning on the 15th day of the month of June. At this Parliament but two dukes came—Suffolk, chamberlain, and basically regent of the whole kingdom of England, and the Duke of Buckingham—because the Duke of Norfolk was held back and excused from the Parliament, and the Duke of York was ordered by the king through the bad counsel of the Duke of Suffolk to enter Ireland and to stay there for ten years or seven. And the Duke of Somerset made delay in Normandy. And thus, under the most noble and most Christian King Henry in England ruled the unfair command of the Duke of Suffolk. And on the ninth day of the month of July, the Duke of York entered Ireland.[2]

And [at Parliament] one fifteenth was conceded to the king. And after this, Lord Jacob,[3] son and heir of the Earl of Salisbury, was made Earl of Warwick, and the son[4] and heir of the Earl of Ormond made Earl of Wiltshire. And in London the archbishop held an invocation which was conceded to the king one tenth, and that each chaplain pay a noble.[5]

And around the feast of the Assumption of the Blessed Mary [August 15] were lost nearly thirty cities with castles in Normandy, on account of which the king had a great council at Sheen, to which came all dukes, earls, barons, knights, and arms-bearers of England, who all gave great support to the king on account of his wars.

And around the feast of the Nativity of the Blessed Mary the king collected 6,000 soldiers for half a year and paid them the first payment, and through the fraud of the Duke of Suffolk and others, the second payment was delayed until the Purification of the Blessed Mary [February 2, 1450]. At which time, through insult, the king of the French obtained the city of Rouen through the fraud of the citizens. And then, he took the Earl of Shrewsbury and others into captivity. And the Duke of Somerset fled into Caen. And also the said king took the town of Harfleur and the land of Anjou in Maine, and all the land in Normandy on the near side of the River Seine.

And after the feast of all Saints, the king held a Parliament at London, which began at Westminster for just one day and several days at the Friars Preachers in London, and it lasted until the Nativity, and then the Parliament was prorogued until the Feast of Saint Vincent the Martyr. And on the fifth ides of January,[6] then a Friday, Master Adam Moleyns, Bishop of Chichester, and accordingly then the clerk of the private seal of the king, was killed at Portsmouth in the God's Hospital by sailors and soldiers, whom the king pardoned, which said bishop before his death accused himself and the Duke of Suffolk and other traitors to the crown.

And on the day of Saint Vincent the Martyr began a Parliament, at which all complained to the king about the Duke of Suffolk, and hearing that, the evil duke came personally to the Commons to excuse himself of many accusations. And on the same day the evil duke seeking license from the king to proceed to the castle at Wallingford, which he set up in the best way, then the commons complained, saying to the king that if the evil duke might go, through his evil advice and fraud he might destroy all England because he is a traitor to the crown, and for this they made judgment on many accusations. And thus on the fourth calends of February,[7] the evil duke was arrested and placed in the Tower of London. And the day before the fourth calends of February,[8] the Archbishop of York was made chancellor of the King of England. And Master Andrew Hulse was made clerk of the private seal of the lord king. And on that day, dragged, hanged, bowels extracted, burned while he lived, decapitated, and quartered was one man from Tyburn on account of his words against the king, and on that same day was captured Thomas Cheyne, who called himself "Bluebeard," in Kent, because he gathered to himself many men to rise up against the traitors against the king, namely against the Duke of Suffolk, the Bishop of Salisbury, and Lord James Fiennes, recently made Lord Saye. And this said Thomas said that he was servant of the King of Faerie, and he gathered many men to himself in Kent and other places for the previously stated cause. And on the fifth ides of February,[9] the traitor, the said Thomas

Cheyne, was hanged, disemboweled and the bowels burnt, beheaded and quartered at Tyburn.

And on the third calends of March,[10] on a Friday, after noon, between the sixth and seventh hour was seen a marvelous thunderbolt, which light lasted for three moments, and around the same time and out of that said thunderbolt were burnt to ashes a storehouse, a hall, the kitchen, and part of the vault in the royal manor of Eltham. And thus was captured the evil duke in the Tower for six weeks, and the king sent him to Westminster, and he was there in the custody of the king for a week and more, and then the king sent him at night into Suffolk to his manor at Eastham. And the evil Duke of Suffolk was exiled on the first day of May until the fiftieth year was completed by the king so far, and on the thirtieth day of March the Parliament ceased and moved to Leicester.

In the year of the Lord 1450, on the twentieth day of April, a Parliament began at Leicester. And on the fifth calends of May, the evil Duke of Suffolk took four or five ships with two hundred men against Brittany. And in the sea opposite Dover certain ships with a great ship named the *Nicholas of the Tower* and other small ships hindered him on the last day of April, and took the evil duke and made judgment and condemned him to death by two inquests, and on the sixth nones of May,[11] on a Saturday, around the tenth hour, they decapitated him in a small skiff and left his body with its severed head on the shore of the sea near Dover. And his body lay in a church unburied for a month and then was buried in Suffolk. And on the sixth day of June, the Parliament at Leicester was dissolved, in which was relinquished to the king by the Lords and Commons that anyone paying out annually £20 give to the king 10*s*. And from any pound beyond £20, give to the king 12*d*. And around the end of the Parliament the men of Kent rose up, choosing for themselves an intensely brave and discrete Captain calling himself John Mortimer, with 50,000 men. And on the day of Saint Barnabas the Apostle,[12] then a Thursday, came the Kentishmen to Blackheath near Deptford, and on the following Saturday, the king came to the house of Saint John near Clerkenwell with a great multitude of men of war from diverse parts of England to subdue the Captain. To whom the king sent the Archbishop Cardinal York, then Chancellor of England, and the Archbishop of Canterbury, and the Duke of Buckingham to take on the Captain and learn the cause of his insurrection, and this Captain proposed to them many articles to be emended on the part of the king and that will benefit the state of the kingdom of England. Hearing these articles, the king refused to emend them. And the Captain lying on Blackheath with all his people for eight days waiting for the will of the king, not intending any prejudice to the king nor to the kingdom of England, nor hurting nor robbing anyone, and this he made be proclaimed. And on the fourteenth calends of July,[13] the king with his own people left London for

Blackheath with 20,000 men excellently armed. However, the Captain, hearing of the arrival of the king and not wishing to resist him if he was able, went from Blackheath in the night before the arrival of the king to the village of Sevenoaks. Following whom Lord Humphrey Stafford, knight, and William Stafford, arms-bearer, fighting with the Kentishmen with four hundred men, knights, and arms-bearers, were killed, and with them forty men were killed and others turned to flight. And the king directed himself to Greenwich. The king and lords and men with him, hearing about the death of Humphrey Stafford and William Stafford and others with them, feared greatly. And the next day all the people proposed to rise up against those lords because held traitors to the king such as the Lord Saye, Baron of Dudley, Daniel, and many others.

The king instructed to arrest the Lord Saye and placed him in the Tower of London. In addition the king made his proclamation that all traitors would be seized wherever they were found, and on the following Saturday, the king came to Westminster. And the king sent secretly for the Lord Say that he would come to him at night. But the Duke of Exeter did not want to free him. Then Daniel raided the churches and killed many men and boys in Kent. Then the king rode with a few to the fort of Berkhamsted. And the Baron of Dudley was captured in the western part of England. And the Bishop of Salisbury headed to the fort of Sherborne, and was captured in the town of Ethlyngton[14] near Frome, and killed by the commons of that country on the day of Saint Peter and Paul, on a Monday, and on that day came the Captain of Kent again to Blackheath on Deptford where he first was with 20,000 men. And out of Essex to Mile End came 6,000 men, and on the following Thursday the Captain came into Southwark with 20,000 men. And on Friday after nine he arrived at London because he had great favor among the commons of London. He may not go further, and came to Cornhill and then to Mile End, and through the way robbed the house of a certain great man named Malpas, and as it is said carried away the value of 20,000 pounds, and thus returned to Southwark to his lodging.

Then the king sent a commission so that the commissioners would enact justice on all those traitors, extortionists, and evil-doers whom the Captain with the Kentishmen was accusing, and justices were scarcely found because the frightened pre-eminent justices fled. Then on Saturday the Mayor of London,[15] the Chief Baron,[16] and Assheton, one of the justices of the Common Bench, sat at the Guildhall over all the evil-doers in order to make peace with the Captain and the Kentishmen. And on that very day of the Translation of Saint Martin,[17] the Captain again entered London, riding his horse through the city with sword drawn and shaking in his hand, and dragging from Fleet [prison] the Sheriff of Kent, named Crowmer, led him to the hill next to the Tower of London, afterward to Mile End, and there beheaded him and another with him and placed their heads on spears and carried them to

Cheap. However, in the midst of that time, nearly twenty men were publicly accused by the justices of treason and extortion, among whom were the Lord Saye, then for a short time, Saye was freed from the Tower and he publicly appeared to the justices and was examined as he responded to his accusations. But he responds, "the king made me Lord and Baron, and according to the laws and statutes, I might not be judged except by my equals." Hearing this, the commons wished that he be killed before the justices. Then one of the lesser captains said that they would allow him to make confession, and after he confessed a few captains surely dragged him from the Guildhall and led him with the Kentish people up to the Standard in Cheap and there decapitated him without delay. Then the Captain came to the two heads on spears and placed the head of the Lord Saye on another higher spear and despoiled the body of the Lord Saye and tied his feet to the horse saddle and with hands unfolded dragged him nude from the Standard outside Newgate and thus through Old Bailey and through Ludgate into Watling Street and thus through Candlewick Street to the bridge, and there went around a large rock, scourging with a sword, and there on the tower placed the three heads, and dragged the body to the House of Saint Thomas in Southwark. And around the ninth hour [the Captain] beheaded a man named Hawarden, a wandering thief and murderer of many men who in the sanctuary of Saint Martin remained for a long time. And on his return he decapitated the custodian of the Castle of Colchester,[18] in Southwark. The Londoners seeing that Captain broke his proclamation were turned against the Captain. And on the following night around the tenth hour, the Lord Scales, knight Matthew Gough, with several London alderman, fought with the Kentishmen on London Bridge until the eighth hour of Monday, and many on each side were killed, among them on the side of London, Matthew Gough was killed, and one alderman named Sutton, a goldsmith, and with them about forty men, and on the side of Kent, two hundred men. Then necessity urged the Kentishmen to accept the royal charter and general pardon, which previously they refused to receive. And thus the Kentishmen went away into Kent and the Essexmen to Essex. However, the Sheriff of Kent, newly created, and many others followed and killed them on the near side of the sea shore on the twelfth of July; he was quartered and decapitated, and thus the quartered body was dragged with the head on the chest from Southwark to Newgate. And afterwards his head was placed on London Bridge, where he would be judged not according to the law but rather according to the will of the king. Then were lost all the cities with castles in Normandy except the city and the castle of Cherbourg.

And on the vigil of Saint James,[19] the king began a council in the city of Saint Alban's, and on the day of Saint Sampson[20] the king came to London and was honorably received and offered in the church of Saint Paul and thus came to Westminster, and intending to go to Eton on the feast of the

Assumption of the Blessed Mary, but when many soldiers came from Normandy, he rejected [that plan].

Then all the people of Kent and Essex and of the Earl of Wiltshire, because of the bad existing governance in this region, intended to make insurrection. Hearing this, the king sent into Kent Rochester, the Archbishop of York, Duke of Buckingham, and others with one justice then newly created[21] because all the justices dared not appear on account of extortion for their own deeds beforehand, and then sat on *oyer et terminer* wishing to satisfy the Kentishmen so that they did not revolt. And around the feast of the Assumption of the Blessed Mary,[22] the city of Cherbourg was returned to the King of France, and thus all of Normandy was lost; the loss to England was irrecoverable. And came the Duke of Somerset into England when he had lost all of Normandy.

And around the feast of the Nativity of the Blessed Mary[23] came the Duke of York from Ireland to England and headed into Wales. Then the Baron of Dudley and the Abbot of Gloucester, greatly frightened by the commons of England, and counselors with the evil Duke of Suffolk came to the Duke of York at the fort of Ludlow for safe custody, and on the Feast of Saint Cosmo and Damian,[24] then on Sunday, came the Duke of York to London with 5,000 men to Westminster to the king by whom he was most gratefully received.

And on the vigil of Saint Michael,[25] the custodian of Newgate, seeing that he was removed from his post, freed all the prisoners there and thus through the whole day of Saint Michael the prisoners were made rebels against the sheriffs, the custodians of prisons, throwing rocks and striking many. And the Duke of York remained in the hospitality of the Bishop of Salisbury until the feast of Saint Denys.[26] And around that time, the King of France began to fight with Gascony. And on the day of Saint Leonard,[27] the king commenced his Parliament at Westminster, to which came all the dukes, earls, and barons, one at a time, with a great multitude of well-armed men. And on the day of Saint Andrew,[28] these men who came with their lords to the Parliament, hearing that nothing was said by the king and his lords about the punishment of those who scandalized all of England by their treason, and especially by the Duke of Somerset, who so negligently and ignominiously lost all of Normandy, made in the royal hall of Westminster three great exclamations over all the dukes, earls, and barons, saying "make justice and punishment on the traitors." Thus the king and his lords were gravely terrified. On the next day, however, after noon nearly a thousand well-armed men rose up against Somerset intending to kill him. But at the request of the Duke of York, the Earl of Devon settled them and prudently captured the Duke [of Somerset] and led him secretly out of Friars on the Thames and thus to the Tower of London on account of fear of the commons, and meanwhile the men pillaged the house of the Friars Preachers. On the next day, however, the Duke of York seized one of the robbers and sent him to the king. And the king instructed the Earl of Salisbury that he have the robber decapitated at the Standard in Cheap, and thus it was done. However, on the third day of the month of December, then a Thursday, the king with all his dukes, earls, barons, knights, and arms-bearers, and others very well armed came through all of London with 10,000. And the Duke of Norfolk and the Earl of Devon with others came before the king with 3,000 men. And then came the king and with him the Duke of York, the Earl of Salisbury, the Earl of Arundel, the Earl of Oxford, the Earl of Wiltshire, the Earl of Worcester, and others with 4,000 men. Afterwards came the Duke of Buckingham and the Earl of Warwick and with them 3,000 other men who all went through London and thus again to Westminster.

And on the fifteenth calends of January,[29] the Parliament was prorogued until the twentieth day of January. And the king and queen held Christmas at Westminster, and the Duke of York at Stafford, and the Duke of Somerset at Friars Preachers in London.

And on the day of Saint Agnes on the following Thursday,[30] the king proceeded toward Canterbury, and with him the Duke of Exeter, the Duke of Somerset, the Earl of Shrewsbury, Lord Roos, Lord Cromwell, Lord Lisle, and others with 3,000 men, and the justices of the Royal Bench and of the Common Bench, who sat all throughout Kent, and thirty-one were hanged, dragged, and decapitated in Kent. And 3,000 on Blackheath in a return to the king received the grace of the king. And on the vigil of Saint Mattias[31] the king came to Westminster to the Parliament.

And on the twelfth calends of May,[32] of course on the third day before Easter, the Parliament was prorogued until after Easter, and the king held Easter at Windsor, and on the feast of the Holy Cross,[33] the king came to Westminster, and on the third nones of May,[34] the Parliament began at Westminster, and few lords and commons appeared at the Parliament because the king many times calmed the commons because they labored so that the king could claim all his property for himself.

And in this year, the feast of Easter occurred on the day of Saint Mark the Evangelist.[35] And the Parliament lasted until Pentecost, and then seemingly suddenly it ended, in which Parliament the king conceded to claim for himself all his properties, few excepted, at which time were acquitted the Baron of Dudley and the Bishop of Hereford by their peers; John Saye, Trevilian and Daniel were acquitted by Londoners.

NOTES

1. 22 April 1449.
2. Richard Duke of York landed in Ireland on 6 July.

3. This should read "Richard," not "Jacob," as Richard Neville was confirmed on 23 July 1449, in this title. James Butler was names Earl of Wiltshire on 8 July 1449.
4. The son is James.
5. The value of a noble coin was 6 shillings and 8 pence.
6. 9 January 1450.
7. 29 January 1450.
8. 29 January 1450.
9. 9 February 1450.
10. 27 February 1450.
11. 2 May 1450.
12. 11 June 1450.
13. 18 June 1450.
14. The manuscript reads "villa de Ethlyngton' iuxta Frome," but no place name called "Ethlyngton" can be located. Hanham, 28, suggests, that this could be "Tytherington."
15. Thomas Chalton.
16. Peter Arden, the Chief Baron of the Exchequer.
17. 4 July 1450.
18. Thomas Mayn.
19. 24 July 1450.
20. 28 July 1450.
21. Robert Danvers was appointed Judge of the Common Pleas on 14 August 1450.
22. 15 August 1450.
23. 8 September 1450.
24. 27 September 1450.
25. 28 September 1450.
26. 28 October 1450.
27. 6 November 1450.
28. 30 November 1450.
29. 18 December 1450.
30. 28 January 1451.
31. 23 February 1451.
32. 20 April 1451.
33. 3 May 1451.
34. 5 May 1451.
35. 25 April 1451.

Chapter 3

From *An English Chronicle, 1377–1461*

OVERVIEW

This chronicle is a continuation of the Middle English Prose *Brut*, a history of England beginning with its "founding" by the Trojan, Brutus. There are at least a hundred and eighty manuscripts that survive of the Middle English prose history. Matheson classifies this chronicle under "Peculiar Texts and Versions," and specifically as "Reworked Texts and Versions." For many years, the manuscript used for this text was Oxford, Bodleian MS Lyle 34 and was edited by John Silvester Davies and published in 1856; it was known as *Davies's Chronicle*. In 2003, William Marx published a new edition of this chronicle, using a different manuscript as the base text, Aberystwyth, National Library of Wales MS 21608. In his edition to the chronicle, William Marx notes how the attitude of the chronicler toward Cade Rebellion is mixed, at first supporting the complaints of the insurgents and then criticizing the leader as tyrannical. According to Marx in his introduction to his edition, this shift in rhetorical strategies is used to "explain and justify the Duke of York's rebellion. [The chronicler] shows that Jack Cade's rebellion is based on sound political principles and sound political analysis, and that it reflects the will of the commons as well as some of the lords" (xcix).

MANUSCRIPT

Aberystwyth, National Library of Wales MS 21608

SOURCE FOR TRANSLATION

Marx, William, ed. *An English Chronicle, 1377–1461: A New Edition*. Medieval Chronicles 3. Woodbridge, UK: The Boydell Press, 2003.

FURTHER READING

Bryan, Elizabeth. "Prose Brut, English." *EMC* 2: 1239–40.
Davies, John Silvester, ed. *An English Chronicle of the Reigns of Richard II, Henry IV, Henry V, and Henry VI*. Camden Society, os, 64. London: J. B. Nichols and Sons, 1856.
Marx, William. "Middle English Manuscripts of the Brut in the National Library of Wales."*Cylchgrawn Llyfrgell Genedlaethol Cymru / The National Library of Wales Journal* 27 (1991–1992): 361–82.
———. "Reception and Revision in the Middle English Prose *Brut*." In "Readers and Writers of the Prose *Brut*," edited by William Marx and Raluca Radulescu, special issue, *Trivium* 36 (2006): 53–69.
Matheson, 290–93.

TRANSLATION

[1449] The twenty eighth year of King Henry on Simon Day and Jude,[1] and other days before and after, the son in his rising and going down appeared as red as blood as men saw, whereof the people had great wonder and deemed that it should betoken some harm soon afterward.

And this same year during the feast of Saint Michael in Monte Tumba,[2] Rouen was lost and yielded to the Frenchmen, those who were there at that being the Duke of Somerset, Edmund, lieutenant of Normandy.[3]

[1450] And this same year, the Friday, the ninth day of January, Master Adam Moleyns, Bishop of Chichester and Keeper of the king's Privy Seal was sent to Portsmouth in order to make payment of money to certain soldiers and shipmen for their wages, fell into disagreement with them, as it was said, and would have reduced their wages. Wherefore they fell on him there and killed him.

And also this same year during the feast of Saint Peter on the Monday, the last day of June, Master William Aiscough, Bishop of Salisbury, was slain at Edington in Wiltshire, by people of the same county where he had said mass, and was drawn from the altar having on him his alb and his stole about his neck.[4] And then they brought him up onto a hill there beside [where he was taken], and they slew him horribly, their father and their bishop, and stripped him to his naked skin and tore his bloody shirt into pieces and bore it away with them in their despite and condemnation of him, and made a boast of their wickedness. And the day before his death his chariot, by men of the same country, was robbed of a huge treasure to the value of ten thousand marks, as they said that knew of it. The two bishops were considered to be extraordinary covetous men and approved of evil among the common people, and, as the people said, were willing and assenting to the death of the Duke of Gloucester.

And this same year in the month of May arose those of Kent and made them a captain, an Irishman, a ribald, called John Cade, who at his start took onto himself and usurped the name of a gentleman and called himself Mortimer in order to get and have more favor of the people. And he called himself also John Amendall, for as much as then and a long time before the realm of England was out of rule and governance and ruled by untrue counsel, wherefore the common good was greatly hurt and decreased so that the common people, with great taxes and great levies and other oppressions done by lords and others, might not [be able to] live by their husbandry and handiwork, wherefore they grumbled greatly against those that had the governance of the land.

Then came the said captain and the Kentishmen and went into Blackheath, and there dwelled a month and more, robbing all about the country, to whom the city of London was at that time very favorable, but they regretted them afterward. In the meantime the king sent notable persons to the said captain and his fellowship in order to know their purpose and the cause of their insurrection. The captain was an articulate[5] man and said that he and his company were gathered and assembled in order to redress and reform the wrongs that were done in the realm, and to withstand the malice of those that were destroyers of the common good, and to correct and to amend the defaults of those that were the king's chief counselors. And [Cade] shared with them the articles of their petitions concerning and in regard to the mischief and misgovernance of the realm; in the same articles was nothing contained but that [which] was rightful and reasonable. Wherefore a copy was sent to the parliament [that was being] held that time as Westminster. Wherefore the said captain desired that such grievance should be amended and reformed by the parliament, and to have a reply [from them] on the same articles.

Soon after the king moved from Westminster to Greenwich, and while he was there he would have sent certain lords with military force in order to attack the Kentishmen, but those that should have gone with the lords answered and said that they would not fight against those that labored in order to amend and reform the common good of the land. And when the lords heard this, they abandoned their intent.

Then cried the Kentishmen and all others against the Lord Saye, the king's Chamberlain, who was one of the king's untrue counselors, as they said. And the king, dreading the malice of the people, commanded him [to be taken] to the Tower.

Then the king went again to London, and within two days after he went toward the Kentishmen with his lords with fifteen-thousand men well-armed into Blackheath. And when they heard of his coming, they fled the night before into the wooded countryside, into a place called Sevenoaks in Kent, the king not knowing where they were.

Then the king returned into London again and sent out a squire called William Stafford and a knight called Sir Humphrey Stafford, his cousin, in order to learn where the Kentishmen were. And when they knew that they were at Sevenoaks, they rode there hastily with a few men, hoping to receive a singular honor. But they had come under the power of the Kentishmen before they knew it, and there they were both slain as were many [who] remained with them.

After this the king dissolved the parliament and departed toward Kenilworth, and as soon as the Kentishmen heard that the king was gone from London, they came down to Sevenoaks, and their captain was lodged at the Hart.[6] And the Thursday after, by the favor of some of them of London, he entered and came into the city, for they of the city were divided among themselves. Nevertheless, the keys of the gates of the city were delivered to the said captain and he kept them two days and two nights. When he had entered into the city, at once he and his people fell into robbery, and robbed certain worthy men of the city and put some of them into prison until they had paid notable sums of money for their lives. And the captain rode about in the city bearing a naked sword in his hand, wearing gilded spurs, and a gilded sallet,[7] having on him a pair of brigandines,[8] a gown of blue velvet, and had a sword brought before him pretending [that Cade was] the rank of a lord, and yet he was nothing but a rascal.[9]

And the Saturday after next, the Lord Saye, by the commandment of the said captain, was brought out of the Tower and into the Guildhall in London before certain justices that were assigned to the king to sit there at that time in order to answer to certain points that he was accused of. And when he was there, the Kentishmen would not allow him to follow the law, but led him into the Standard in Cheapside, and there his head was cut off and his body was drawn naked behind a horse's tail upon the street so that the flesh stuck to the stones, from Cheapside to Southwark, to the said captain's inn. Also a squire named [William] Crowmer, who was the sheriff of Kent, who had wed Lord Saye's daughter, was brought by the commandment of the said captain out of Fleet prison, who was imprisoned there for certain extortions that he had done in his office, and was led into a place that was called Mile End, outside of

London.[10] And there, without any judgment, his head was cut off and brought to the [Standard] in Cheapside, and afterward Lord Saye's head and his were born on two long shafts onto London Bridge and there set upon [it].

The next Sunday, men of London, seeing the tyranny and robbery of the cursed captain and of his men, and when it was evening, they laid their hands on those that were scattered about the city, and drove them out at the gates. And when the captain heard this, who [at the time] was in his inn in Southwark, he quickly with his men made a raid toward London Bridge and would have come in and pillaged the city. And the Lord Scales with his men and the men of the city fought with him from nine o'clock in the evening until ten o'clock in the morning, and many men were slain on both parties and greatly wounded. And there were slain Matthew Gough, a squire of Wales, and John Sutton, alderman of London. And in the end, one of them from Kent set the bridge [made] of wood on fire so that none might come to the others.

And then those of Kent withdrew themselves a little and a little, and the captain put all his spoils and stolen goods into a barge and sent it toward Rochester. And he went by land, and would have gone in with his said spoils into the castle of Queenborough with a few men that were left with him, but he was impeded from his goal. And then he fled into the wooded countryside beside Lewes, and the Sheriff of Kent—by commandment of Master John Kemp, Archbishop of York and Cardinal of Rome and Cardinal of England that lived in London all this time, and Master John Stafford, Archbishop of Canterbury, in order to assist and counsel the city and to withstand by their wisdom the malicious purpose of the said rebels—pursued the said captain, and there he was mortally wounded and taken and carried in a cart toward London. And along the way he died, but he was shriven as grace would [allow].[11] And then his head was cut off and set on London Bridge, and his body quartered and sent to different towns of England. This captain in his tyranny slew many men without judgment, and would not allow them to be shriven. And his madness and tyranny endured from Trinity Sunday to the eve of the Feast of Saint Thomas of Canterbury.[12] And thus ended the captain of mischief.

And this same year the commons arose in different parts of England, as in Sussex, Salisbury, Wiltshire, and other places, and did much harm to many persons.

NOTES

1. The Feast of Saint Simon and Saint Jude takes place on 28 October.
2. "Monte Tumba" is the sanctuary of Saint Michael in Mont-Saint-Michel in the Diocese of Coutances; the feast is on 16 October.

3. Rouen was surrendered on 29 October 1449.

4. "Alb" refers to the ecclesiastical vestments, usually made of white linen, that the bishop wore that would have reached his ankles. The "stole" refers to the robe that he wore.

5. The chronicler here describes Cade as a "sotellmon." The *MED* has a wide range of definitions for "sotil" (adj.), any of which could correspond with Cade's temperament and personality at this moment in the episode, including 1. (a): "Of a person, the intellect, etc.: penetrating; ingenious; perspicacious; sophisticated, refined; of the sight: sharp, keen; of a speaker: articulate, persuasive."

6. This is the White Hart Inn.

7. A sallet is a light helmet.

8. Brigandines are body armor that protects the chest and back. It is typically made of heavy cloth or leather onto which small steel plates are attached.

9. The chronicler, at the end of this sentence, calls Cade a "lurdeyne," from the Old French "lordin." In the *MED* "lurdan" (n.) has many colorful meanings, any one of which could apply to Jack Cade: "(a) An evildoer, wicked person, criminal; (b) as a term of abuse: good-for-nothing, rascal; (c) a spiritless person, lazy person; coward; (d) a low-born person, an ill-mannered person, an ugly person, a fool; (e) an unfortunate wretch."

10. The chronicler writes "myles Ende, withoute London," (Marx 69.20-1), which suggests that this execution takes places outside the walls of London.

11. With the ecclesiasts in his presence, Cade was shriven, that is, he confessed his sins. We do not know if Cade was absolved of his sins and received the sacrament of penance, or if he died with the works of satisfaction being incomplete.

12. In 1450, Trinity Sunday would have taken place on 31 May. The Feast of Saint Thomas of Canterbury takes place on 29 December.

Chapter 4

From *A Short English Chronicle*

OVERVIEW

This London chronicle, written in Middle English and referred to as *A Short English Chronicle*, was written shortly after 1465. It provides valuable information on Edward IV's reign and the events of the Cade Rebellion. McLaren classifies the manuscript, a commonplace book that contains this London chronicle, as part of the Harley Roll C 8 group. This chronicle begins at 1189 and the final entry is for the year 1465.

MANUSCRIPT

London, Lambeth Palace MS Lambeth 306

SOURCE FOR TRANSLATION

Gairdner, James, ed. *A Short English Chronicle* in *Three Fifteenth-Century English Chronicles*. Camden Society, ns, 28. Westminster: Camden Society, 1880. Pp. 66–68.

FURTHER READING

Kennedy, 2651.
McLaren, 113–15.
Radulescu, Raluca. "London Chronicles." In *EMC* 2: 1042–43.

TRANSLATION FROM MIDDLE ENGLISH

[1450] This year the king held his parliament at Westminster. And that same year was all of Normandy lost. And also during Christmas while the parliament was at Westminster the Duke of Suffolk was arrested and sent to the Tower of London. And within a month after, the king sent for the Duke to move from the Tower to the Tower at Westminster, and shortly before Easter the parliament was adjourned to Leicester, and the king took with him the Duke of Suffolk. And when the king and the commons came to Leicester, the commons said that they would have execution done upon the traitors that had sold Normandy, Guyenne, and Gascony, who were the causes of the death of the Duke of Gloucester, for which the Duke of Suffolk was named chief, and the Lord Saye and Daniel, squire, and many others. And so the commons cried so sore on the Duke of Suffolk that at last the king did exile him out of the land. And so the duke embarked and was further in the sea, and there met with him a ship called the *Nicholas of the Tower* that took the duke and cut off his head in the see on the first day of May. And so he was brought to Dover on land, and immediately the parliament was ended. And then the commons of Kent arose and had chosen for themselves a captain, who named himself John Mortimer, whose very true name was John Cade, and he was an Irishman; and so he came to Blackheath with the commons of Kent. And the king with all of his lords made themselves ready with all their power in order to withstand him. And the captain, hearing that the king was coming, the night before the he withdrew himself and his people; and so the eighteenth day of June the king made his way toward Blackheath. And Sir Humphrey Stafford, knight, and John Stafford, squire, with their people went forward, and they were slain and much of their people. And the king came to Blackheath with his lords. They, hearing of this battle, the lords' troops went together and said [to the king], and the king would execute such traitors that they named, otherwise they would turn to the captain of Kent. And the king granted them that they should have their intent, and told them to name such traitorous persons, and they should have as the law would allow. And then the lords' men said that the Lord Saye was one, the Bishop of Salisbury, the Baron of Dudley, the Abbot of Gloucester, and Daniel, and many more. And the Lord Saye was arrested in the king's presence and sent to the Tower of London. And so the king went to Greenwich, and then to London by water, and was there two or three days, and then made himself ready to depart to Kenilworth. And the mayor of London with the commons of the city came to the king, beseeching him that he would remain in the city and they would live and die with him, and pay for his household costs for one half year; but he would not, and instead took his journey to Kenilworth. And when the king was gone the captain with the commons of Kent came toward Blackheath.

And the third day of July he came to London, and as soon as they entered London they robbed Philip Malpas. And the fourth day of July he beheaded Crowmer and another man at Mile End; and the same day in the afternoon the Lord Saye was brought out of the Tower to the Guildhall for the mayor to sit in judgment, and when he came before the mayor he said he would be judged by his peers. And then the commons of Kent took him from the officers and led him to the Standard in Cheap and there cut off his head. And then the captain dragged him through London and over to London Bridge and to Saint Thomas Watering, and there he was hanged and quartered, and his head and Crowmer's head and another man's head was set on London Bridge. And after that he cut off two other men's heads in Southwark. And the fifth day of July at night (and being Sunday) the commons of London set upon the commons of Kent, for they began to rob. And all the men of Kent that were in London that night they went to their captain and into Southwark. And the same night the mayor and the sheriffs and my Lord Scales and Matthew Gough and the commons of London went to London Bridge, and there they fought from nine o'clock at night until eleven o'clock in the morning, and in the end the captain set fire to the drawbridge. And right away the Chancellor went to the captain and seized him and gave him a charter and his men another, and so they withdrew themselves homeward. Then on the twelfth day of July it was proclaimed in every shire that whatever man could take the aforesaid captain should have 1,000 marks, for it was openly known that his name was not Mortimer, his name was John Cade, and therefore his charter was not valid. And so one Alexander Iden, a squire of Kent, captured him in a garden in Sussex on the thirteenth day of July. And in the capturing of him he was hurt and died that same night, and in the morning he was brought in to the King's Bench, and after he was drawn through London and his head set on London Bridge.

Chapter 5

From *A Chronicle of London* in Oxford, Bodleian Library MS Gough London 10

OVERVIEW

This Middle English chronicle of London beings in 1189 and ends in 1470, with a lone entry for 1495 after a break in the manuscript. McLaren places this chronicle within the Harley Roll C 8 Group of manuscripts. The manuscript that contains this chronicle is a commonplace book, which also includes "items of interest to a London citizen: ordinances, oaths to be taken by the city chamberlains; oaths of wardens and of members of the goldsmiths' company; and indices to some of the letter books [of the city of London]" (McLaren 114). This London chronicle, in the earlier entries, contains entries not found in the other two manuscripts in this group: London, British Library MS Harley Roll C 8; and London, Lambeth Palace, MS Lambeth 306. Beginning with the coronation of Richard II in 1377, the content all three manuscripts deviate, and in 1435 they "deviate dramatically" (McLaren 115).

MANUSCRIPT

Oxford, Bodleian Library MS Gough London 10

SOURCE FOR TRANSLATION

Flenley, Ralph, ed. *Six Town Chronicles of England*. Oxford: Clarendon Press, 1911. Pp. 153–57.

FURTHER READING

Kennedy, 2647–50.
Kingsford, 103.
McLaren, 113–15.
Radulescu, Raluca. "London Chronicles." In *EMC* 2: 1042–43.

TRANSLATION

This year [1450] was the battle at the bridge. And this year, the largest part of Normandy was lost. Also in February, the same twenty-eighth year that the parliament began at the Blackfriers and continued until the following Easter, but they were not harmonious. In the meantime, the Duke of Suffolk was arrested and put in the Tower and a great watch was made in the city of London during the time of the parliament, and after Easter the parliament was adjourned to Leicester and was there until after Whitsuntide and nothing was carried out. In the meantime, the Duke of Suffolk was going over in the sea was taken by a ship called the *Nicholas of the Tower* and his head was cutoff on Mayday and the body and the head cast on the sands beside Dover.

And soon after the commons of Kent arose with great power and came down to Blackheath on the ninth day of June and there assembled themselves and readied themselves all around with stakes and ditches and stayed there seven days. And when the king heard this while he was in Leicester, he made all the lords gather all the armed men that could go with him against the Kentishmen, and so they did and came to London and sent many lords to Blackheath to find out what they meant to do. And they said they were petitioners and asked from the king that certain things that they felt aggrieved with might be amended. But the king would not grant them. The captain of them they called John Mortimer. And many appointments were taken with him but they would not hold them. Wherefore, on Thursday, the twenty-ninth day of June, the king took all of his lords with all their people in good array in the manner of war and rode to Blackheath, but the captain and his army were gone the night, but no man knew to what place.

Wherefore, certain lords that kept the forward position followed their trace. And it happened that Sir Humphrey Stafford, knight, and Sir William Stafford, squire, and another squire with all of their army met with the Kentishmen near Sevenoaks and there fought with them, and there were slain the aforesaid Sir Humphrey and William and many of their men. And on the Friday after, several lords' men gathered together in Blackheath, and said that they saw their friends slain and that they were likely to be slain also if they followed the king and his traitors. And when the Duke of Buckingham heard that he went to the king, to Greenwich, and told him that his people would forsake him if he would not execute his traitors. Wherefore, at once the king ordered Lord Saye to be arrested and brought to the Tower by the Duke of Exeter, and on the morning after Midsummer Day, the king departed from Westminster to the castle of Kenilworth. But before he went, it was told to him that the Kentishmen would come again. Wherefore, he sent for the mayor and aldermen and Council of London and commanded them to keep them out of the city. And the morning after Saint Peter's Day, the captain of Kent came to Blackheath again and there beheaded one Parys, a captain of his. And on the same day there came tidings to London that the Bishop of Salisbury was slain in Wiltshire. And on the Thursday, the first day of July, the captain with his army came into Southwark and encamped there all night and the gates of the bridge were shut, save the wicket,[1] and that was kept with armed men. However, with permission, men went out, but the Kentishmen would not allow men to pass the farthest post of the bridge after they had come out.

And the same day, the commons of Essex came down to Mile End to the said captain, and on the morning after the commons of London went to the Guildhall because of a summons made by a commission that was sent from the king to certain lords and to the mayor and certain justices in order to inquire about all of those persons that were traitors, extortioners, and oppressors of the king's people, but the justices would not be found. Wherefore, the commons of London were very angry. Nevertheless, certain inquests were called and while the mayor sat, the commons complained loudly to alderman Malpas, and this caused him to be relieved of his duties. And Robert Horne and other aldermen, because of the outcry of the people, was arrested there and put in Newgate.

And the same day at five o'clock in the afternoon the said captain came into London over the bridge and cut the ropes asunder so that the drawbridge was brought down. And when he was at Saint Magnus, he made a declaration that no man in his army upon the pain of death should despoil no man in London, and again at Leadenhall [he made that declaration]. And forthwith he went to Malpas' place and despoiled all that was therein and after rode out to Mile End to the army of Essex men, and from there went into Southwark the same night. And in the morning the mayor and the aldermen and two justices sat at the Guildhall and charged ten inquests, which indicted the Lord Saye and others of treason, and before the mayor went to the hall he sent Horne to the captain and he ransomed him and many other men of the city.

And while the mayor was at the hall the captain came again into London and went to the Fleet and from there to one Crowmer, a squire, that had wedded the Lord Saye's daughter and had been sheriff of Kent and had done much extortion there as they said, and he beheaded him at White Chapel without respect with another man that was called Bailey and a clerk and brought the heads on stakes through London, and the same day the said captain dined at Gest's place by Tower Street and took from him great goods.

And the same day in the afternoon, the Lord Saye was sent forth to the Tower by several aldermen and men, harnessed, and brought him to the Guildhall and there was arraigned at the bar, and after he was delivered to the commons and led to the Standard in Cheap, and there he was beheaded and his body drawn through London to Saint Thomas-a-Watering and there hanged and then [they] carried him toward and into Southwark. And the next day that was Sunday at night the said captain made a declaration in Southwark that every man of the city should bring themselves into the city, and that all his men should bring themselves to him in their best array, for it was told that the mayor and the aldermen of London would secure the city. And so it happened that about nine o'clock in the evening the Lord Scales and Matthew Gough, squire, who was a noble warrior, with their army went against the said captain and his men and fought from that time until eight o'clock in the morning, and many people [were] slain on both sides. And those who were slain were the said Matthew Gough and Sutton, alderman, and other worthy men of the city, and then the Kentishmen set fire to the drawbridge so that men might not come to them, and shortly after eight the Archbishop of Canterbury and the Cardinal of York, Chancellor of England, and others went between [them] and made a truce. And the day after, which was Saint Thomas' Day of Canterbury, the said captain withdrew to Blackheath with all of his people and forward into Kent, and on Thursday, the tenth day of July, the said captain's goods were taken at Rochester.

And on the following Sunday Alexander Iden, who was Sheriff of Kent, with others took the said captain beside Maidstone, and he was badly hurt and he was so taken that he died as a result, and on the following Monday he was brought down to Southwark in a little cart that was open down the middle so that men might see him, and he was left in the king's bench. And on the next Wednesday he was beheaded and quartered, and on Thursday he was drawn from the king's bench to Newgate, and on Friday the head was set on London Bridge and the quarters still remained in Newgate and after they were displayed in many parts of Kent.

And the same year a little before Michaelmas the Duke of York came out of Ireland.

NOTE

1. A wicket is a small door that is built into the gate.

Chapter 6

From *Gregory's Chronicle*

OVERVIEW

The Middle English London chronicle known as *Gregory's Chronicle* (at times, also, *"Gregory's" Chronicle*) is found within a fifteenth-century commonplace book attributed to William Gregory (d. 1467), skinner, sheriff of London (1436–1437), and later mayor (1451–1452), on the basis of an entry for the years he was mayor. McLaren convincingly argues that Gregory is not the author of the work, noting that, in addition to inconsistencies with the content of the chronicle and Gregory's life, the chronicle itself does not "indicate a type of person interested in writing and keeping London chronicles" and "has a particular interest in the feelings of uprisings and the feelings and injustices that cause them" (32). The chronicle can be divided into two parts, written by two different persons: 1189–1453 and 1454–1470. In addition to the London chronicle, the commonplace book contains the *Siege of Rome*, John Lydgate's "Verses on the Kings of England," and other, mostly secular, items.

MANUSCRIPT

London, British Library MS Egerton 1995

SOURCE FOR TRANSLATION

Gairdner, James, ed. *The Historical Collections of A London Citizen of the Fifteenth Century.* Camden Society, ns 17. Westminster: Nichols and Sons, 1876. Pp. 190–94.

FURTHER READING

Gransden, 229–35.
Kennedy, 2651–52.
Kingsford, 95–98.
McLaren, 29–33; 104–6.
Radulescu, Raluca. "London Chronicles." In *EMC* 2: 1042–43.

TRANSLATION

And that same year [1450] was the greatest part of Normandy lost, and a parliament was at Westminster. In the same time was Roen, Montivilliers, and Harfleur lost before Christmas, and then the parliament was prolonged until after Saint Hilary's Day.[1] And at the same time were many soldiers at Portsmouth, who had taken the king's pledge to pass over the sea. And soon after Christmas was sent toward the seashore the [keeper of the] privy seal, who was called Master Adam Moleyns, to seize the monster at the seashore, he being that time the Bishop of Chichester. And for his covetousness, as it was reported, shipmen put him to death, and some unwise men of the soldiers helped as well, too. And this was done at Portsmouth.[2]

And after Saint Hilary's Day the parliament was moved to Leicester. And in the meantime Caen was lost, and all the remnants of Normandy, save Cherbourg. And the Duke of Suffolk was impeached at that parliament, he being at London, of very serious treason, and of many charges; among all other, for that he should have sold Normandy, and also for the death of that noble prince the Duke of Gloucester, and for many other charges of treason, for which he was expelled out of England for certain years. And at his passing over the sea he was met between Dover and Calais by several ships, one of which was called the *Nicholas of the Tower*. And in that ship, being in the sea, they smote off his head of the aforesaid Duke of Suffolk, and they cast both body and his head into the sea. And after that [his body] was taken up and brought into the town of Dover, and after from there brought into Wingfield in Suffolk, and there it was buried, whose name was Sir William [de la] Pole.

And after that the commons of Kent arose with certain other shires, and they chose them a captain, the same captain compelled all the gentry to arise with them. And at the end of the parliament they came with great might and a strong army into Blackheath, beside Greenwich, to the number of 46,000. And there they made a field of battle, ditched and staked well about it, as it would be in the land of war, save they only kept order among themselves, for all good was Jack Robin as John at the Nook, for all were as high as pigs feet, until the time that they should come and speak with such status and messengers as were sent to them. Then they put all their power into the man that named himself captain of all their army. And there they remained for a certain time for the coming of the king from the parliament at Leicester. And then the king sent to the captain several lords, both spiritual and secular, to learn and to have knowledge of that great assembly and gathering of that great and misadvised fellowship. Their captain sent word to the king that it was for the good of him, our sovereign Lord, and of all the realm, to destroy the traitors being about him, with other numerous charges that they would see that they were in a short time amended. Upon which answered the king, sent by his lords to that place, and did make a proclamation in the king's name of England that all the king's liege men of England should avoid the field. And upon the night after they were all departed and gone.

The morning after, the king rode armed all the way from Saint John's Priory, which is beside Clerkenwell, through London, and with him the majority of secular lords of this land of England in their best array. After that, there was every lord with his retinue, to the number of ten-thousand persons, ready as if all should have gone into battle in any land of Christendom, with bands above their harnesses so that every lord should be known from the other. And in the destruction, as they would have followed the captain, were slain Sir Humphrey Stafford and William Stafford, squire, one of the manliest men of all this realm of England, and with them many more others of common persons at Sevenoaks, in Kent, in their unruliness from their host against our sovereign lord the king, Henry VI. And the king lodged that night at Greenwich, and soon after every lord with his retinue rode home into their country.

And after that, upon the first day of July, the captain came again, as the Kentishmen said, but it was another that named himself the captain, and he came to Blackheath. And upon the morning, he came with a great host into Southwark, and at the Whote Hart he took his lodging. And upon the morning, that was Friday, toward evening, they smote asunder the ropes of the drawbridge and fought hard, boldly. And many a man was murdered and killed in that conflict, and I know not what to name it for the multitude of riff-raff. And then they entered into the city of London as men that had been half beside their wits. An in that fury they went, as they said, for the common good of the realm of England, straight toward a merchant's place, named Philip Malpas of London. If it were true as they surmised after their doing, I commit myself to writing: "God knows and I do not."[3] But well I know that every ill beginning must commonly have an ill ending, and every good beginning has the truly good ending. Proverb: "A happy beginning makes for a good end."[4] And that Philip Malpas was alderman, and they looted him and bore away much goods of his, and especially much money, both in silver and gold, the value being a notable sum, and especially of merchandise, of tin, woad,[5] madder dye,[6] alum,[7] and with a great quantity of woolen cloth and many rich jewels, with other notable stuff of feather beds, bedding, napery, and many a rich cloth of arras, to the value of a notable sum—"I know not, but God knows all."[8]

And in the evening, they went with their simple captain to his lodging, but a certain [number] of his simple and rude retinue stayed there all night, presuming that they had the wit and wisdom to guide or put in guidance all England. As soon as they had gotten the city in a mishap by cutting two sorry cords that now are altered, [they] made two strong chains of iron onto the drawbridge of London. But they had other men with them as well of London as part of their own party. And those of one party and of that other party they left no thing unsought,[9] and they searched all that night.

And in the morning he came again, that sorry and simple and rebellious captain with his retinue. That was Saturday, and it was also Saint Martin's Day,[10] the dedication of Saint Martin in the Vintry,[11] the fourth day of July. And then diverse inquests were summoned at the Guildhall, and there Robert Horne, being alderman, was arrested and brought into Newgate. And that same day, William Crowmer, squire and Sheriff of Kent, was beheaded in the field outside Aldgate at the Mile End besides Clopton's Place. And another man that was named John Bailey[12] was beheaded at the White Chapel.

And that same day [in the] afternoon was beheaded in Cheap before the Standard, Sir James Fiennes, being that [same] time the Lord Saye and Great Treasurer of England was brought out of the Tower of London into the Guildhall, and there of diverse treasons he was examined, particularly his knowledge of the death of that notable and famous price, the Duke of Gloucester. And then they brought him into the Standard in Cheap, and there he received his misery and his death. And so, all the three heads that day smote were set upon the Bridge of London, and the two other heads taken down that stood upon the London Bridge before. And at the coming of the captain into Southwark, he cut off the head of a strong thief that was named Hawarden.

And upon the morrow, the Sunday at high mass time, [Cade] permitted to behead a man of Hampton, a squire, who was named Thomas Mayn. And that same evening, London did arise and came out upon them at ten o'clock, being that time their captains the good old lord Scales and Matthew Gough. And from that time until eight o'clock in the morning they were continually fighting upon London Bridge, and many a man was slain and cast in the Thames, harness, body, and all. And among the crowd was slain Matthew Gough and John Sutton, alderman. And the same night, soon after midnight, the captain of Kent did fire the drawbridge of London. And before that time he broke both King's Bench and Marshalsea, and let out all the prisoners that were in them.

And upon the morning, early, came my lord the Cardinal of York,[13] and my lord of Canterbury,[14] and the Bishop of Winchester,[15] and they mediated between the Lord Scales and that captain, that the sore conflict and skirmish was ceased, and gave the captain and his retinue a general charter[16] for him and all his company in his name, calling himself John Mortimer, and through that mean they were for the most part cleared.

And the sixth day after that, the Saturday at evening, the three heads were taken down from London Bridge, that is to say, the Lord Saye's head, Crowmer's and Bailey's, and the other two heads set up again that stood upon London Bridge before, and the bodies with the heads were buried at the Grey Friars at London.

And upon the twelfth day of July, the year aforesaid, the said captain was cried and proclaimed traitor, by the name of John Cade, in diverse places of London, and also in Southwark, with many more, and that what man might or would bring the said John Cade to the king, quick or dead, should have of the king a thousand marks. Also, whosoever might bring or would bring any of his chief counselors, or of a companion that kept any state or rule or governance under the said false captain, John Cade, he should have to his reward of the king five hundred marks. And that day was the false traitor, the captain of Kent, taken and slain in the Weald of the country of Sussex. And upon the morning he was brought in a cart all naked, and at the Hart in Southwark there the cart was made to stand still, so the wife of the house might see him, if it were the same man or not that was named the captain of Kent, for he was lodged within her house in his perverse time of his misrule and rising.

And then he was brought into the King's Bench, and there he lay from Monday at evening until the Tuesday following at evening. And within the King's Bench the said captain was beheaded and quartered. And the same day he was drawn upon a sledge in pieces, with the head between his breast, from the King's Bench throughout Southwark, and then over London Bridge, and then through London into Newgate, and then his head was taken and set upon London Bridge.

NOTES

1. 13 January 1450.
2. Moleyns was killed 9 January 1450.
3. Latin: "Deus scit et ego non."
4. Latin: "Proverbium: Felix principium finem essebeatum." This was a popular proverbial saying in grammar books in the Middle Ages.
5. The leaves of the wode plant were used to make blue dye, so this could refer to either the dye or the plant itself.

6. The dye made from the madder plant is red in color.
7. A common ingredient in dying fabrics.
8. Latin: "nescio, set Deus omniascit."
9. The word here in the manuscript and Gairdner's edition is "unsoffethe," which could be "unsought."
10. This is the Translation of Saint Martin of Tours.
11. The parish church of Saint Martin Vintry was in the Vintry ward of London; it was destroyed in the Great Fire London in 1666.
12. *Bale's Chronicle* records his name as William Bailey.
13. John Kemp, who afterwards is the Archbishop of Canterbury.
14. John Stafford.
15. William Waynflete.
16. This is the general pardon.

Chapter 7

From *Ingulph's Chronicle of the Abbey of Croyland*

OVERVIEW

Croyland (Crowland) was a Benedictine Abbey in Croyland, Linconshire. There, a Latin chronicle was composed by its monks, a work that contains a number of continuations. The earliest portion of the chronicle spans the years from the founding of the abbey in 655 to 1089 and is ascribed to Ingulf, the Abbot of Croyland from 1085/1086 to 1089, though this portion of the chronicle is a medieval forgery and composed sometime in the fourteenth century. Peter of Blois (ca. 1130–1211), a well-known French poet, theologian, cleric, and diplomat was linked to the continuation, to 1148, but this too is spurious. At times the chronicle, especially these early parts, is referred to as the *Pseudo-Inglulf Chronicle*. The multiple fifteenth-century continuations of the chronicle (1144–1469, 1459–1468, and 1485–1486), however, are authentic and valuable sources, especially regarding events related to Richard III.

SOURCE

The Latin translation of the chronicle is from *Ingulph's Chronicle of the Abbey of Croyland*. Translated by Henry T. Riley. London: Henry G. Bohn, 1854. Pp. 413–14.

FURTHER READING

Edwards, J. G. "The 'Second' Continuation of the Crowland Chronicle: Was It Written in 'in ten days'?" *Bulletin of the Institute of Historical Research* XXXIX (1966): 117–29.

Gransden, 400; 490–92.

Pronay, Nicholas, and John Cox, ed. *The Crowland Chronicle Continuations: 1459–1486*. London: Richard III and Yorkist History Trust, 1986.

TRANSLATION

In this year, also being the year from the Incarnation of our Lord, 1448, upon Saint George's night,[1] towards daybreak, there happened a violent and terrible earthquake, respecting which, some teachers, remarkable for their knowledge, publicly prophesied that it was a prognostic of sinister events. Nor were they deceived in this presage. For, in the following summer, there was an extensive rising of the commons throughout nearly all of England, and a most dreadful commotion. But the common people of Kent, who had become quite used to attempts at change, showed much greater violence than all the rest. For, having first appointed over them a captain and leader,[2] they encamped upon the plain of Blackheath, and, in warlike form, fortified their position with pitfalls and embankments, and stakes driven into the ground. After this, presuming to make stull further rash attempts, they assaulted the citizens upon London Bridge, and, by force, entered the city; upon which, their said captain became elated to a pitch of extreme vanity, and being honored by the frantic mob as though he had been a king, fancied that there was no one to resist him, and that he was at liberty to do just as he pleased; and, accordingly, dragged the prisoners forth from the Tower, and, at the prompting of the clamorous multitude, had them beheaded, without any form of trial whatever. Besides this, turning his hand to rapine, and attended by a band of his satellites, he stripped one of the richest citizens to his utmost farthing, and plundered him of the whole of his property and goods; upon which, the rest of his fellow-citizens were greatly apprehensive for themselves, and, conjecturing for certain that he would be guilty of the like conduct towards them, speedily collected troops of armed men from every quarter, and manfully drove him out of the city. After the lapse of a short space of time he was caught, and, in conformity with the laws of the realm, was condemned to be beheaded and quartered as a traitor; and thus, did he unhappily terminate an unhappy existence.

NOTES

1. April twenty-third.
2. Jack Cade.

Chapter 8

From *John Stone's Chronicle*

OVERVIEW

John Stone (John of Canterbury, d. 1481) was a Benedictine monk of Christ's Church, Canterbury, where he served for over twenty-six years. He began writing his Latin chronicle in 1467, the fifteenth year of his life as a monk. The years of his chronicle are from 1415 to 1471/1472; he wrote about his duties within the convent as well as the liturgical life of the church. Many of the later entries in his chronicle reflect first-hand accounts told to him as well as personal observations.

MANUSCRIPT

Cambridge, Corpus Christy College Cambridge MS 417

SOURCE FOR TRANSLATION

John Stone's Chronicle: Christ Church Priory, Canterbury, 1417–1472. Selected, Translated, and Introduced by Meriel Connor. TEAMS Documents of Practice Series. Kalamazoo, MI: Medieval Institute Publications, 2010. Pp. 87–89. Used with permission. I have maintained Connor's footnotes, though for this volume the numbering begins with "1."

FURTHER READING

Connor, Meriel. "Brotherhood and Confraternity at Canterbury Cathedral Priory in the Fifteenth Century: The Evidence of John Stone's Chronicle." *Archaeologia Cantiana* 128 (2008): 143–64.

———. "Fifteenth-Century Monastic Obituaries: The Evidence of Christ Church Priory, Canterbury." In *Memory and Commemoration in Medieval England: Proceedings of the 2008 Harlaxton Symposium*, edited by Caroline M. Barron and Clive Burgess, 143–58. Harlaxton Medieval Studies 20. Donington: Shaun Tyas, 2010.

———. "The Political Allegiances of Christ Church Priory 1400–1472: The Evidence of John Stone's Chronicle." *Archaelogia Cantiana* 127 (2007): 393–406.

Gransden, 412–17.

Kaufman, Alexander. "Stone, John (John of Canterbury)." In *EMC* 2: 1393.

TRANSLATION

[1450]

The Duke of Suffolk

On the vigil of the apostles Philip and James [30 April] this year, which was a Friday, William de la Pole, duke of Suffolk, was captured at sea. And the following day, at dawn, he was beheaded at sea, and they threw his body together with [his] head onto the seashore, near the town of Dover. And the following day, the mayor of the town of Dover, and others, took up his body and carried it to the church of Saint Martin, and there he had exequies and three masses with music. The third Mass was celebrated by the prior of Dover in the parish church.

On the twenty second day of May, the Friday before Pentecost, Suffolk's body was carried to the church of Canterbury, and there he had exequies with three lessons.

His body was then carried to the church at Rochester.[1]

Jack Cade

On the third day of June this year, namely, on the vigil of Corpus Christi, a certain unknown person rose up in Kent who was called John Mortimer. And on the eighth day of June, he came close to Canterbury with four thousand men in a great camp between the church of Saint Michael at Harbledown and the church of Saint Dunstan [in Canterbury]. They waited for three hours, and afterwards he departed for Blackheath, and there he waited.[2]

William Ayscough, Bishop of Salisbury

On the twenty ninth day of June following, master William Ayscough, bishop of Salisbury, was killed close to Edington in the diocese of Salisbury in the county of Wiltshire.[3]

[Cade's Entry to London]

On the third day of July following, the aforesaid captain entered the city of London and accepted the keys to the gates of the city.[4] The following day, Sir James Fiennes, Lord Saye [and Sele], knight, and [gap in text—William] Crowmer, sheriff of Kent, and the clerk of the said sheriff, and another, were beheaded in a street called Cheap.[5]

Matthew Gough

And the following day, outside the walls of London, there was a battle and Matthew Gough was killed.[6]

On the twelfth day of July, the aforesaid captain [Jack Cade] was killed in the county of Sussex, in the parish of Heathfield.

NOTES

1. Rochester Cathedral Priory—a Benedictine foundation. By 1450, England was effectively ruled by Queen Margaret and the duke of Suffolk. In March 1450, growing discontent with the regime lead to Suffolk's impeachment for conspiracy, misuse of funds, misconduct in the French war, etc. He was on his way to exile when his ship was intercepted.

2. Cade's pseudonyms were John Mortimer and John Amend-All. Stone refers to him as *homo ignotus*, which could mean "unknown" or vulgar, base, or of low birth. Stone's careful choice of ambiguous wording on more than occasion may conceal sympathy for the supporters of the anointed king, Henry VI. Following Suffolk's murder, there was a popular rising in Kent petitioning for changes in government. Dissent was intensified by the passage of Suffolk's funeral cortege through the county. There was a fear that the king would take steps to punish the citizens of Kent for the murder of Suffolk. The Kentish rebels came to Canterbury to seek additional support. On 7 June, Cade was refused entry into Canterbury, and an attempt was made to negotiate access to the city.

3. As Cade's insurgents surrounded London, Ayscough, the king's confessor, retreated to Wiltshire, where he probably expected to be more secure. His baggage

train was plundered on the night of 28 June 1450, and the following day, a band of men took him from the monastery of the Bonhommes at Edington and killed him.

4. Cade gained entry into London by threatening to set fire to the bridge. In spite of his good intentions, disorder and violence resulted from the rebels' entry.

5. Fiennes's name was linked with those of Suffolk, Moleyns, and Ayscough. His son-in-law, William Crowmer, was a retainer of the late duke of Suffolk.

6. Gough, a Welsh captain, had a distinguished career in France and was involved in the negotiations with the French delegation led by the Bastard of Orléans. He was killed 5 July, during the battle on London Bridge.

Chapter 9

From the Middle English Prose *Brut*

OVERVIEW

The Middle English prose *Brut* is the title assigned to some 180 surviving texts that describe the history of England from its founding by Brutus to the concluding date of the chronicle. The earliest of the manuscripts that contain a Middle English prose *Brut* text is ca. 1400, but the majority of extant chronicles in this group are from the fifteenth and early sixteenth centuries. It was a popular work in the Middle Ages, for the Middle English version of the prose *Brut* survives in more manuscripts, except for two Wycliffite translations of the Bible. There are other *Brut* traditions, in Latin and Anglo-Norman; all told, there are over 240 manuscripts that contain *Brut* texts. The development of the texts of the *Brut* is complicated, but Lister Matheson has provided a magisterial study of the Middle English version that classifies the chronicles that have survived into six versions: The Common Version, The Extended Version, The Abbreviated Version, Peculiar Texts and Versions, Unclassified Texts, and Early Printed Editions; each of the first four versions also contain subcategories that divide the main version into more discrete units. The Middle English prose *Brut* texts of the fifteenth century were, and remain, an important resource for the learning and dissemination of the history, culture, and literature of England.

MANUSCRIPT

London, British Library MS Additional 10099

SOURCE FOR TRANSLATION

Brie, Friedrich W. D., ed. *The Brut or The Chronicles of England*. Part II. EETS, os 136. London: Oxford University Press, 1908. Pp. 516–20.

FURTHER READING

Bryan, Elizabeth. "Prose Brut, English." *EMC* 2: 1239–40.
Kennedy, 2611–47.
Kingsford, 113–39.
Marx, William, and Raluca Radulescu, ed. "Readers and Writers of the Prose *Brut*." Special issue, *Trivium* 36 (2006).
Matheson, 159–61.
———. "Printer and Scribe: Caxton, the *Polychronicon*, and the *Brut*." *Speculum* 60 (1985): 593–614.
Rajsic, Jaclyn, Erik Kooper, and Dominique Hoche, ed. *The Prose Brut and Other Late Medieval Chronicles: Books Have Their Histories: Essays in Honour of Lister M. Matheson*. Manuscript Culture in the British Isles 8. Woodbridge, UK: York Medieval Press, 2018.

TRANSLATION

How this year the was insurrection in Kent of the commons, of whom Jack Cade, an Irishman, was captain.

This year of our Lord, 1450, was the great grace of the Jubilee at Rome, where there was a great pardon, in so much that, from all places in Christendom, a great multitude of people went there.

This year was a great assembly and gathering together of the commons of Kent in great number, and [they] ordained themselves a captain called John Cade, an Irishman, who named himself Mortimer, cousin to the Duke of York. And this captain held these men together and made ordinances among them, and brought them to Blackheath, where he made a bill of petitions to the king and his council, and showed what injuries and oppressions the poor commons suffered. And all came under cover to his success. And he had a great multitude of people.

And on the 17th day on June, the king, many lords, captains, and men of war, went towards him to Blackheath. And when the captain of Kent understood the coming of the king with so much power, he withdrew himself with his people to Sevenoaks, a little village. And on the 28th day of June, he, being withdrawn and gone, the King came with his army set in order and arrayed to Blackheath. And by the advice of his council, [the king] sent Sir Humphrey Stafford, knight, and William Stafford, squire, two valiant captains, with certain people, to fight with the captain and to take and bring him and his accessories to the king, who went to Sevenoaks. And there the captain, with his fellowship, met with them and fought against them, and in conclusion slew them both, and many remained and would not surrender themselves nor flee. During this skirmish fell a great variance among the lords' men, and the common people, being at Blackheath against the lords and captains, saying plainly that they would not go to the captain of Kent, to assist and help him, if they might have the execution of the traitors being about the king, to which the king said "nay." And they said plainly that the Lord Saye, Treasurer of England, the Bishop of Salisbury, the Baron of Dudley, the Abbot of Gloucester, Daniel, and Trevilian, and many more, were traitors and worthy to be dead. Therefore, in order to please the lords' men and also some of the king's house, the Lord Saye was arrested and sent to the Tower of London.

And then the king, hearing the tidings of the death and overthrowing of the Staffords, withdrew himself to London, and from there to Kenilworth, for the King nor the lords did not trust their own household people.

Then, after the captain had his victory over the Staffords, quickly he took Sir Humphrey's sallet[1] and his brigandines,[2] struck full of gilded nails, and also his gilded spurs and arrayed himself like a lord and a captain and returned to Blackheath. To [Cade] again came to Blackheath the Archbishop of Canterbury and the Duke of Buckingham and spoke with him. And it was said they found him witty in his talking and request, and so they departed.

And on the third day of July he came and entered into London with all his people, and there did make a cry in the king's name and in his name that no man should rob nor take no man's goods but if he paid for it. And [he] came riding through the city in great pride and smote his sword upon London Stone in Canwikstrete.[3]

And he, being in the city, sent [men] to the Tower in order to have Lord Saye. And so they moved him and brought him to the Guildhall before the mayor and the aldermen, where he was examined. And the lord said that he would and ought to be judged by his peers. And the commons of Kent took him by force from the mayor and officers that kept him, and took him to a priest to make confession. And before he might have been half confessed, they brought him to the Standard in Cheapside and there smote off his head. And thus died the Lord Saye, Treasurer of England. After this, they set his head on a spear and carried it about in the city. And the same day, around Mile End, Crowmer was beheaded.

And the day before, at afternoon, the captain, with certain [persons] of his company, went to Philip Malpas' house and robbed him and took away many goods. And from there he went to Saint Margaret Pattens, to one Cherstis' house, and robbed him and took away many goods. Also, at this robbing, diverse men of London of their neighbors were at it, and took part with him. Because of this robbing, people's hearts fell from him, and every thrifty man was arrested[4] before he acted in the same manner. And there was many a man in London that [were] incited and would have delightfully seen a common robbery, which almighty God forbid! For it is to suppose that, if he had not robbed, he might have gone far before he had been resisted, for the king and all the lords of the realm of England were departed, except the Lord Scales, that was kept the Tower of London.

And on the fifth day of July he struck off a man's head in Southwark. And the night after, the mayor of London, the aldermen and the commons of the city concluded to drive away the captain and his host, and sent for Lord Scales in the Tower and to Matthew Gough, a captain of Normandy, that they would that night assail the captain and with those of Kent. And so they did. And [they] came to London Bridge, into Southwark, before the captain had any knowledge thereof, and there they fought with those that kept the bridge. And the Kentishmen went to arms and came to the bridge and attacked and fought with them, and took the bridge, and made those of London flee, and slew many of them. And this endured all night, to and fro, until nine o'clock in the morning. And at last they burnt the drawbridge, where many of those of London were drowned. In that night, Sutton, an alderman, was slain, [as was] Roger Heysant, and Matthew Gough, and many others.

And after this, the Chancellor of England sent to the captain a general pardon for him, and another for all of his company. And then they departed from Southwark, every man to his house. And when they were all departed and gone, there were proclamations made in Kent, Southsea, and in other places, that whatever man could take the captain, alive or dead, should have 1,000 marks.

And after this, one Alexander Iden, a squire of Kent, took him in a garden in Sussex, and in the taking of the captain, John Cade was slain, and after beheaded, and his head set on London Bridge.

And then quickly after, the king came into Kent, and ordered his justices sit at Canterbury and inquire who were the accessories to and the chief cause of this insurrection. And there were eight men judged to death in one day, and in other places more. And from there the king went into Sussex, and so into the west country, where a little before was slain the Bishop of Salisbury. And this year so many were judged to death that twenty-three heads stood upon London Bridge.

NOTES

1. A sallet is a light helmet.
2. Brigandines are body armor that protects the chest and back. It is typically made of heavy cloth or leather onto which small steel plates are attached.
3. Now Cannon Street; the name has undergone numerous name changes. London Stone is kept in an alcove at 111 Cannon Street.
4. The manuscript here reads "A-forde," but another Prose *Brut* manuscript, London, British Library MS Harley 53, here reads "Arested," which is a preferred reading.

Chapter 10

From *A Chronicle of London* in London, British Library MS Cotton Vitellius A XVI

OVERVIEW

The manuscript London, British Library MS Cotton Vitellius A XVI is made up of three different chronicles, written by several scribes. The section of the Cade Rebellion, below, comes from the second Middle English London chronicle in the manuscript, which covers the years of 1440 to 1496. McLaren places this chronicle in The Egerton 1995 Group, which includes *Gregory's Chronicle* (a selection from this chronicle is in this volume), although she notes that "there are more variations between these manuscripts" than between other groups of London chronicles (104). Kingsford notes that the portion of this chronicle devoted to the Cade Rebellion is "a long and valuable account" (102).

MANUSCRIPT

London, British Library MS Cotton Vitellius A XVI

SOURCE FOR TRANSLATION

Kingsford, Charles Lethbridge, ed. *Chronicles of London*. Oxford: Clarendon Press, 1905. Pp. 158–62.

FURTHER READING

Kennedy, 2647–50.
Kingsford, 101–3.
McLaren, 105–6.
Radulescu, Raluca. "London Chronicles." In *EMC* 2: 1042–43.

TRANSLATION

In this year, there was a parliament held at Westminster, and from there [it] adjourned to the Blackfriars, and after Christmas to Westminster again. During that parliament the Duke of Suffolk was arrested and put into the Tower, and a great watch was made in the city all the time of the parliament. And after Easter the parliament was adjourned to Leicester, and there continued until after Whitsuntide. In that time, the aforesaid Duke was delivered out of the Tower, for which delivering all the commons of England were in a great tumult for the losing of Anjou and Maine, but most especially for the death of the good Duke of Gloucester. Inasmuch that in some places they assembled them together, and made them captains, as Bluebeard and others, which were resisted, taken, and put to death.

And during this parliament the Duke of Suffolk was banished [from] the land for five years; and shortly after this he went into Norfolk, and took ships there. And a ship called the *Nicholas of the Tower* met with him upon the sea, and took him and brought him to Dover, and there struck off his head, and laid the body upon land upon the sands. Moreover, this year was a great assembly of the commons of Kent, which came down to Blackheath in June, and there made their field, abiding there seven days.

When the king heard about this, being at Leicester, he assembled his lords, and [they] came all in haste against the Kentishmen, and at his coming sent several lords to them to know their intent. And when these lords came to their captain, named Jack Cade, otherwise Mortimer, cousin to the Duke of York as the said captain named himself, he said he and his people had come to redress many points whereby the king's subjects and commons were grievously wronged; but his final purpose was to rob, as after it shall appear. Therefore, it was agreed that Sir Humphrey Stafford, knight, and Sir William Stafford, esquire, and another squire with them, should follow the chase. And at Sevenoaks in Kent they met and fought with the captain and his company, where the said Sir Humphrey and his company lost the field, and Sir Humphrey Stafford and William his brother with many others there were slain.

And in this season, the king's people were laying still upon the heath, several of the commons and of the lords' men said plainly, if they might not have the execution of certain traitors about the king's person, they would leave their masters and go unto the captain and take his side; which [traitors] were the Lord Saye, that time treasurer of England, the Bishop of Salisbury, the Abbot of Gloucester, Daniel, Trevilian, and many more. Therefore, the king sent Lord Saye into the Tower. And then the king, hearing of this attack on the Staffords, removed [himself] from Greenwich to London, and from London to Kenilworth, for the king nor his lords did not trust their own household servants. And when the captain had thus, as you have heard, attacked the Staffords, right away he took the sallet and the brigadiers of Sir Humphrey, set full of gilded nails, and also his gilded spurs, and arrayed himself like a lord. And after [he] returned to Blackheath with more people than he had before, which was upon Saint Peter's Day.

Then came to the captain the Bishop of Canterbury and the Duke of Buckingham, and there spoke with him, whom they found very wise and well advised among his commons. And the first day of July he with his people came into Southwark, and because he might not enter the city, he lay there that night.[1] And the same day the commons of Essex came to Mile End to accompany the said captain. And upon the morning the commons of the city went into the Guildhall by a summons made by a commission, which was sent from the king to certain lords, and to the mayor and to several justices to inquire of all persons who were traitors, extortioners, or oppressors of the king's people; but the justices would not be found. Therefore, the citizens were fully content toward evil. Nevertheless, certain inquests were called; and while the mayor sat, the commons shouted angrily upon Philip Malpas to have him discharged of his duty, and so he was immediately; and Robert Horne, another alderman, by instigation of the people, was arrested there and committed to Newgate.

And the same day at five in the afternoon the captain came into the city by force. And in his entrance at the bridge he hewed the ropes of the drawbridge asunder. And when he came to Saint Magnus he a made a proclamation upon pain of death, that no man of his army should rob nor despoil no man within the city. An in the same manner [he declared this] at Leadenhall and so through the city with great pride. And at London Stone he struck upon it like a conqueror, and so being in the city sent into the Tower for the Lord Saye, and he was obtained and brought into the Guildhall, where he was indicted with others for treason. And upon the same day the captain sent for Robert Horne, alderman, where with great labor of his friends he escaped with his life, and ransomed at a great sum of money; and so were others deal with in like manner.

And while the mayor was at the hall the captain came again into the city and went into Fleet [Street], and from there toward one Crowmer, a squire, that had wedded the Lord Saye's daughter and had been Sheriff of Kent, and had done much extortion there, as they said. Meanwhile the Lord Saye, being there at the Guildhall before the mayor and the king's justice, desired to be judged by his peers; but the Kentishmen would not allow that, but by force and strength took him out of the Guildhall and brought him into the Standard in Cheap, and there smote off his head, and after set it upon a spear and bore it about the city. And the same day at Mile End, Crowmer, before named, was beheaded, upon whose soil Jesus have mercy. And the same day, before the beading of Crowmer, the captain with a certain [number of persons] with him went into Philip Malpas' house, and robbed him of many goods. And from there he went into one Gest's house, beside Tower Street, and there dines, and in the like manner robbed him. And it is to be remembered that when Crowmer was beheaded that same season was also beheaded a man that was called Bailey; and after they brought the heads of the Lord Saye and of Crowmer upon two stakes or poles, and in several places of the city put them together, causing one to kiss the other. And when the citizens saw that he had robbed Philip Malpas and Gest, those that were supportive [now] doubted. As such, in case afterward he would rob them in the same manner, they withdrew hearts and love from him. For if he had not fallen to robbery, it is to assume he might have gone far in the land, for the king and all the lords were departed, except for Lord Scales that kept the Tower.

Then the fifth day of July he smote off a man's head in Southwark, and the same night following the mayor, the aldermen, with the thrifty commons of the city concluded to drive away the captain and his army. Wherefore they sent for the Lord Scales and to one Matthew Gough, a Captain of Normandy, that they would that night assail the captain and his people. So they did, and at the Bridge was a sore and long fight, where sometime the city had the better and sometime the Kentishmen. And thus they fought all the night until nine o'clock the next morning. And lastly they burnt the drawbridge, and in doing so many men of the city were drowned. And in that fight an alderman named Sutton was slain, Roger Heysant, and Matthew Gough, and many others.

And after this the Chancellor of England, upon the morning after, granted all the Kentishmen with their captain a general pardon. And so they departed every man to his own [dwelling]. And when all were departed and gone there were made proclamations, that what man could take the captain, quick or dead, should have one-thousand marks for his labor; after which proclamations [were] made one Alexander Iden, gentleman of Kent, took him in a garden in Sussex; but in the taking the captain was slain. And so [he was] brought into Southwark so that all men might see him, and that night [he was] left in the king's bench, and from there he was drawn to Newgate, and then beheaded and quartered; and his head set upon London Bridge. And his four quarters were sent to several towns in Kent. And shortly after the king rode into Kent and commanded his justices to sit at Canterbury to inquire who were the accessories and causers of this insurrection. And there eight men [were] judged to death in one day, and in other places more. And from there the king rode into Sussex, and from there into the west country, where a little [time] before was slain the Bishop of Salisbury. And this year, so many were judged to death that twenty-three heads stood upon London Bridge. Upon whose souls Jesus have mercy. And the same year a little before Michaelmas the Duke of York came out of Ireland.

NOTE

1. The suggestion here is that the city officials had not given Cade and his company permission to enter into London.

Chapter 11

From *The Great Chronicle of London*

OVERVIEW

The Great Chronicle of London survives in a single manuscript: London, Metropolitan Archives CLC/270/MS03313. It was formerly known as London, Guildhall Library, MS Guildhall 3313; and before that, the Baginton Hall Manuscript. Charles Lethbridge Kingsford assigned to the Middle English chronicle the current title of the volume, and he made known that it was "the best representative of the [now lost] Main City Chronicle" (100). McLaren places this manuscript and its text within the Saint John's 57 Group of London chronicles. The manuscript had a number of prominent owners: John Stow, the chronicler; John Foxe, the martyrologist; and perhaps the chronicler Edward Hall. Two scribes copied the manuscript, which is in two parts. Robert Fabyan wrote the second half, though McLaren disagrees with Stow's, Kingford's, the Thonleys', and Boffey's assessment that he is the author of the manuscript. *The Great Chronicle of London* also includes numerous annotations by later, sixteenth-century owners, John Stow being one such industrious annotator. At 369 folios, it is one of the longest of the chronicles of London. The chronicle covers the years from 1189 to 1512, and it provides lengthy and fascinating details of life in medieval London: pageants and processions, uprisings, trials, accounts of battle, events related to local and national government, guild activities, weather, and prophecies. In short, this chronicle is a treasure-trove of information about life in medieval London.

MANUSCRIPT

London, Metropolitan Archives CLC/270/MS03313

SOURCE FOR TRANSLATION

Thomas, A. H., and I. D. Thornley, ed. *The Great Chronicle of London*. London: The Sign of the Dolphin, 1939; repr., Gloucester: Alan Sutton, 1983. Pp. 181–85.

FURTHER READING

Boffey, Julia. *Manuscript and Print in London c. 1475–1530*. London: The British Library, 2012.
———. "Robert Fabyan's Two Hats: Compiling *The Great Chronicle of London* and *The New Chronicles of England and France*." In *Editing and Interpretation of Middle English Texts: Essays in Honour of William Marx*, edited by Margaret Connolly and Raluca Radulescu, 171–88. Texts & Transitions 12. Turnhout: Brepols, 2018.
Gransden, 227–32.
Kennedy, 2647–52.
Kingsford, 100–101.
McLaren, 26–28; 100–103.
Radulescu, Raluca. "London Chronicles." In *EMC* 2: 1042–43.

TRANSLATION

This year [1449] the king called a parliament at Westminster, and from there convened to the Black Friars at London where it continued until Christmas. After that feast [1450], it was again convened to Westminster, and while it continued the Marquis of Suffolk was arrested and placed under protection. And a great watch was kept both day and night for the duration of the session of this parliament. And after Easter, the court was removed to Leicester, and there it continued until Whitsuntide.[1]

At this time the Marquis of Suffolk was released to the great resentment of the commons of this land. Thus, shortly after a company assembled themselves and chose a captain whom they named Bluebeard. But they were quickly opposed, rounded up, and all punished.

And the above named Marquis of Suffolk was deemed by the authority of the parliament to be banished from this land for five years, whereupon he rode into Norfolk, where he intended to board a ship so as to sail to France. But as he kept his course on the sea, a ship named the *Nicholas of the Tower*, which was manned with English men, took him and brought him back to Dover Road, and there on the ship's side struck off his head and after laid the body with the head upon the land and then departed again to the sea.

It was not long after that the commons of Kent assembled themselves in great number and chose for themselves a captain and named him Jack Cade. And afterward they traveled toward the city and into Blackheath, and there they mustered in the month of June in great number. How plentiful they were but poorly dressed in armor.

In this season, the king being at Leicester and hearing of the rebellion, departed quickly to London and lodged within the Tower. And from there he made provisions to push back Jack Cade and his company. As such, understanding this and of the king's great power, they withdrew backward to a town named Sevenoaks. Then the king with his host approached onwards to Blackheath, and seeing that the rebels were departed was advised by such lords who were then about him, considering that they were but commons and not one noble man among them, that his grace nor none of his lords should take no further action, but to appoint some petty captain with a sufficient power to follow them, and to disperse and break them up. Whereupon, a knight named Sir Humphrey Stafford and his brother William Stafford were finally assigned, with other petty captains and with them a number of soldiers such that the king and his lords were thought to be sufficient for that journey. And so they departed toward the rebels, and at the aforesaid village of Sevenoaks encountered the said rebels and there engaged them in battle.

But fortune was so badly on the Staffords' side, for they were slain there and much of their people, and the rest fled and were chased. This victory gave the rebels great boldness and comfort, insomuch that many who before had withdrawn from them now returned, and with them many more, so that after this fighting this captain Jack Cade was hugely fortified. And then to advance his pride he put on himself the armor of the aforesaid Sir Humphrey, of velvet garnished with gilded nails and his salet[2] and gilded spurs. And so a knave was made a king. Afterward, he with his people then marched again toward London. Then the king, hearing of the defeat of the Staffords, left Greenwich for London, and from London [traveled] to Kenilworth. During that time certain captains with an effective army controlled the field of Blackheath for the king's use, but among them was such a murmur of words that the captains feared their own warriors but were afraid to say that the captain of Kent was in a just and rightful quarrel. For the king was ruled by flattery and false counsel from Lord Saye, then Treasurer of England, the Bishop of Salisbury, the Abbot of Gloucester, Daniel, Trevilian, and others. The people, except those who were removed from the king's office, would assist the said captain and take his side. After this news was disclosed, and learning of the increasing [size] of the captain's company, and of his returning to London, the said captains of the king's people ceased their battle and returned toward the king.

And Jack Cade with his followers came to Blackheath upon Saint Peter's day, or upon the twenty-ninth day of June, at which time the intent was that he would be made famous as a true and good justice. He there beheaded a petty captain named Parys, but for what offence it is not showed. And all such proclamations that were made by him were proclaimed in the name of King Henry VI, and he called himself John Mortimer, cousin to the Duke of York, and there he fortified himself and his [assembly] with a strong army.

When the king and his counsel were advised of all of these things, they feared the followers of him, and all the more so because they mistrusted their own household servants. As such, in redress of this mischief, by the king's commandment the Archbishop of Canterbury and the Duke of Buckingham were sent to the said captain, who handled him in a courteous and loving manner and offered to him in the king's name a special pardon for himself and a general [pardon] for all his company with other things that he would lawfully desire that were not contrary to the king's honor. But when he had heard with good manner and discretion all that the lords would say, he answered with good deliberation that he and the others of his company were coming as the king's true subjects to reform the well being of this land, which had been long disorderly by a few persons about the king, to the great dishonor of the king and his nobles of the realm as those two and others were, and to the utter impoverishing and undoing of all the king's true commons, as many things it appeared were daily put into execution by the said few persons. Therefore, he entreated the said lords that they and others, who were his true counselors, would be a good representative of the king's grace, and that the said few persons might be removed from the king and have such lawful punishment as they greatly deserved, for he said that he knew well that the said commons would not return until they had seen the said few persons executed. And to justify his speech, he then asked those who stood near about whether they would return or not, and they cried exceedingly "Nay Nay" in such a passionate manner that it was long before he could quiet them of their outcry.

And so as soon as the lords had inquired about him, what few persons he and his company had discovered to be disrespectful he immediately entreated the said lords that they would not command him to disclose their names, for they knew well that if their names were known the parties would withdraw themselves to such places that they should not lightly be captured. With that answer the lords departed, except that this desire of the captain was thought not to stand with the king's honor that such mean persons should take upon themselves the king's authority, and their request was not considered. Afterward, the said captain with his accomplices came upon the first day of July into Southwark, and thereafter he was denied by the mayor to enter the city, and he lodged himself there and much of his people. And the same day the commons of Essex in a great number came into Mile End to support the said captain. At this time the king and all the lords left from their lodgings close to London and left the city without aid except for themselves, which was not of one mind nor will. Then upon the third day of July the citizens by virtue of a commission authorized by the king, where, before the mayor and other commissioners, they were charged to inquire about all traitors, extortioners, and oppressors of the king's people, during which business the commons cried out excessively against Philip Malpas to have him discharged from his cloak, and so he was immediately, and Robert Horne and other aldermen by instigation of the people were there arrested and committed to Newgate, and the same day at five in the afternoon the captain came into the city with an equal force [to the king's], and during his entrance at the Bridge he cut the ropes at the drawbridge asunder. And when he came to Saint Magnus he made a proclamation, upon pain of death, that no man of his host should rob nor despoil no man within the city, and in a similar manner [he proclaimed this] at Leadenhall and throughout the city with great pride. And at London Stone he struck upon it like a conqueror. And as he was in the city he sent for Lord Saye from the Tower, and he was taken and brought into the Guildhall where he was indicted with others of treason. And upon the same morning the captain sent for Robert Horne, alderman, where with great labor of his friends he escaped with his life and was ransomed at a great sum of money, and so were others dealt with in a similar manner. And while the mayor was at the hall, the captain came again into the city and went into the hall, and from there [to find] one Crowmer, a squire who had married Lord Saye's daughter and had been sheriff of Kent and had done much extortion there as they said. In the meantime, the Lord Saye was at the Guildhall before the mayor and the king's justices, who desired him to be to be judged by his peers, but the Kentishman would not allow that, and by force and strength brought him to the Standard at Cheap and there smote off his head, and after set his head upon a spear and carried it about the city. And the same day before the beheading of Crowmer the captain with a certain number of persons with him went into Philip Malpas' house and robbed him of many goods. And from there he went to one Gest's house beside Tower Street and dined there and robbed him in the same manner. And it is to be remembered that when Crowmer was beheaded at the same time a man who was called Bailey was also beheaded, and after they brought the heads of the Lord Saye and Crowmer upon two stakes or polls, and in many places in the city put them together causing one to kiss the other. And when the citizens saw that he had robbed Philip Malpas and Gest, those who were wealthy believed very strongly that afterward he would rob them in the same way, and they withdrew their hearts and love from him, for if he had not been tempted by robbery it is believed that he might have gone far in the land, for the king and all the lords were departed, except the Lord Scales who kept the Tower.

Then the fifth day of July he smote off a man's head in Southwark, and the same night following [this] the mayor, the aldermen, and the honorable commoners of the city decided to drive away the captain and his host. Therefore they sent [word] to Lord Scales and to one Matthew Gough, a captain of Normandy, that they would that night assail the captain and his people. And so they did, and at the Bridge was a sore and a long fight where sometimes the city had the better and sometimes the Kentishmen, and thus they fought all the night until nine o'clock in the morning. And in the end, they burned the drawbridge by intent, from which many men of the city were drowned. And in that fight an alderman named Sutton was slain, Roger Heysant, and Matthew Gough, and many others. And after this the Chancellor of England on the morning after granted all the Kentishmen with their captain a general pardon. And so they departed, every man, to his own [dwelling]. And when all were departed and gone, there were made proclamations that whatever man could take the captain quick or dead should have 1,000 marks for his labor. After those proclamations were made one Alexander Iden, gentleman of Kent, took him in a garden in Sussex, but in the taking the said captain was slain, and so brought to Southwark so that all men might see him and that night left [him] in the King's Bench. And from there he was drawn to Newgate and then beheaded and quartered and his head set upon London Bridge. And his four quarters were sent to four separate towns in Kent. And soon after the king rode into Kent and commanded his justices to sit at Canterbury to inquire who were the accessories and causers of this insurrection. And then there were seven men judged to death on one day and in other places more. And from there the king rode into Sussex, and from there to the west country, where a short time before the Bishop of Salisbury was slain. And this year there were so many judged to death that twenty-three heads stood upon London Bridge, upon whose souls and all Christians, God, to his pleasure, have mercy. Amen.

NOTES

1. This is the festival week that begins on the seventh Sunday following Easter. It is also known as "Whitsun," "Whitsunday," or more commonly nowadays, "Pentecost." It celebrates the descent of the Holy Ghost to his apostles.

2. A sallet is a light helmet that is in the shape of a bowl that extends in the back. Sometimes it contains a visor.

Chapter 12

From Robert Fabyan's *The New Chronicles of England and France*

OVERVIEW

Robert Fabyan (d. 1513) was a London draper and alderman of the ward of Farrington Without in 1494. He served as an auditor of the city accounts from 1496 to 1487, and was the city's sheriff in 1493. He is someone who knew municipal life and work quite well and had access to records that informed his writing. Fabyan was the author of the *New Chronicles of England and France*, written in Middle English, a seven book chronicle of England that commemorates the seven joys of Mary. The first book begins with the founding of England by Brutus, while the final book is a chronicle of London that begins in 1189 with the ascension of Richard I; Fabyan completed his work in 1504. Kennedy observes that the history does not "have the Yorkist bias of the London chronicles, but is hostile to Edward IV and Richard III and sides with Henry VII" (2654). Fabyan was one of the two scribes of *The Great Chronicle of London* (a selection of which is included in this volume). Julia Boffey's study of Fabyan's two chronicles provides a valuable discussion of the authorial and editorial decisions that the chronicler made, especially in regards to different reading audiences that he may have had in mind.

MANUSCRIPTS

London, British Library MS Cotton Nero C XI
Norfolk, Holkham Hall MS 671

SOURCE FOR TRANSLATION

Fabyan, Robert. *The New Chronicles of England and France, in Two Parts.* Edited by Henry Ellis. London: F. C. and J. Rivington, et al., 1811. Pp. 622–25.

FURTHER READING

Boffey, Julia. *Manuscript and Print in London c. 1475–1530.* London: The British Library, 2012.
———. "Robert Fabyan's Two Hats: Compiling *The Great Chronicle of London* and *The New Chronicles of England and France*." In *Editing and Interpretation of Middle English Texts: Essays in Honour of William Marx*, edited by Margaret Connolly and Raluca Radulescu, 171–88. Texts & Transitions 12. Turnhout: Brepols, 2018.
Gransden, 245–48.
Kennedy, 2654–55.
McLaren, M-R. "Fabyan, Robert." In *ODNB*.
Neumaier, Marco. "Fabyan, Robert." In *EMC* 1: 604–5.

TRANSLATION

In the month of June this year [1450] the commons of Kent assembled themselves in great multitude, and chose for them a captain, and named him Mortimer, and cousin to the Duke of York. But to most he was named Jack Cade. This kept the people wondrously together, and [he] made such ordinances among them that he brought a great number of people of them into Blackheath, where he devised a bill of petitions to the king and his council, and showed therein what injuries and oppressions the poor commons suffered by such as were about the king, a few persons in number, and all under color to come to his office. The king's council, seeing this bill, disallowed it, and counselled the king, which, by the seventh day of June, had gathered to him a strong host of people, to go against his rebels, and to give unto them battle. Then the king, after the said rebels had held their field upon Blackheath seven days, made toward them. Thus, hearing [this], the captain drew back with his people to a village called Sevenoaks, and there made ready for battle.

Then it was agreed by the king's council that Sir Humphrey Stafford, knight, with William, his brother, and other certain gentlemen, should follow the chase, and the king and his lords should return to Greenwich, presuming that the rebels were fled and gone. But as before I have showed, when Sir

Humphrey with is company drew near toward Sevenoaks, he was warned that the captain remained there with his people. And when he had counselled with the other gentlemen, he, like a courageous knight, set upon the rebels and fought with them long. But in the end, the captain slew him and his brother, and many others, and caused the rest to retreat. All during this season the king's host lay still upon Blackheath, being among them sundry opinions, so that some and many favored the captain. But finally, when word came of the overthrow of the Staffords, they said plainly and boldly, that except the Lord Saye and others before reported were committed to confinement, they would take the captain's party. For the appeasing of this rumor, the Lord Saye was put into the Tower, but those others at that time were not at hand. Then the king, having knowledge of the defeat of his men, and also of the rumor of his encamping people, removed from Greenwich to London, and there with his host rested himself awhile.

And so, soon as Jack Cade had thus overcome the Staffords, he at once appareled himself with the knight's apparel, and placed on himself his brigadiers set with gilded nails, and his sallet[1] and gilded spurs. And after he had refreshed his people, he returned again to Blackheath, and there prepared his field, as before he had done, and lay there from the 29th day of June, being Saint Peter's Day, until the first day of July. At this time the Archbishop of Canterbury came toward him, and the Duke of Buckingham, with whom they had long communication, and found him truly discreet in his answers. Nevertheless, they could not cause him to lay down his people and to submit himself unto the king's grace.

In this time, the king and queen, hearing of the increasing of his rebels, and also the lords fearing their own servants, lest they would take the captain's party, removed from London to Kenilworth, leaving the city without aid, except only the Lord Scales, who was left to keep the Tower, and with him a manly and wary man named Matthew Gough. Then the captain of Kent, thus standing at Blackheath, intending to blind more of the people, and to bring himself in fame that he kept good justice, beheaded there a petty captain named Parys,[2] for so much as he had offended again such ordinances as he had established in his host. And hearing that the king and all of his lords were thus departed, [he] drew himself near into the city, and upon the first day of July he entered the borough of Southwark, being then Wednesday, and lodged himself there that night, for he might not allowed to enter that city.

And upon the same day, the commons of Kent, in great number, prepared themselves a field upon a plain at Mile End. Upon the second day of the said month, the mayor called a common council at the Guildhall to discuss the withstanding of these rebels and other matters, in which assembly were diverse opinions, so that some thought good that the rebels should be received into the city, and some otherwise. Among the which, Robert Horne, stockfish monger,[3] then being an alderman, spoke sore against those that would have him enter. For these sayings, the commons were very annoyed against him, that they ceased not until they had taken him into custody.

And the same afternoon, about five o'clock, the captain with his people entered by the bridge. And when he came upon the drawbridge, he cut the ropes that drew the bridge in sunder with his sword, and so passed into the city, and made in sundry places proclamations in the king's name, that no man, [upon] pain of death, should rob or take anything by force without paying for it. By this reason he won many hearts of the commons of the city. But all was done to beguile the people, as after shall evidently appear. He rode through diverse streets of the city, and as he came by London Stone, he struck it with his sword and said, "Now is Mortimer lord of the city." And when he had thus showed himself in diverse places of the city, and showed his intention to the mayor for the receiving of his people, he returned to Southwark, and there stayed as he before had done, his people coming and going at lawful hours when they would. Then upon the morning, being the third day of July and Friday, the said captain entered again the city, and caused the Lord Saye to be brought from the Tower and led into the Guildhall, where he was arraigned before the mayor and others of the king's justices. Previously, he intended to have brought before the said justices the aforesaid Robert Horne, but his wife and friends made to him such urgent distress, that finally, for 500 marks, he was released on his liberty. Then the Lord Saye being, as before is said, at the Guildhall, desired that he might be judged by his peers. Whereby hearing [this], the captain sent a company of his into the hall, and by force took him from his officers and so brought him into the Standard in Cheap where, before he was half confessed, they struck off his head. And that done, placed it upon a long pole, and so bore it about with them.

In this time and season had the captain caused a gentleman to be taken, named William Crowmer, who before had been sheriff of Kent, and engaged, as they said, in some extortions. For which cause, or because he had favored the Lord Saye, by reason that he had married his daughter, he was harried to Mile End, and there, in the captain's presence, beheaded. And the same time was there also beheaded another man, called [William] Bailey, the cause of whose death was this, as I have heard some men report. This Bailey was an associate and old acquaintance of Jack Cade. Thus, as soon as he learned of him coming to him protected, he cast in his mind that he would discover his life and old manners and show of his vile kin and lineage. Thus, knowing that the said Bailey used to bear scrolls and prophecy about him, showing to his company that he was an enchanter and all ill disposition, and that they should well know by such books as he bore upon him, and bade them search, and if they found as he said, that they should put him to death, which all was done according to his commandment.

When they had thus beheaded these two men, they took the head of Crowmer and put it upon a pole, and so entered the city with the heads of the Lord Saye and Crowmer. And as they passed the streets, [they] joined the poles together and caused either dead mouth to kiss the other many different times.

And the captain, the very same day, went into the house of Philip Malpas, draper and alderman, and robbed and pillaged his house, and took from there much property. But he was before warned, and thereby conveyed much of his money and plate,[4] or else he would have been done.

Then, toward night, he returned to Southwark, and upon the morning reentered the city and dined that day at a place in Saint Margaret Pattens Parish, called [John] Gest's house. And when he had dined, like an uncourteous guest, [he] robbed him, as the day before he had Malpas. For these two robberies, albeit, that the poor and needy people drew unto him and were partners in that ill, the honest and thrifty commoners cast in their minds the consequence of this matter and feared that they should be dealt with in a like manner. In this manner, thus, he lost the people's favor and hearts. For it was to be thought, if he had not executed that robbery, he might have gone far and brought his purpose to good effect, if he had intended well. But it is to demean and presuppose that the intent of him as not good. Therefore, it might not come to any good conclusion. Then the mayor and aldermen, with assistance of the worshipful commoners, seeing this bad demeanor of the captain, for the safeguarding of themselves and of the city, got counsel on how they might drive the captain and his adherents from the city, because their fear was great, for the king and his lords with their powers were far from them. But yet, in avoiding the apparent peril, they consented that they would withstand any more entrance of his into the city. For the accomplishment of this, the mayor sent for Lord Scales and Matthew Gough, [who] then held control of the Tower, and had them assent to accomplish the same.

Then upon the fifth day of July, the captain, being at Southwark, caused more to be beheaded, for the cause of displeasure done to him, as the report went. And so [he] kept himself in Southwark all that day. Nevertheless, he might have entered the city if he had the ability.

And when night was coming, the mayor and citizens, with Matthew Gough, in favor of their former appointment, kept the passage of the bridge, being Sunday, and defeated the Kentishmen, which made a great force to reenter the city. Then the captain, seeing this fighting begin, went to arm himself and called his people about him, and attacked so fiercely upon the citizens that he drew them back from the gateposts in Southwark and the bridge foot, into the drawbridge. Then the Kentishmen set fire upon the drawbridge. In defending [the drawbridge], many a man was drowned and slain, among whom of men of status was John Sutton, alderman; Matthew Gough, gentleman; and Roger Heysant. And thus continued this skirmish all night until nine o'clock in the morning, so that sometime the citizens had the better, and thus sometimes the Kentishmen were on the better side. But always they kept themselves upon the bridge, so that the citizens never passed more than the bulwark at the bridge foot, nor the Kentishmen much farther than the drawbridge. Thus continuing this cruel fight, to the destruction of much people on both sides, lastly, after the Kentishmen were given the worst of the battle, a truce was agreed for a certain time. During this truce, the Archbishop of Canterbury, then Chancellor of England, sent a general pardon to the captain for himself, and another for the people. By reason whereof, he and his company departed the same night out of Southwark, and so returned every man to his own [place].

But it was not long after that that the captain with his company was thus departed that proclamations were made in diverse places of Kent, Sussex, and Southery, that who might take the foresaid Jack Cade, either alive or dead, should have a thousand marks for his travail. After this proclamation [was] thus published, a gentleman in Kent, named Alexander Iden, awaited so his time that he took him in a garden in Sussex, where in the taking of him the said Jack was slain. And so being dead [he] was brought into Southwark the . . . day of the month of September and there left in the king's bench for that night.[5] And upon the morning, the dead corpse was drawn through the high streets of the city into Newgate and there beheaded and quartered. [Cade's] head was then sent to London Bridge and his four quarters were sent to four sundry towns of Kent.

And this [being] done, the king sent his commissions into Kent and rode after himself, and caused an inquiry be made of this riot in Canterbury, where for the same eight men were judged and put to death. And in other towns of Kent and Sussex, diverse others were executed for the same riot.

NOTES

1. A sallet is a light helmet.
2. Griffiths notes that a "John Parys was living at Rye on the eve of the revolt," 652n32.
3. Stockfish is dried fish.
4. "Plate" here refers to works of gold or silver used in the house, such as pitcher, dishes, and candlesticks.
5. Fabyan does not include a specific date in "September"; moreover, his timeline is too late as by 17 July 1450 the "mayor and sheriffs of Norwich were sent a quarter [of Cade's body] to place on their city gate," Harvey, 100.

Chapter 13

From John Mair's *Historia Maioris Britanniae tam Angliae quam Scotiae* (History of Greater Britain)

OVERVIEW

John Mair/Major (ca. 1467–1550) was a Scottish theologian, philosopher (especially ethics, logic, and metaphysics) and historian. His chronicle is the history of Scotland, Ireland, and England from their beginning through the reign of Henry VIII, and it is the representative of Renaissance humanism. Mair taught theology at le collège de Robert Sorbon, (which later was named le Collège de Sorbon, and finally La Sorbonne). He spent almost twenty five years there, writing at least forty six books, many of which were issued in multiple editions and served as textbooks in leading theological programs. In 1518, Mair left Paris and returned to Scotland, where he became the principal of the University of Glasgow; in 1523, he became dean of the faculty of theology at University of Saint Andrews. Mair returned to Paris in 1526 to teach and to write, and his final book, a commentary on Aristotle's *Nicomachean Ethics*, was published in 1530. Mair returned to Scotland (and to Saint Andrews) in 1531, where he lived for the rest of his life. As a humanist, a key theme in Mair's *History* is a desire for balance in both political thoughts and actions.

SOURCE FOR TRANSLATION

Major, John. *A History of Greater Britain As Well England and Scotland.* Translated and edited by Archibald Constable. Scottish History Society. Vol. 10. Edinburgh: Edinburgh University Press, 1892. Pp. 374–77. Reprinted by permission of The Scottish Historical Society.

FURTHER READING

Broadie, Alexander. *The Circle of John Mair: Logic and Logicians in Pre-Reformation Scotland*. Oxford: Clarendon Press, 1985.

———. *A History of Scottish Philosophy*. Edinburgh: Edinburgh University Press, 2009.

———. "Mair [Major], John." In *ODNB*.

Kaufman, Alexander L. "John Mair's Historiographical Humanism: Portraits of Outlaws, Robbers, and Rebels in His *Historia Maioris Britanniae tam Angliae quam Scotiae* (*History of Greater Britain*)." *Enarratio* 19 (2015): 104–18.

———. "Mair, John [John Major]." In *EMC* 2: 1060.

Mason, Roger A. "From Chronicle to History: Recovering the Past in Renaissance Scotland." In *Building the Past/Konstruktion der eigenen Vergangenheit*, edited by Rudolf Suntrup and Jan R Veenstra, 53–66. Medieval to Early Modern Culture/Kultureller Wandel vom Mittelalterzur Frühen Neuzei 7. Frankfurt am Main: Peter Lang, 2006.

———. *Kingship and the Commonweal: Political Thought in Renaissance and Reformation Scotland*. East Lothian: Tuckwell Press, 1998.

TRANSLATION

In the year 1448, in Henry's reign, did the duke of Somerset and the earl of Shrewsbury altogether abandon Rouen and Normandy; and in as much as the duke of Suffolk was reckoned to be the cause of this action of theirs, he was kept as a prisoner in the tower of London; and when he had been there for a month, he was set at liberty. There was a mighty stir among the people at this and also at the death of the duke of Gloucester. A parliament, however, was continued to be held in the presence of the king, but the place of its meeting was changed to Leicester, and the duke of Suffolk was present at this parliament. The commonalty, however, did not cease from their murmurs and their complaints against the duke of Suffolk, the lord Saye, and the bishop of Salisbury; and to appease the people, a decree of banishment for a period was passed against Suffolk; but while he was on board ship, he was taken as a prisoner by someone and was killed.

In the year 1450, the same when the jubilee was held at Rome, the people of Kent rose against the king, and, as they were drawing near to London, routed the king's army that had been sent out to meet them. And when the servants of the noble families—for these men belong to the common people—saw this, they too rose in rebellion, and demanded that those who were traitors to the kingdom should be slain, otherwise they too would join

From John Mair's Historia Maioris Britanniae tam Angliae quam Scotiae

the Kentish mob in their rising. They also made a petition for the sentence of death upon the lord of Saye, treasurer of England, the bishop of Salisbury, and the baron of Dudley; therefore, the lord Saye was arrested and carried to the tower of London, in hopes to appease the people. When the king's army had been defeated, the mob, under its Irish leader, made for London, and there on the third day of July, did that same Irishman, in his own name and the king's made proclamation of many things, and this amongst the rest, that under pain of death, no man should take for himself meat or drink or aught else without he paid for it. Afterward, they marched to the tower of London and demanded that lord Saye should be handed over to them; and when this was done, and when he had been brought to trial before the mayor of the city and the leader of the common people, he refused to acknowledge their right to sit in judgment upon him, and declared that it was his due to be judged by his peers and the nobility, and not by the common people. And when the people heard these words, their rage had no bounds, and without further inquiry they ordered him to make his last confession, and before he got half way through they cut off his head.

Hereafter, did that Irish leader of the common people begin to rob many wealthy merchants of London of their goods; and for this, the sensible men amongst the common people held him in detestation, and the chief citizens, along with the lord of Scales, captain of the Tower of London, gathered together a large number of men of London, and went out against the Irishman and the rabble, who made a stubborn resistance. Round about London Bridge the fighting went on all night long, the rabble fighting outside the city, the London men within. And when the chancellor of England, who was a man of sense, saw how matters went, he sent to the Irish captain of the rabble and promised him for him and his a general pardon for all that he had done in the past; and forthwith the rabble dispersed, and every man returned to his own house. Proclamation was made a short while afterward that whoever should take that captain, John Cade the Irishman, living or dead, should be rewarded with one thousand pounds of sterling money. And without delay he was taken, and other along with him who had taken part in that conspiracy.

And here, I may say that that there is nothing more unprofitable than a rebellion of the common people and government at their hands; for they make a general unreasoning overturn of everything: when they have to pass judgment or sentence upon men, 'tis without discrimination that they do so. As well in fact be governed by brute beasts as by them; and, to say truly, they are but a beast with many heads. And this is plain enough from a consideration of that thrice-damnable rabble that when John, the French king was a prisoner, violated many noble women of France—whom afterward they murdered. There is nothing for it but the sword when the common people rise in wanton insolence against the state; otherwise they will confound in one common ruin themselves and all else. For that reason, Henry the Sixth went into Kent, and at Canterbury did justice upon his pestiferous people. After that, he went into Sussex, and executed like judgment there. I have nothing but approval for the zeal for justice of this king, as he showed the same in curbing this unruly rabble and severely punishing them for their evil deeds, to the end that there should be less likelihood in time to come of such frivolous insurrections; for facile pardon gives not seldom the occasion to offend.

Chapter 14

From *Hall's Chronicle*

OVERVIEW

Edward Hall (1497–1547) was a chronicler, a lawyer, a member of parliament, common sergeant of London and under sheriff. He is most well known as the author of *The Union of the Two Noble and Illustre Families of Lancastre and Yorke*, which is most commonly referred to as *Hall's Chronicle* and which he completed around 1532; it was printed in 1548 by William Grafton (himself a chronicler). Hall's chronicle, like Fabyan's, was divided into seven parts; however, his were secular in nature and corresponded to the reigns of seven monarchs, from Henry IV to Henry VIII. Gransden notes how Hall's work is a renaissance history that favors the Tudor monarchs, though one that relies on medieval histories, especially fifteenth-century London chronicles, for content (471). *Hall's Chronicle* is one of the primary sources that Shakespeare used for his history plays, including *1 Henry IV* and *Richard III*.

SOURCE FOR TRANSLATION

Hall, Edward. *Hall's Chronicle*. Edited by Henry Ellis. London: J. Johnson, et al., 1809. Pp. 219–22.

FURTHER READING

Gransden, 470–71.
Herman, Peter C. "Hall, Edward." In *ODNB*.

McKisack, May. *Medieval History in the Tudor Age*. Oxford: Clarendon Press, 1971.

Pollard, A. F. "Edward Hall's Will and Chronicle." *Bulletin of the Institute of Historical Research* IX (1932): 171–77.

Rissanen, Matti. *Studies in the Style and Narrative technique of Edward Hall's Chronicle*. Mémoires de la Sociéténéophilologique de Helsinki 40. Helsinki: SociétéNeophilologique, 1973.

TRANSLATION

But the death of this disobedient person and ungrateful patron [William de la Pole, the Duke of Suffolk] brought not the realm quiet nor deliver it from all inward grudges and internal division, which to all realms is more pestiferous and harmful than outward war, daily famine, or extreme pestilence. For although Richard Duke of York was in prison (as the king's deputy) in the realm of Ireland, continually residing there, yet his breath puffed and his wind blew daily in many parts of the realm. For many of the nobility, and more of the lower ranks, wisely pondering the state and condition of the realm, perceiving more loss than increase, more ruin than advancement, daily to ensue. Remembering also that France was conquered and Normandy gained by the French people in a short space, [they] thought to themselves and imagined that the fault of all these miserable chances happened either because the king was not the true inheritor to the crown, of that he or his council were not able of wit, policy, and circumspection to rule and govern so noble a realm or so famous a region.

Upon this conjecture, the friends, kinsmen, and allies of the Duke of York, which were of no small number, began to practice the governance of his title: infusing and putting into men's heads secretly his right to the crown, his political governance, his gentle behavior, to all the Irish nation, affirming that he, who had brought that rude and savage nation to civil fashion and English urbanity would (if he once ruled in the realm of England) depose evil counselors, correct evil judges, and reform all matters [that were] amiss and not mended. And to set open the flood gates of these devices, it was thought necessary to cause some great commotion and rising of people to be made against the king, so that if they prevailed then the Duke of York and his accomplices had their appetite and desire. And because the Kentishmen are impatient regarding wrongs and disdain too much oppression, and very desirous on new change and new fangledness, the overture of this matter was put forth first in Kent, to intent that is should not be known that the Duke of York or his friends were the cause of the sudden rising.

A certain young man of good stature and pregnant wit was enticed to take upon himself the name of John Mortimer, although his name was John Cade, and not for a lack of wisdom, thinking that by that surname, the line and lineage of the attendant house of the Earl of March, which were no small number, should be to him both adherent supportive and favorable. The captain not only suborned by teachers, but also enforced by secret schoolmasters, assembled together a great company of valiant personages, assuring them that their attempt was both honorable to God and the king, and also profitable to the commonwealth, promising them that if wither by force or policy they might once take the king, queen, and others [who were] their counselors into their hands and governance, that neither fifteenth[1] should hereafter be demanded, nor another impositions or tax should be spoken of.

These persuasions, with many other fair promises of liberty (which the common people more affect and desire, rather than reasonable obedience and due conformity) so animated the Kentish people that they with their captain above named in good order of battle (not in great number) came to the plain of Blackheath, between Eltham and Greenwich. And to the intent that the cause of this glorious captain's coming there might be shadowed from the king and his council, he sent to him a humble supplication, with loving words but with malicious intent, affirming his coming, not to be against him but against [persons] disagreeable to his counsel, lovers of themselves and oppressors of the poor commons, flatterers to the king and enemies to his honor, suckers of his purse, and robbers of his subjects, partial to their friends, and extreme to their enemies, for rewards corrupted, and for indifference doing nothing.

This proud bill was both for the king and his council disdainfully taken, and thereupon a great consultation [was] had, and after much debating it was concluded that such proud rebels should rather be suppressed and tamed with violence and force than with words or an amicable answer. Whereupon the king assembled a great army and marched toward them, which had encamped on Blackheath over the space of seven days. The subtle captain named Jack Cade, intending to bring the king farther within the compass of his net, broke up his camp and retreated back to the town of Sevenoaks in Kent, and there, expecting his prey, encamped himself and made his abode. The queen, who maintained control, being well advised of his retreat, sent Sir Humphrey Stafford, knight, and William, his brother, with many other gentlemen to follow the chase of the Kentishmen, thinking that they had fled but verily they were deceived. For at the first skirmish both the Staffords were slain and all the company shamefully discomfited.

The king's army, being at this time [had] come to Blackheath, hearing of this discomfiture, began to grudge and murmur among themselves: some wishing to the Duke of York at home to aid the captain, his cousin; others openly crying out to the queen and her accomplices. This rumor openly spoken and commonly published caused the king and certain [members] of his council not led by favor nor corrupted by rewards (to the intent to appease the furious rage of the inconstant multitude) to commit the Lord Saye, Treasurer of England, to the Tower of London. And if others against whom like displeasure was born had been present, they [would] have likewise been served. But it was necessary that one should suffer rather than all the nobility should then perish.

When the Kentish captain, or the covetous Cade, had thus obtained victory and slain the two valiant Staffords, he appareled himself in their rich armor, and so with pomp and glory returned again to London, to which retreated diverse idle and vagabond persons returned to him from Sussex and Surrey and from other parts in a great number. Thus, the glorious captain compassed about and encircled with a multitude of evil, rude, and rustic persons and came again to the plain of Blackheath, and there strongly encamped himself. To whom were sent by the king the Archbishop of Canterbury and Henry Duke of Buckingham to discuss with him his grievances and requests.

These lords found him sober in his communication, wise in disputing, arrogant in heart, and stiff in his opinion, and by no ways possible to be persuaded to dissolve his army, except if the king would come to him in person and assent to all things, which he should require. These lords, perceiving the willful pertinence and manifest arrogance of this rebellious javelin, departed to the king, declaring to him his reckless and rash words and presumptuous requests. The king somewhat hearing but more marking the sayings of this outrageous rouge, and having daily reports of the gathering and approaching of people, which continually resorted to him, doubting as much his familiar servants as his unknown subjects (which spared not to speak that the captain's cause was profitable for the common good) departed in all haste to Kenilworth in Warwickshire, leaving only behind the Lord Scales to keep the Tower of London.

The captain, being informed of the king's absence, came first into Southwark and there lodged at the White Hart, prohibiting to all men murder, rape, or robbery, by which argument he allured to him the hearts of the common people. But after that he entered into London and cut the ropes of the drawbridge, striking the sword on London Stone, saying, "Now is Mortimer lord of the city," and rode in every street like a lordly captain. And after a flattering declaration was made to the mayor of the city and his coming thither, he departed again into Southwark.

And upon the third day of July, he caused Sir James Fiennes, Lord Saye and Treasurer of England, to be brought to the Guildhall of London to be arraigned there. And being brought before the king's justices to answer to the charges, [Saye made it known that he] desired to be tried by his peers for the longer delay of his life. The captain, perceiving his dilatory plea,[2] by force took him from the officers and brought him to the Standard in Cheapeside, and there before his confession ended caused his head to be cut off and pitched it on a high pole, which was openly born through the streets. And this cruel tyrant, not content with the murder of the Lord Saye, went to Mile End and there apprehended Sir [William] Crowmer, then Sheriff of Kent and son-in-law to the Lord Saye, and he, without confession or excuse heard, caused [him] there likewise to be beheaded and his head fixed on a pole. And with these two heads, this bloody butcher entered into the city again, an in spite caused them in every street to kiss together, the great detestation of all the beholders.

After this shameful murder, open rapine and manifest robbery succeeded in diverse houses within the city, and especially in the house of Philip Malpas, alderman of London, and diverse others. Additionally, the ransoming and fining [occurred] of diverse notable merchants for the protection and security of their lives and goods, such as Robert Horne, alderman, who paid five hundred marks, and yet neither he nor any other person [who] was either of life or substance in a surety of safeguard. He also put to execution in Southwark diverse persons, some for infringing his rules and precepts, because he would be seen as indifferent. Or he tormented his old acquaintances, lest they should grow angry and declare his base birth and lousy lineage, disparaging him from his usurped surname of Mortimer, for which he thought and doubted not to have both friends and deceivers, both in London, Kent, and Essex.

The wise mayor and sage magistrates of the city of London deliberated [among] themselves, whether or not that goods or lives were guaranteed protection, determined with fear to repel and expel this mischievous head and his ungracious company. And because Lord Scales was ordained keeper of the Tower of London, with Matthew Gough, the often named captain in Normandy (as you have heard before), they proposed to make themselves privy both of their intent and enterprise. Lord Scales promised them his aid, with shooting and ordinance, and Matthew Gough was appointed by him to assist the mayor and the Londoners because he was both of manhood and experience greatly renowned and celebrated.

So the appointed captains of the city took it upon themselves in the night to keep the Bridge of London, prohibiting the Kentishmen either to pass or approach. The rebels, which never soundly slept for fear of sudden circumstances, hearing the bridge [was] to be kept and manned, ran with great haste to open their passage, where between both parties was a fierce and cruel encounter. Matthew Gough, more expert in martial feats than the other chieftains of the city, perceiving the Kentishmen [were] better to withstand their weaponry, advised his company to proceed no further toward Southwark until the day appeared, the intent being that the citizens hearing where the place of the jeopardy rested might make a gain upon[3] their enemies and relieve their friends and companions.

But this counsel came to small effect, for the multitude of the rebels drew the citizens from the gateposts at the foot of the bridge to the drawbridge began to set fire in diverse houses. Alas, what sorrow it was to behold that miserable chance, for some [person] desiring to eschew the fire leapt on his enemies weapon and so died. Fearful women with children in their arms, bewildered and frightened, leapt into the river. Others, doubting how to save themselves between the fire, water, and sword, were suffocated and smoldered in their houses. Yet the captain's awareness, regarding these chances, fought on the drawbridge all night valiantly, but in conclusion the rebels captured the drawbridge and drowned many, and slew John Sutton, Alderman, and Robert Heysant, a hardy citizen, with many others besides Matthew Gough, a man of great wit, much experience in feats of chivalry, the which in continual wars had valiantly served the king and his father in the parts beyond the sea (as before you have heard). Yet it is often seen that he, which many times had vanquished his enemies in strange countries and returned again as a conqueror, has afterward been shamefully murdered and brought to death by his own nation.

This hard and sore conflict endured on the bridge until nine o'clock in the morning, in doubtful chance and fortune's balance. For some times the Londoners were beat back to the gateposts at Saint Magnus' corner, and suddenly again the rebels were repelled and driven back to the gateposts a Southwark, so that both parties, being faint, weary, and fatigued, agreed to desist from the fight and to cease battle until the next day, upon the condition that neither Londoners should pass into Southwark nor the Kentishmen into London.

After this abstinence of war [was] agreed, the lusty Kentish captain, relying on more friends, broke open the jails of the king's bench and Marshalsea and set free a swarm of rakes,[4] both suitable for his service and apt for his enterprise. The Archbishop of Canterbury, being then Chancellor of England and for his surety staying in the Tower of London, called to him the Bishop of Winchester, who also for fear lurked at Holy Well.[5] These two prelates, seeing the fury of the Kentish people, by reason of their being beaten back, to be mitigated and diminished, passed the Thames River from the Tower, into Southwark, bringing with them under the King's Seal a general pardon to all the offenders, which they caused to be openly proclaimed and published. Lord, how glad the poor people were of this pardon (even more than the Great Jubilee of Rome)[6] and how they accepted the same in so much that the whole multitude, without bidding farewell to their captain, retired the same night, every man to his own home, as men amassed and stricken with fear.

But John Cade, desperate of succor, which by the friends of the Duke of York were promised to him, and thus seeing his company without his knowledge suddenly departed, mistrusting the consequences of the matter, departed secretly in disguised clothing into Sussex. But for all of his metamorphosis or transfiguration little prevailed. For after a proclamation [was] made that whosoever could apprehend the said Jack Cade should have for his pain one-thousand marks. Many looked for him, but few spied him, until one Alexander Iden, esquire of Kent, found him in a garden, and there in his defense manfully slew the coward Cade[7] and brought his dead body to London, whose head was set on London Bridge. This is the success of all rebels, and this fortune happens always to traitors. For when men strive against the stream, their boat never comes to their feigned port.

After this commotion, the king himself came into Kent and there sat in judgment upon the offenders, and if he had not mitigated his justice with mercy and compassion, more than five-hundred [persons] by the rigor of his law [would] have been justly put to execution. But he considered both their fragility and innocence and how they with perverse people were seduced and deceived. And so [he] punished the stubborn heads and delivered the ignorant and miserable people, to the great rejoicing of all of his subjects.

NOTES

1. Hall writes that "neither fiftenes should hereafter be demauded," (220), where "fiftenes" here refers a "tax of one-fifteenth levied on property by parliament as a temporary aid to the King"; see *MED* "fīf-tēne (card. num.)."

2. See *MED* "dīlātōrīe" (adj.(2)), "~ plea, a formal objection or plea that tends to retard the progress of an action."

3. Hall here states "might occurre their enemies," (222), with the verb used figuratively. See *MED* "okoren" (v.): "(a) To lend (money, goods) at interest; (b) to make a loan (to sb.) at interest; (c) to practice usury (with sb.);—used *fig.*; increase, as with interest;—used *fig.*"

4. Hall here writes that these men are a "swarme of galātes" (222). See *MED* "galaunt" (n.), which includes both our modern equivalent of a "gallant" man but also the now obsolete pejorative meaning: "(a) A man of fashion; esp., one who dresses showily or extravagantly; a fop; (b) a dissolute man, a rake; (c) a gentleman."

5. Now Sadler's Wells.

6. Jubilees, in Judaism and later Christianity, were official events where sins were universally forgiven under the auspices of a general pardon. A jubilee was first recorded in the Hebrew Bible (Lev. 25:10). This "Great Jubilee of Rome" more than likely refers to Pope Boniface VII's first Christian Jubilee, published in 1300. Subsequent jubilees take place every 25 or 50 years.

7. The phrase that Hall uses here to describe Cade is "the caitife Cade" (222). By Hall's account, Cade is not truly a prisoner yet (he will be once Alexander Iden kills him) but instead an enemy combatant. See *MED* "caitīf" (n.): "1. A captive, prisoner;

a slave," and also "2. (a) A miserable or unfortunate person, a wretch; a poor man, one of low birth; (b) a wicked man, scoundrel, one who is cowardly or covetous." Hall, like other medieval chroniclers, were fond of alliterative phrases, which were used for poetic effect and emphasis. The *OED* notes that "catiff" is now obsolete. William Martyn, in his *History and Lives of the Kings of England* (1615) also calls Cade a "caitiffe" (248); see chapter 18.

Chapter 15

From Polydore Vergil's *Anglica Historia*

OVERVIEW

Polydore Vergil/Polidoro Virgili (ca. 1470–18 April 1555) was an Italian humanist born in Urbino or, as Connell states, at Fermignano near Urbino. His grandfather taught medicine and astrology. Vergil studied at the University of Padua and was employed by the Church and Pope Alexander VI. As a papal employee, he traveled first to England in 1502 as a subcollector of Peter's pence, the annual collection by the Church of one pence per English household; it was discontinued in 1534. He traveled again to England in 1505, and that is when he probably befriended Erasmus. It was through Henry VII's encouragement that Vergil began his Latin history of England, the *Anglica Historica*, and a manuscript was completed in 1512–1513. He continued to work on his history, and it was first printed in 1534 at Basel. Revised and expanded editions continued to be published in 1546 and 1555. This final edition was composed of physical descriptions of Britain, a chronological history of England up to 1066, and then chapters that focus on the reigns of individual monarchs, concluding in 1538. As Dana F. Sutton observes, the aim of Vergil's *Anglica Historica* positions itself within the humanistic belief in the function of written history: "[I]t should reinforce moral philosophy by providing a storehouse of positive and negative moral examples, so that history was regarded as a special branch of moral philosophy." To this end, his history compliments John Mair's, a selection of which is in this volume.

MANUSCRIPTS

Vatican, BAV, MS Codices Urbinates Latini 497 and 498

London, British Library MS Royal 18 C VIII/IX

SOURCE FOR TRANSLATION

Ellis, Henry, ed. *Three Books of Polydore Vergil's English History Comprising the Reigns of Henry VI, Edward IV, and Richard III*. Camden Society, os 29. London: J. B. Nichols and Sons, 1844. Pp. 84–86.

NOTE ON TRANSLATION

A critical edition of Vergil's Latin history does not exist. Ellis' edition, the source for my translation, is from London, British Library MS Royal 18 C VIII/IX, which is an English translation that was made during the latter part of Henry VIII's reign.

FURTHER READING

Carley, J. P. "Polydore Vergil and John Leland on King Arthur: The Battle of the Books." *Interpretations* 15, no. 3 (1984): 86–100.
Connell, William J. "Vergil, Polydore [Polidoro Virgili]." In *ODNB*.
Freeman, T. S. "From Catiline to Richard III: The Influence of Classical Histories on Polydore Vergil's *Anglica Historia*." In *Reconsidering the Renaissance: Papers from the Twenty-First Annual Conference*, edited Mario A. Di Cesare, 191–214. Medieval and Renaissance Texts and Studies 93. Binghamton: Medieval and renaissance Texts and Studies, 1992.
Hay, Denys. *Polydore Vergil: Renaissance Historian and Man of Letters*. Oxford: Clarendon Press, 1952.
Neumaier, Marco. "Vergil, Polydore [Virgilio, Polidoro]." In *EMC* 2: 1427.
Sutton, Dana F. Polydore Vergil, *Anglica Historia* (1555 version). http://www.philological.bham.ac.uk/polverg/. Last modified 25 May 2010. 27 February 2018.

TRANSLATION

But when William Duke of Suffolk was dead, peace could in no better manner be preserved, by reason of civil dissension, the beginning whereof sprung through contention of factions, as before is said, which always have been and ever will be more hurtful to commonwealths then foreign wars, than famine, or sickness. Whereunto the Kentish people were most prone, as well for that they can hardly bear injuries, as for that they are desirous of novelties, for whether it were by the instigation of Richard, Duke of York, who, aspiring to the crown, sought to make innovations, his policy tending to this end, that by occasion of discord amongst the commons he might procure himself authority, and become the head of some faction. Or else that they were desirous to revenge injuries done unto them, especially by the king's officers. So it was they took weapon in hand, made one John, by surname Cade, their captain, and gathering a great power together marched toward London, where as soon as they approached they encamped themselves upon the next hill toward it.

Here, consulting deeply upon the matter, certain [persons] were chosen to present their supplication full of complaints unto the king and to declare that those who assembled there in this forcible manner was for the liberty of their country, against certain counselors of his, who molested his people with intolerable exactions of money. And it might please him to cause them to be duly punished, they were ready to lay weapons down. The king, thinking it unworthy to give audience to the messengers of this rebellious group, but rather with speech to repress the fury of their enraged commotion, sent forth against them Humphrey Stafford, knight, with a chosen band of men, upon whom they gave charge as he came, and at the first encounter put him to flight.

After that happy attempt, they enticed unto them on every side, in hope of spoils, a huge number, citizens[1] as well as country people, and so together in a warlike manner marched toward London, where they first entered without doing any harm. But afterward, moved by covetousness, they looted the houses of certain wealthy citizens. And yet, because they would not be reported to seek out spoils, they announced that the same was done in revenge of wrongs committed by the same citizens. But that dealing in the end turned to their own damage, for many of good calling, who were privately well pleased with that rebellion, in hope of some reformation that might grow thereby, when they saw the Kentish men fall to lootings the town, fearing what may happen to themselves, they thought it not suitable to expect any longer the event of that furious enterprise.

But all this while that the Kentish commons raged with cruelty upon the citizens, none went about to withstand them before that John Saye, Lord Treasurer of England, with sundry other gentlemen, were beheaded. Then Thomas Chalton, lord mayor of the city, and the sheriffs, Thomas Canynges and William Hulyn, determined by one way or another to make headway against such great mischief, levied quickly a mighty force of soldiers. And because John, captain of the commons, kept his men beyond the Thames, at the village of Saint George, in the suburbs, and repaired himself there every night, therefore, under the conduct of Matthew Gough, they set upon the rebels about midnight and took the bridge, killing the watch and the ward.

But they found the Kentish men not unprepared, for as soon as they, who for fear lay in armor both day and night, understood by the clamor of their company that the citizens were upon the bridge, by and by they rushed upon them, and the fight was immediately fierce and cruel. After that, Matthew Gough saw the Kentishmen might make a mighty resistance, for he would have believed otherwise. He at once advised his people to proceed no further, but only contended to keep the place which he had taken until it were day, so that the rest of the city, hearing the noise, might certainly know to what place they should return for relieving their fellows. But the commons so forcibly pressed onward, that the citizens were compelled first to give a little ground, and after, with great slaughter, to forsake the bridge.

The Kentishmen at once supplied their placed, and being masters of the bridge set fire on both sides in the houses built there upon [it]. Then might one behold a lamentable sight, for some fleeing the fire ran headlong upon the weapons of their enemies to their own destruction. Others, alas, with horrible shrieks and cries, were suffocated in the flames. Many, moreover, valiantly fighting, were killed in the conflict itself, and among them [was] Matthew Gough, a man of surpassing prowess, very dutiful to his country, and of great renown in martial affairs, who had served beyond the seas with great commendation more than twenty years. But finally, such was the chance that he who was invincible in so many conflicts with foreign enemies was, in the end, by his own countrymen rewarded with death.

But when the king perceived that the Kentish people could not be subdued by force, thinking to pacify them with leniency, he proclaimed a pardon to all of them that were in that rebellion, only except John Cade, their captain, who, being the head of that heinous enterprise, that fact alone [he] by no means would suffer unpunished. Whereupon the people, as having that which they desired, hasted home immediately with the spoils they had gotten, leaving their captain, who was taken soon after, and lost his life for his labor.

NOTE

1. By "citizens," the chronicler is referring to the more established persons of the area, especially the freemen.

Chapter 16

From George North's *A Brief Discourse of Rebellion and Rebels*

OVERVIEW

George North (fl. 1561–1581) was an English diplomat, who served in Sweden, and author of three translations of political discourse: *The Description of Sweden, Gotland, and Finland* (1561), *The Philosopher of the Court* (1575), and *The Stage of Popish Toys* (1581). North wrote *A Brief Discourse of Rebellion and Rebels* in 1576 at Kirtling Hall, Cambridgeshire; he signed it, and dedicated and presented it to Roger, 2nd Lord North. The manuscript had not been studied until McCarty and Schlueter's edition of it in 2018. The text is important not only for Cade studies but also for Shakespeare scholarship. Indeed, North's remarks on Cade's deadly fight with Alexander Iden and the rebel's soliloquy confirm that this is the source of Shakespeare's scene in *2 Henry VI* 4.10. In studying North's manuscript, the scholars have traced over twenty of Shakespeare's monologues back to this work, shedding new light on sources for *Richard III*, *Macbeth*, *Coriolanus*, and *King Lear*, among others. Besides verses on Cade, the discourse includes political verses on Owain Glyndwr. Following the verses on Cade, North presents a biting critique of the rebel leader and of rebellion in general.

MANUSCRIPT

London, British Library MS Additional 70520

94   *Chapter 16*

SOURCE FOR TRANSCRIPTION

McCarthy, Dennis and June Schlueter. *"A Brief Discourse of Rebellion and Rebels" By George North: A Newly Uncovered Manuscript Source for Shakespeare's Plays*. Cambridge: D. S. Brewer in association with the British Library, 2018. Pp. 134, 136–39, 142–43.

I would like to thank the authors, D. S. Brewer, the British Library, and Rachel Reeder for granting permission to reproduce the below pages from their volume. I have not altered their text; as such, all internal references to chapters refer to McCarthy and Schlueter's book.

FURTHER READING

Eklund, Hillary. "Revolting Diets: Jack Cade's 'Sallet' and the Politics of Hunger in *2 Henry VI*." *Shakespeare Studies* 42 (2014): 51–62.
Fitter, Chris. "'Your Captain is Brave and Vows Reformation': Jack Cade, the Hacket Rising, and Shakespeare's Vision of Popular Rebellion in *2 Henry VI*." *Shakespeare Studies* 32 (2004): 173–219.
Kennedy, Ross. "North, George." In *ODNB*.

TRANSCRIPTION

44v

I will remember Owen Glendor, Jack Cade, and the Black Smith,[1] whose repenting (though over late) opinions you shall have, as true testimonies of their own fruitless follies. But you must imagine that you hear Owen howling from the high mountains in Wale and that you can see Jack Cade and the Black Smith preaching on a ladder, shrouded with the Tyburn[2] and shrined with a halter, a meet stage for all traitors

46

to make their last triumph on.

Jack Cade

If trundle tail of currish kind
with greyhound may compare

Or mastie made to hunt the hog
with spaniel have his share.

46v

Then wordly whelps account of me
that durst presume to run;
With swiftest dog and Phaeton like
to soar so near the sun.

Till scorching heat, deciphered plain
my birth and beastly trade
That would have him Prince Mortimer[3]
and yet but poor Jack Cade.

For when I had by Kentish cloynes
the Staffords[4] overthrown:
I climed aloft and thought the King
and crown to be my own.

But little know we traitors all,
what we do take in hand:
When rebel like, in deed we dare,
against our Prince to stand.

Was never traitor yet prevailed,
but came to shameful end:
Nor never shall attain his will
till God be forced to bend.

47

He has appointed Princes sure,
to sit in Kingly seat:
He fights for them, he them defends,
though traitors' force be great.

The wisdom rebels seem to have,
he turns to doltish dreams:
And in the top of hoped joy,
he drives them to extremes.

No subject ought, so God commands,
for any kind of cause:

To dare his Prince, or to resist,
but yield him to his laws.

Though Fortune favor fools awhile,
and lend some happy days:
Yet usance great, for shameful death,
to shameless life she pays.

For I that durst at first presume,
in field with Prince to fight:

47v

And then by name of Mortimer,
to claim the crown for right:

Was served of trust by rebel mates,
for they fled every man:
And let me post alone at length
Jack Cade as I began.

What should I do, but run also,
myself in hole to hide:
Where lurk I did, till Iden's search,
my miching place had spied.

There he bereft me of my life,
and horst me like a hog:
And brought me back through London streets,
drawn like a mastie dog.

My cursèd carcass quartered was,
parboiled and trimly dight:
And after at tower gates on poles,
they were as comely pight.

48

Then in the sun a roasting set,
because I should not smell:
For carrion crows and worm's meat
to eat me flesh and fell.

What better tomb or meeter place,
would rascal rebels have:
Than in the bowels of such beasts,
to find their fairest grave.

50

What should be said touching the rebels of our time, whose follies with their punishments is well known to us: perdition to themselves, their friends, and posterity is the best grain can be gathered of seditious seed, the same they sow, the same they reap, as they manure their matters with treason and mischief, so they mow their own faults with endless sorrow

50v

and shameful death. Ourselves have seen in sundry their sudden rising and momentary falling, even now triumphing multitudes to be feared and straight miserable captives to be pitied, even now shapes and bodies of substance and straight shadows of no value or countenance. So hateful is treason, so loathed is licentious liberty, so embraced is obedience, and so liked is loyal duty, as the rebel's own conscience (which is a near accuser to the best and uprightest liar) will not suffer him to enjoy one minute's quietness.

If therefore in all our actions (before the beginning) we retire our roaming judgment into the bosom of his breeder and look into our own selves, weighing our state, calling, and condition, in the obedient balance of wisdom, fore-

51

sight, and discretion, we shall find such security in subjects' duty, such comfort in loyal concord, such joy in common quietness, such delight in mutual dealing, such gain in public, such profit in private, (and specially) such fruits and felicity in Princes' safety, as nothing more.

Where the Sovereign stands, his Majesty honored, his person loved, his presence desired, his absence feared, his laws observed, and his word obeyed, there the subjects live, the nobility prosper, the commons increase, the commonwealth flourishes, and virtue triumphs, to the thrice fortunate fame both of King and country.

Is not the rebel then (that by his sedition seduces many thousands unto him, and by

51v

his traitorous attempt bereaves them, the blessing of God, the favor of their Prince, the joy of their wives and children, the use of their goods, and sweet comfort of their country and friends) worthy a well framed gibbet, a pliant halter, and a nimble hangman to send him swinging to the Devil in the midst of his misery?

Such is the fruits and fine of them, such is their reward, and such is the tried treasure that time brings them to.

NOTES

1. Glendor = Glendower; see chapter 3, "The Final Hours of Jack Cade."
2. Tyburn was the traditional place of execution, near Marble Arch in present-day London.
3. In 1450, Jack Cade asserted his right to the crown by claiming Edmund Mortimer as ancestor. See chapter 3, "The Final Hours of Jack Cade."
4. The Stafford brothers, Sir Humphrey and William, killed in a battle with the rebels.

Chapter 17

From *Holinshed's Chronicle*

OVERVIEW

Raphael Holinshed (ca. 1525–1580) published his first edition of the *Chronicles of England, Scotland, and Ireland* in 1577, though the initial impetus for the project was from Reginald (Reyner) Wolfe, a Dutchman who moved to London around 1553 and became a successful bookseller and printer. Wolfe, around 1548, decided to undertake an ambitious project, a "Universall Cosmographie," a history of the known world, complete with maps; Holinshed was his assistant. Wolfe died ca. 1573, and Holinshed soldiered on with the project, which was still ongoing after twenty-five years of work. The executors of Wolfe's will decided that Holinshed should focus the volume just on England, Scotland, and Ireland; this was done, and the two volumes were published: 2,835 folio pages, plus prefatory remarks and indices. In 1587, a second edition of *Holinshed's Chronicles* appeared, which benefitted greatly from a royal privilege (under the guidance of Henry Denham) to help fund the project, as well as the significant contributions of Abraham Fleming, who edited, revised, and extended the history to 1586. The second edition was published in three volumes, with some additional text written by John Stow. Holinshed was one chronicler who believed in the importance of written history, for it was, "next unto holy scripture" (1: 766), the ideal mean to teach moral lessons. William Shakespeare relied on Holinshed's work for a significant number of his history plays—roughly one-third of them—to supply plot points, character development, and specific phrases. Some of the plays that benefitted greatly from Holinshed include *Macbeth*, *King Lear*, *Edward II*, and *Richard III*.

SOURCE FOR TRANSLATION

Holinshed, Raphael. *Holinshed's Chronicles of England, Scotland, and Ireland*. 6 vols. London: J. Johnson, et al., 1807–1808. 3: 220–27.

NOTE ON TRANSLATION

Holinshed frequently included content enclosed within parentheses as well as brackets, and both sets of characters, below, are Holinshed's. Those words I supply are italicized in brackets.

FURTHER READING

Clegg, Cyndia Susan. "Holinshed [Hollingshead], Raphael." In *ODNB*.
———. *Press Censorship in Elizabethan England*. Cambridge: Cambridge University Press, 1997.
Djordjevic, Igor. *Holinshed's Nation: Ideals, Memory and Practical Polity in the Chronicles*. Farnham: Ashgate, 2010.
The Holinshed Project. http://www.cems.ox.ac.uk/holinshed/. 2008–2013. Accessed 20 November 2018.
Kewes, Paulina, Ian Archer, and Felicity Heal, ed. *The Oxford Handbook of Holinshed's Chronicles*. London: Oxford University Press. 2013.
Patterson, Annabel. *Reading Holinshed's Chronicles*. Chicago: University of Chicago Press, 1994.
Woolf, D. R. *The Idea of History in Early Stuart England: Erudition, Ideology and 'The Light of Truth' from the Accession of James I to the Civil War*. Toronto: University of Toronto Press, 1990.
———. *Reading History in Early Modern England*. Cambridge Studies in Early Modern British History. Cambridge: Cambridge University Press, 2000.

TRANSLATION

Soon after another disquiet befell here. Those that favored the Duke of York and wished the crown upon his head, for that (as they judged) he had more right thereto than he that wore it, procured a commotion in Kent on this manner. A certain young man of a goodly stature and right pregnant of wit was enticed to take upon him the name of John Mortimer, cousin to the Duke of York (although his name was John Cade, or, for some, John Mend-all) [*an Irishman as the* Polychronicon *says*] and not for a small policy, thinking by that surname that those that favored the house of the Earl of March would be assistant to him. And so indeed it came to pass (as in such cases there is no breeder of a broil, but he shall find adherents enough, no less forward to further his pernicious enterprise by their foolhardiness, than himself was in the plot of his devise) though in fine (as in the unlucky lot of such tumults) their attempts were withstood, and their offence duly rewarded, as in the process of the story shall more at large appear. According to the wise man's sentence, "Often, the master returns to his crimes."

This captain, assembling a great company of tall personages, assured them that the enterprise that he took in hand was both honorable to God and the king, and profitable to the whole realm. For if wither by force or policy they might get the king and queen into their hands, he would cause them to be honorably used, and take such order for the punishing and reforming of the misdemeanors of their bad counselors, that neither the fifteen[1] should hereafter be demanded, nor once any impositions or taxes be spoken of. The Kentish people moved at these persuasions and other false promises of reformation, and in good order of battle (though not in great number) came with their captain into the plain of Blackheath, between Eltham and Greenwich, and there kept the field more than a month, robbing about the country, to whom the city of London at that time was very favorable.

And the said captain, (as I find recorded by John Stow) sent for such citizens of London as it pleased him to command to go to him, under letters of safe conduct, as follows.[2]

. . .

And to the intent and the cause of this glorious captain's coming thither might be shadowed under a cloak of good meaning (though his intent nothing so) he sent to the king, a humble supplication, affirming that his coming was not against his grace but against such of his counselors, who were lovers of themselves and oppressors of the poor commonwealth, flatterers of the king and enemies to his honor, suckers of his purse and robbers of his subjects, partial to their friends and extreme to their enemies, through bribes corrupted, and for indifference doing nothing.

Here, because a full report of this insurrection may pass to the knowledge of the readers, it is necessary to set down the articles of the commons' complaints, touching the aforesaid matters, whereof a copy was sent to parliament, then held at Westminster, with their bill of requests concerning abuses to be reformed.[3]

. . .

These bills, when the council had well perused [them], they did not only disallow and condemn them and the authors as proud and presumptuous but also persuaded the king rather to suppress those rebels by force than by fair promises. Whereupon the king removed from Westminster to Greenwich, from whence he would have sent certain lords with a power to have distressed the Kentishmen, but the men said to their lords they would not fight against them that labored to amend the commonweal. Wherefore, the lords were driven to leave their purpose. And because the Kentishmen cried out against the Lord Saye, the king's chamberlain, he was by the king committed to the Tower of London. Then went the king again to London, and within two days after went against the Kentishmen with 15,000 men, well prepared for war. But the said Kentishmen fled the night before his coming into the wooded country, near to Sevenoaks. Whereupon the king returned again to London.

The queen (that bare rule) being of his retreat advertised, sent Sir Humphrey Stafford, knight, and William, his brother, with many other gentlemen to follow the Kentishmen, thinking that they had fled. But they were deceived, for at the first skirmish both the Staffords were slain and all their company defeated. The king's army by this time had come to Blackheath, and hearing of this defeat began to murmur amongst themselves. Some wishing the Duke of York at home to aid the captain, his cousin. Some undoubtedly coveting the overthrow of the king and his council. Others openly crying out at the queen and her accomplices.

This rumor, published widely, caused the king and certain of his council (for the appeasing thereof) to commit the Lord Saye, treasurer of England, to the Tower of London. And if others (against whom like displeasure was born) had been present, they [would have] been likewise committed. Jack Cade, upon victory against the Staffords, appareled himself in Sir Humphrey Stafford's brigandine set, full of gilded nails, and so in some glory returned again toward London. Diverse idle and vagrant persons out of Sussex, Surrey, and other places [were] still increasing his number. Thus the captain, guarded with a multitude of rustic people, came again to the plain of Blackheath, and there strongly encamped himself. To whom were sent from the king; the Archbishop of Canterbury; and Humphrey, Duke of Buckingham, to discuss with him his griefs and requests.

These lords found him sober in talk, wise in reasoning, arrogant in heart, and stiff in opinion. As one that by no means would grant to dissolve his army, except if the king in person would come to him and assent to the things he would require. The king, upon the presumptuous answers and requests of this villainous rebel, beginning as much to doubt his own menial servants, as his unknown subjects (which spared not to speak, that the captain's cause was profitable for the commonwealth) departed in all haste to the castle of Kenilworth in Warwickshire, leaving only behind him the Lord Scales to keep the Tower of London. The Kentish captain, being advertised of the king's absence, came first into Southwark, and there lodged at the White Hart, prohibiting all to his retinue murder, rape, and robbery. By which color of well meaning, he more allured to him the hearts of the common people.

After that, he entered into London, cut the ropes of the drawbridge, and struck his sword on London Stone, saying, "Now is Mortimer lord of the city. And after a flattering declaration, made to the mayor touching the cause of his thither coming, he departed again into Southwark, and upon the third day of July he caused Sir James Fiennes, Lord Saye and Treasurer of England, to be brought to the Guildhall and there to be arraigned. Who, being before the king's justices put to answer, desired to be tried by his peers for the longer delay of his life. The captain, perceiving his dilatory plea, by force took him from the officers and brought him to the Standard in Cheap, and there (before his confession ended) caused his head to be stricken off, and pitched it upon a high pole, which was openly born before him through the streets.

And not content herewith, he went to Mile End and there apprehended Sir [William] Crowmer, the sheriff of Kent and son-in-law to the said Lord Saye, causing him likewise (without confession or excuse heard) to be beheaded, and his head to be fixed on a pole. And with these two heads this bloody wretch entered into the city again, and as it were by spite cause them in every street to kiss together, to the great detestation of all the beholders. After this succeeded open rapine and manifest robbery in diverse houses within the city, and especially in the house of Philip Malpas, aldermen of London, and diverse others. Additionally [*there was*] ransoming and fining of diverse notable merchants, for the surety of their lives and goods, such as Robert Horne, alderman, who paid five-hundred marks. He also put to execution in Southwark diverse persons, some for breaking his ordinance, and others being of his old acquaintance, lest they should reveal his base lineage, disparaging him from his usurped surname of Mortimer.

The mayor and the other magistrates of London, perceiving themselves neither to be sure of goods nor of life well warranted, determined to repel and keep out of their city such a mischievous wretch and his wicked company. And to be better able to do so, they made the Lord Scales and that renowned captain Matthew Gough privy both of their intent and enterprise, beseeching them of their help and furtherance therein. The Lord Scales promised them his aid, with shooting off the artillery in the Tower. And Matthew Gough was by him, appointed to assist the mayor and Londoners in all that he might [*do*], and so he and other captains, appointed for the defense of the city, took it upon themselves in the night to keep the bridge and would not suffer the

Kentishmen once to approach. The rebels, who never soundly slept for fear of sudden assaults, hearing that the bridge was thus kept, ran with great haste to open that passage, where between both parties was a fierce and cruel fight.

Matthew Gough, perceiving the rebels to stand to their weaponry more manfully than he thought they would have done, advised his company not to advance any further toward Southwark until the day appeared, so that they might see where the place of jeopardy rested and so to provide for the same, but this little availed. For the rebels with their multitude drew back the citizens from the stoops of the bridge's foot to the drawbridge and began to set fire to diverse houses. Great pity it was to behold the miserable state, wherein some desiring to eschew the fire died upon their enemies' weapons. Women with children in their arms leapt for fear into the river. Others in deadly grief [*debated*] on how to save themselves, between fire water and sword, were in their houses, choked and smothered. Yet the captains, not sparing, fought on the bridge all night, valiantly. But in conclusion, the rebels got the drawbridge and drowned many, and slew John Sutton, alderman, and Robert Heyssant, a hardy citizen, with many others beside Matthew Gough, a man of great wit and much experience in feats of chivalry, for which in continual wars he spent his time in service of the king and his father.

This sore conflict endured in a doubtful manner on the bridge until nine o'clock in the morning. For some time, the Londoners were beaten back to Saint Magnus' corner. And suddenly again, the rebels repelled to the stoops in Southwark, so that both parts being faint and weary agreed to leave off from fighting until the next day, upon condition that neither Londoners should pass into Southwark nor Kentishmen into London. Upon this abstinence, this reckless captain, for making himself more friends, broke up the prisons of the King's Bench and Marshalsea, and so were many mates set at liberty, verily engaged for his matters in hand.

The Archbishop of Canterbury, being Chancellor of England, and as then for his surety laying within the Tower, called to him the Bishop of Winchester, who was for some safeguard staying then at Holy Well. These two prelates, seeing the fury of the Kentish people, by their late repulse, to be somewhat assuaged, passed by the River of Thames from the Tower into Southwark, bringing with them under the king's great seal a general pardon for all the offenders and caused the same to be openly published. The poor people were so glad of this pardon, and so ready to receive it, that without bidding farewell to their captain they withdrew themselves that night, every man, towards his home.

But Jack Cade, despairing of succor, and fearing the reward of his lewd dealings, put all his pillage and goods that he had robbed into a barge and sent it to Rochester by water, and [*he*] himself went by land and would have entered into the castle of Queenborough with a few men that were left with him, but he was there let of his purpose. Wherefore, he disguised in strange attire, privately fled into the wooded country besides Lewes in Sussex, hoping to escape. The captain and his people, being thus departed, not long after proclamations were made in diverse places in Kent, Sussex, and Southery, that whoever could take the aforesaid captain alive or dead should have a thousand marks for hos travail. A copy of that proclamation, touching [*upon*] the apprehension of the said captain and his accomplices, hereafter follows.[4]

. . .

After that proclamation [*was*] thus published, a gentleman named Alexander Iden waited his time so that he took the said Cade in a garden in Sussex, so that there he was slain at Hothfield and brought to London in a cart, where he was quartered, his head set on London Bridge, and his quarters sent to diverse places to be set up in the shire of Kent. After this, the king himself came into Kent, and there sat in judgment upon the offenders. And if he had not mingled his justice with mercy, more than five-hundred by rigor of law [*would*] have been justly put to execution. Yet he punished only the stubborn heads and disordered ringleaders, pardoned the ignorant and simple persons, to the great rejoicing of all his subjects. But says another [*authority*], the king sent commissioners into Kent and caused inquiry to be made of this riot in Canterbury. Wherefore, the same eight men were judged and executed, and in other towns of Kent and Sussex was done the like execution.

NOTES

1. See *MED*, "fīf-tēne," (c ard. num.), "4. A tax of one-fifteenth levied on property by parliament as a temporary aid to the King."

2. Holinshed includes two items, which I omit here as they appear elsewhere in this volume. The first is the letter of safe conduct issued by Jack Cade to Sir Thomas Cook. The second are orders from jack Cade to Cook. John Stow copied this both items, London, British Library MS Harley 545, fol. 138 and included it in his *Annales* (1600), 640. Both items also appear in John Vale's commonplace book, London, British Library MS Add. 48031A, fol. 136v; see Kekewich, et al., 206–7. For translations of these two items in this volume, please see chapter 21.

3. Holinshed then includes the first version of the rebel's bills of complaint, which Stow included in his *Chronicles of England* (1580), 654–56, and which is found among his historical writings in London, British Library MS Harley 545, fol. 136v–137v. Immediately following this bill of complaint, Holinshed includes the third version of the bills of complaint, which is found in Stow's *Annales* (1580), 656–58; it is also in Harley 545, fol. 137v–138r. For translations of these two items in this volume, please see chapter 19.

4. Holinshed here includes a copy of the proclamation of Henry VI for the taking of Jack Cade. John Stow copied this item into London, British Library MS 545, fol. 138r–138v, and he printed it in *Annales* (1600), 646–47. It also appears in John Vale's commonplace book, London, British Library MS Add. 48031A, fol. 136v–137; see Kekewich, et al., 207–8. For a translation of this item in this volume, see chapter 20.

Chapter 18

From William Martyn's *The Historie, and Lives, of the Kings of England*

OVERVIEW

William Martyn was born in Exeter in 1562 and called to the bar in 1589. He published his *Historie, and Lives, of the Kings of England* in 1615, which spans the years of all of England's monarchs from William I up to the death of Henry VIII. Martyn was one who did not hold back his criticisms of past kings, notably Edward II, Richard III, and the Stuarts. Woolf, in his study *The Idea of History in Early Stuart England*, notes a "certain provincialism" in Martyn's history, that includes a "discernible hostility towards centralizing forces" as well as an "unequivocal condemnation of any kind of rebellion" (72, 74). Martyn died in 1617, but his *Historie* remained popular; it was reprinted in 1638 with additional material that expanded the history to the death of Elizabeth I. His entry on Cade, the last in this volume, demonstrates his reliance on other chroniclers, notably Holinshed and Hall, but Martyn, nevertheless, imprints his own views on Cade, the rebels, and Henry VI.

SOURCE FOR TRANSLATION

Martyn, William. *The Historie, and Lives, of the Kings of England*. London: W. Stansby for Henrie Fetherstone, 1615. *STC* 17526.

FURTHER READING

Woolf, D. R. *The Idea of History in Early Stuart England: Erudition, Ideology, and the 'Light of Truth' from the Accession of James I to the Civil War.* Toronto: University of Toronto Press, 1990.
———. "Martyn, William." In *ODNB*.

TRANSLATION

The king (to pacify this broil, and to weaken their importunity, by doing something wherewith he thought he should please them) exiled the said Duke [of Suffolk] for five years. But as he sailed toward France, he was taken by an English man of war,[1] who landed him upon Dover Sands, and chopped off his head on a boat's side. And thus was the guiltless blood of Humphrey the good Duke of Gloucester in some measure revenged. And the rest of those delinquents were sequestered from their offices and imprisoned by the king.

While these things were thus in handling, the Duke of York (albeit residing in Ireland) solicited and procured his allies and friends in England (by some secret plotting, pretending some other ends) to set on foot his claim and title to the crown, he being lineally descended from Philippa the daughter, and heir of George Duke of Clarence, who was the elder brother of John of Gaunt, great grandfather to King Henry VI. And first of all it was whispered, and privately reported, that the king's wits were weak, the queen's heart ambitious, the king's counselors of state not wise enough to rule, and that all France, Normandy, and Aquitaine were lost, because God blessed not the usurped succession of King Henry.

Upon these speeches, too commonly divulged, a Kentish rebel named Jack Cade, but falsely nominating himself John Mortimer, made an insurrection in that country, and with his rudely armed crew, and banners displayed, he marched towards the king, who was at Greenwich. But before he came unto him, by messengers he informed him that he intended not any hurt against his royal person, but would displace and punish some of his evil counselors, who were his flatterers, and partial to their own friends, bitter to their enemies, enrichers of themselves, oppressors of the common people, greedy of too much honor, and who for rewards corruptly ordered (or rather disordered) all things as they pleased.

When the king and his council had maturely considered of this individual and insolent message, he was advised to encounter them, not with fair words, which might breed further contempt, but with the sword, for example's sake, that others might (by their punishment) afterwards take better heed. And thereupon a strong army was suddenly prepared, of which when the rebels were informed (to gain advantage by their valor, under a false pretense of cowardly fear), they retired many miles. The queen (who was resolved that this retreat rather proceeded from baseness, rather from policy and wit), sent after them Sir Humphrey Stafford and William Stafford, his brother, they being accompanied with many lusty gentlemen and brave soldiers. But most of them were quickly slain by the rebels, who boldly and courageously confronted them when opportunity and place gave them good advantage to return.

This victory being thus obtained, Jack Cade (to whom multitudes of rude and graceless people from many shires daily resorted) pressed forth again and boldly came into Blackheath, and from thence to London, where they did much harm. But at length the king's general pardon was proclaimed by the Archbishop of Canterbury and by the Bishop of Winchester, to all such as were not the ringleaders of that ungodly rebellion, by means whereof the inconstant and fearful multitude left their captains and returned home. Then was Jack Cade proscribed by the king, and a proclamation was made, by which a reward by the gift of one-thousand marks was promised to him that could take him alive or dead. The hope of this payment occasioned very many to make good inquiries and narrow searches after him. So that in the end being found, he was slain as he fought desperately for his life, and his head was presented to the king, who willingly paid the reward that was promised. This coward[2] destroyed, and thus this commotion appeased, which threatened destruction to the king and the common good.

NOTES

1. The "man of war" here is the ship the *Nicholas of the Tower*.
2. Martyn, following perhaps Edward Hall in his chronicle, calls Cade a "caitiffe," a "coward."

Part II

DOCUMENTS OF THE GOVERNMENT AND REBELS, PERSONAL CORRESPONDENCES

Chapter 19

The Rebels' Bills of Complaint of 1450

OVERVIEW

Three different versions are extant of the Middle English rebels' bills of complaint all from the fifteenth and sixteenth centuries. Harvey (186–191) provides transcriptions of the three versions as well as notes on the manuscripts of the extant copies. Moreover, Kekewich (204–205) includes transcriptions of two versions that are included in John Vale's commonplace book. The order in which these complaints are presented below reflect Harvey's assessment of their order of production during the events of the rebellion. These petitions bring us closer to the language of the revolt and its participants than any surviving document. These are documents that are powerful in their rhetorical strategy, for they argue that that commonwealth was being misgoverned by corrupt officials and that they, the rebels, have a plan to ameliorate the situation. David Grummitt observes how these petitions were "essentially subversive, rehearsing one again that the king's counselors were traitors forced to flee the realm by the rebels and the claims Cade had made to be defender of the commonwealth" (118). While aspects of these complaints echo past accusations of rebels, most notably those who participated in the Peasants' Revolt of 1381, Griffiths points out how this was the "first popular rebellion in English history to produce a coherent program of grievances, requests, and remedies in the form of written, publicized manifestos" (628). In many ways, these documents can be read as formal proposals, where problems are identified and solutions are suggested. That the rebel host is speaking on behalf of the commons (especially the commons of Kent) in these documents calls to question the true participatory nature of politics, government, and action in fifteenth-century England.

SOURCE FOR TRANSLATIONS

Harvey, 186–91.

NOTE ON TRANSLATIONS

These written petitions point to a more literate public in the fifteenth century. Nevertheless, the syntax and semantics of these three versions are the result of individuals who were not fully competent in English composition. As such, these translations attempt to remain true to the language, style, and tone of the Middle English while also making them comprehendible to modern readers.

FURTHER READING

Caldwell, Ellen C. "Jack Cade and Shakespeare's *Henry VI, Part 2*." *Studies in Philology* 92, no. 1 (1995): 18–79.
Griffiths, 628–40.
Grummitt, David. "Deconstructing Cade's Rebellion: Discourse and Politics in the Mid Fifteenth Century." In *The Fifteenth Century VI: Identity and Insurgency in the Late Middle Ages*, edited by Linda Clark, 107–22. Woodbridge: Boydell Press, 2006.
Harvey, 73–101.
Kekewich, 204–5.

TRANSLATIONS OF THE THREE BILLS OF COMPLAINT

I. From London, British Library Cotton Roll IV 50. A fifteenth-century copy, perhaps the first one written by the rebels.

The complaints and causes of the assembly on Blackheath. First, it is openly rumored that Kent should be destroyed with a royal power and made a wild forest for the death of the Duke of Suffolk, of which the commons never did this deed.

Moreover, that the king is steered and moved to live only on his commons, and other men have the revenues of the crown, which has caused poverty in his excellence, and great payments of the people given to the king, granted in his parliaments.

Moreover, that the lords of his royal blood being denied of his daily presence, and other mean persons of lower nature exalted and made chief of the Privy Council, which stops wrong matters done in his realm from his excellent audience and may not be redressed as lawful, unless bribes and gifts be the messenger to the hands of the said people.

Moreover, the people of his realm are not to be paid from the debts [of persons] that they owe for the stuff and purveyance[1] taken to the king to use for the undoing of said people.

Moreover, the menial men of household and other persons asking daily goods and lands of people impeached or indicted for treason, which the king granted at once or before they are endangered of being convicted, which causes the receivers thereof to enforce labors applied to the death of people by subtle means of covetous of the said grant.

Moreover, the people so impeached and attached though it be untrue may not be committed to the law for their deliverance but hold still in person to their utter undoing for covetous of goods.

Moreover, it is noticed by the common voice that the king's lands in France are alienated[2] and put away from the crown and his lords and people there destroyed by untrue men of treason, of which now it is desired that inquiries be made through all the realm how and by whom, and if such traitors may be found guilty then [they are] to have execution by law without any pardon as an example.

Moreover, though many of the people have never had much right to their land, yet by untrue claims fiefdoms have been made to diverse estates and gentry to maintain so that the true owner of it dare not pursue his right.

Moreover, the collectors of the fifteen penny[3] in Kent, being greatly vexed and hurt in paying great sums of money to the Exchequer to sue to recover in a writ called *quorum nomina*[4] for the allowance of the barons of the Cinque Ports, which now it is desired that hereafter in relief of the said collectors the aforesaid barons may recover for their ease at their own cost.[5]

Moreover, the sheriffs and undersheriffs are allowed to rent their offices and bailiwicks, taking great severance. Therefore, this causes extortions to be done to the people.

Moreover, simple people that do not hunt are greatly oppressed by indictments feigned and done by the said undersheriffs and bailiffs and others of their assent to cause their fees to increase for payment of the said use.[6]

Moreover, they turn in names of inquests by writing to diverse courts of the king's where [the persons are] not summoned nor warned, whereby the people lose daily great sums of money or the value of their undoing.

Moreover, they make levy of penalties[7] called the "green fine"[8] in more sums of money than can be found recorded in the king's books.

Moreover, the people may not have their free election in choosing knights of the shire, but letters are sent from diverse estates to the great rulers where they embrace their tenants and other people chose other persons than they like.

Moreover, wherein knights of the shire should choose the king's collectors indifferently without taking any bribes, or let them have noted certain persons in feigning to be collectors, whereupon some have made a fine to them to be discharged, and so the collector's office is bought and sold exorbitantly as they desire.

Moreover, the ministries of the court of Dover in Kent vex and arrest the people there throughout the entire shire out of the castle tax,[9] overstepping their boundaries used in olden time and taking great fees of the people at their desire, exorbitantly, too much hurt to them.

Moreover, the people are very vex in the costs and labors called to the sessions of the peace, appearing from the farthest parts of the west into the east, which causes a five day journey to some people, wherefore they desire that appearance to be divided in two parts, of which one part to appear in one place and another part in another place of the shire in relieving of the vexation of the people.

II. From Oxford, Magdalen College MS Misc. 306. This is a sixteenth-century copy made by John Stow. The manifesto carries the date 4 June 1450.

These are the points, problems, and causes of the gathering and assembling of us, your true liegemen of Kent, which we trust to God to remedy with the help of our king, our sovereign lord, and all of commons of England and to die therefore.

1. First, we are considering the king, our sovereign lord, by the false and untrue covetous desires and malicious presumptions brought up daily and nightly about his highness, the same daily and nightly is informed that good is evil, and evil is good, as the scripture says, *Ve vobis qui facitis de bono malum*.[10]
2. Moreover, they say that our sovereign lord is above the law, and that the law is made to his pleasure, and that he may break it as often as he likes without any destruction. The contrary is true, otherwise he should have not been sworn at his coronation to keep it, which we conceive as the highest point of treason that any subject may do against his prince so as to make him reign in perjury.
3. Moreover, they say the king should live upon his commons, and that their bodies and goods are his. The contrary is true, on account that [they] never needed him to set parliament and to ask for goods from them.

4. Moreover, they inform the king that the commons would first destroy the king's friends and afterward himself, and then bring in the Duke of York to be king, so that by their false means and lying they make him to hate and destroy his very friends and to cherish his false traitors that called themselves his friends. And if there were no more reasons by which to know a friend, he may be known by his own covetousness.
5. They say it was a great reproof to the king to reassume that he has given his livelihood, so that they neither allow him to have his own nor keep lands or tenements forfeited, nor no other goods but that they ask it from him, or else they take money in order to get it themselves.
6. Moreover, it is to be remembered that these false traitors will suffer no man to come to the king's presence for no cause without a bride, whereas there ought no bribe to be, but that every man might have his due coming in due time to him to ask for justice or grace as the cause requires.
7. It is a heavy thing that the good Duke of Gloucester [was] impeached for treason by one false traitor alone, how soon he was murdered, and [one] never might come to answer [for this crime]. And the false traitor [William de la] Pole [was] impeached by the commonwealth of England, which number passed an inquest of twenty-four thousand, might not be suffered to die as the law would [allow], but rather these said traitors, at Pole's assent, that was as false as Fortiger,[11] would that the king our sovereign lord would battle in his own realm to the destruction of all his people and toward himself.
8. Moreover, they whom the king wills shall be traitors, and whom he wills not shall be none, and that appears well up to now. For if any of the traitors malign against any man, high or low, they will find false means so that they may die as a traitor, to have lands and goods. But they will not in such a case allow the king to have him pay either his debts or for his victuals therewith, nor to be richer than one penny.
9. Moreover, the law serves [that which is] right, but in these days [it serves] nothing else but to do wrong, which nothing succeeds but false matters by the color of the law for reward, dread, or favor, and no remedy is had in the Court of Conscious nor elsewhere.
10. Moreover, we say that out sovereign lord may well understand that he has had false counsel, for his lords are lost, his merchandise is lost, his commons destroyed, the sea is lost, France is lost, himself so poor that he may not pay for his meat nor drink. He owes more than [any] king ever did in England, and yet daily his traitors that have been about him wait wherever a thing should come to him by his law, and they ask for it from him.

11. Moreover, they ask for gentlemen's lands and goods in Kent, and call us risers and traitors and the king's enemies, but we shall be found to be true liegemen and his best of friends with the help of Jesus, to whom we cry daily and nightly, with many thousand more, that God by his righteousness shall take vengeance on the false traitors of his royal realm that have brought us into this mischief and misery.
12. Moreover, we wish that all men know that we will neither rob nor steal, but if these faults are amended we shall go home. Wherefore, we exhort all the king's true liegemen to help us, for whomever is he that wishes these faults not be amended, he is falser than a Jew or Saracen, and we shall will a strong desire live, and kill him [as one would] either a Jew or Saracen. Whoever is against this, we will mark him, for he is not the king's true liegeman.
13. Moreover, we wish it to be known that we blame not all the lords nor all that have been about the king's person, nor all gentlemen, nor all men of law, nor all bishops, nor all priests, but such [persons who] may be found guilty by a just and a true inquiry by the law. Wherefore, we move and desire some true judge with certain true lords and knights may be sent into Kent to inquire about all such traitors and bribers, and that justice may be done upon them, whomever they be. And that our sovereign lord direct official letters to all his people, to be openly read and cried that it is our sovereign lord, his will, and he desires all his people truly to inquire of everyman's governance and of the defaults that reign, not letting for love, for dread, nor for hate, and that justice be done forthwith. And thereupon, the king is to keep in his own hands their lands and goods and not give them to any man but to keep them for his own riches, or else to muster his army toward France, or else to pay his debts therewith. By our writing you may conceive we are the king's friends or his enemies. Those foresaid mischiefs thus duly remedied, and that from henceforth no man upon pain of death being about the king's person take any bribe for any bill of supplication or reputation, or cause succeeding or impeding, our sovereign lord shall reign with great worship, love of God and his people, that he shall be able with God's help to conquer where he wishes. And as for us, we shall be ready to defend our country from all nations and to go with our sovereign lord where he will command us.
14. Moreover, he that is guilty will writhe against this, but [we] shall bring them down, and they should be ashamed to speak against reason. They will perhaps say to the king that they should be taken from him, that they will then put down the king, for the thieves would live longer. And if we were disposed against our sovereign lord, as God forbids, how might his traitors help him?

God be oure gyde, and then schull we spede,
Who so evur say nay, ffalse for their money reulethe.¹²
Trewth for his tales spellethe.
God seende vs a ffayre day! Awey, traytors, awey!

[God, be our guide, and then shall we succeed. Whosoever says "no", they are false, for it is their money that governs. His tales speak for truth. God, send us a fair day! Away, traitors, away!]

III. London, British Library Cotton II 23. This copy is from the fifteenth century. In this manuscript, the poem "Verses Against the Duke of Suffolk," which is included in this volume, follows immediately after these complaints.

These are the desires of the true commons of your sovereign lord the king.

First, the captain of the same commons desires the welfare of our sovereign lord the king, and all of his true lords, spiritual and temporal, desiring of our sovereign lord and all his true council to take again all his demesne,¹³ and he shall then reign like a royal king, as he is born our true, anointed Christian king. And who says the contrary we will all live and die in that quarrel.

Also desiring of his true commons is that he will void all the false progeny and affinity of the Duke of Suffolk, who are openly known traitors, and they are to be punished after the custom and law of the land. And to take about him a noble person, the true blood of the realm, that is to say the high and mighty prince, the Duke of York, lately exiled from our sovereign lord's presence by the false traitor, the Duke of Suffolk and his affinity, and take to you, the mighty prince, the Duke of Exeter, the Duke of Buckingham, the Duke of Norfolk, and the earls and barons of this land, and then shall he be the richest king christened.

His true commons also desire the punishment of his false traitors, who have contrived and devised the death of our excellent prince, the Duke of Gloucester, which is too much to rehearse, for the Duke was openly proclaimed at the parliament of Bury¹⁴ a traitor, upon that quarrel we declare to live and die that it is false.

Also, the Duke of Exeter, and our holy father the Cardinal of Winchester, the noble princes the Duke of Somerset, the Duke of Warwick, were delivered and destroyed by the same means.

Also, the realm of France, the duchy of Normandy, Gascony, Guyenne, Angers, and Maine, were lost by the same traitors, and our true lords and knights, squires, and yeomen were lost or sold before they went over the sea, which is a great pity and a great loss to our sovereign lord and destruction to his realm.

120   *Chapter 19*

Also, the captain with the commons of Kent desires that all the extortions may be laid down, that is to say, the great extortion of the green wax, that is falsely used to the perpetual destruction of the king's liege men and the commons of Kent without provision. [Also, the king's bench, which is grateful to the shire of Kent without the provision of][15] our sovereign lord and his true council.

Also, in taking wheat, grain, beef, mutton, and other victuals, which is burdensome to the commons, without a brief provision of our sovereign lord and his true council, they may no longer bare it. And also unto the Statute of Laborers and great extortionists being in Kent, that they be punished, and that is to say, the traitors Slegge,[16] Crowmer,[17] Isle,[18] and Est.[19]

NOTES

1. The word "stuff" (Harvey, 187) here can refer to military supplies or, more generally, provisions or any time of moveable goods.

2. "Alienated," (Harvey, 187) here meaning "surrendered" or "lost."

3. See *MED*, "fīf-tẹne," (card. num.), "4. A tax of one-fifteenth levied on property by parliament as a temporary aid to the King."

4. Latin for "their names." Tomlins and Granger comment thus on *quorum nomina*: "In the reign of Henry VI. the king's collectors and other accountants were much perplexed in passing their accounts by new extorted feed and forced to procure a then late-invented writ of *quorum nomina* for the allowing and suing out of their *quietus* [a discharge that settles a debt] at their own charge, without allowance of the king." In *The Law-Dictionary, Explaining the Rise, Progress, and Present State of the British Law*, Vol. 2, s.v., "Quorum Nomina."

5. Harvey, regarding this describes how the writers of this bill "wanted something done about the inconvenience and nuisance caused to the tax collectors in Kent by the requirement that they sue out writs of exemption for the barons of the Cinque Ports (the Cinque Ports having to provide properly manned vessels were exempt from the subsidies but the people of Kent thought that the ports should claim such an exemption at their own costs)" (80).

6. As A. J. Pollard observes, this complaint and the one before it relate to the modes of extortion that the sheriffs and undersheriffs used. Their income was generated out of the "profits of his office, fees, sweeteners and bribes." Regarding the phrase "usith not huntyng" and that which follows, Pollard notes that "false accusations of poaching were made for the kickback," (104). Harvey, "Poaching and Sedition in Fifteenth-Century England," argues that this this section was drafted on behalf of those who could not afford to hunt, as the supporters of the rebellion were "the village notables," and that those who did draft the complaint "were unlikely to see themselves as simple people and knew themselves to be hunters," (176).

7. Specifically, the bill notes that these types of penalties were "amerciements" (187). See *MED* "amerciment" (n.), "(a) A penalty imposed upon an offender or defaulter, esp. one imposed 'at the mercy', i.e. at the discretion, of the court (as distinct from a statutory fine); amercement ; (b) the income from such penalties; also, a record of such penalties; (c) a penalty or mulct inflicted, as upon a tenant."

8. These fines are called in the complain the "grene wexe" (187). See *MED* "grēne-wax," (n.) "(a) An estreat; notice of a fine, amercement, etc., sealed with the green wax seal of the Exchequer."

9. The "caste-ward" tax was a tax paid in lieu of the feudal service of supplying guards for a castle.

10. "Woe to you that make evil from good." A scriptural reference to Isaiah 5:20: "Woe unto them that call evil good, and good evil."

11. The text here reads "ffortegere," (Harvey, 189), which suggests a reference to the Arthurian character Fortiger in the Middle English poem *Arthur and Merlin*, a poem found in the Auchinleck Manuscript; this poem is itself a translation of the long Old French poem *Estoire de Merlin*. Fortiger, early in *Arthur and Merlin*, usurps the throne of England and allies himself with the Saracens, whom he invites to England to aid in the killing of many nobles. In other works of Arthurian literature he is known as "Vortigern."

12. Here, British Library Harleian MS 543 has "pillith" (plunders) in place of "reulethe."

13. See *MED* "dēmeine" (n.(1)), 2.(a): "Land directly attached to the possessor's dwelling; land retained by the lord of the manor and managed by himself or a steward rather than by tenants, demesne; similar lands belonging to a king."

14. This parliament was held in February 1447, in present day Bury Saint Edmonds. The Duke of Gloucester is arrested en route to the parliament by men of the king's and is dead five days later.

15. This section is omitted in the manuscript but is found in Stow's version and printed in Kingsford, 362.

16. Stephen Slegge, a high ranking royal official in Kent during the 1440s who is much hated.

17. William Crowmer, the Sheriff of Kent from 1444 to 1445 and 1449 to 1450.

18. William Isle, of Sundridge. Harvey notes that he is "among the most notorious office-holders in Kent during the 1440s, abusing his position again and again by extortion and the violent taking of land and property," 39. Furthermore, Harvey states that during the 1440s, "Slegge had stood witness to Saye in his transactions, acted as his co-feoffee, collaborated with him in crime, and was generally one of his most frequent associates. He was lucky to survive him," (39).

19. Robert Est, of Maidstone. Harvey comments thus on this person: "In October 1449 [Slegge] and Robert Est, a gentleman from Maidstone, together with a great gang, allegedly 200 strong, broke into the close of Edward Neville, Lord Abergavenny, at Singlewell, two miles south of Gravesend, looted his granary, and assaulted his servants. And this was not, the allegation revealed, the first time he had raided Lord Abergavenny in this way," (39).

Chapter 20

The Proclamation by King Henry VI Authorizing the Taking of John Cade

With Latin Translations by Evan Golightly

OVERVIEW

This item appears in the commonplace book of John Vale (who was a servant to alderman and mayor of London, Sir Thomas Cook), and John Stow copied it into London, British Library MS 545 and printed it in his *Annales* (1600). John Watts, in Kekewich, observes how this proclamation by King Henry VI and the charge against Cade—as one who deceived the king's people and convinced them (through deception) to rise up against the king's laws and his right to the throne—resembled the charged brought against the Duke of York in 1460; however, this link between the two individuals to "reassert the royal authority of the government . . . did nothing to convince the public that the authority was . . . justly, reasonably, or even royally exercised" (11–12). This undated document is one that should be read in conjunction with the rebels' bills of complaint and as an answer to the rebels' words as well as their actions.

MANUSCRIPTS

London, British Library Additional MS 48031A
London, British Library MS Harley 545

SOURCE FOR TRANSLATION

Kekewich, 207–8.

NOTE ON TRANSLATION

The second and fourth paragraphs are in Latin, which Evan Golightly has translated; the remainder of the document is translated from Middle English.

FURTHER READING

Harvey, 97–98.
Kekewich, 11–12.
Peverley, Sarah L. "Vale, John." In *EMC* 2: 1466.

TRANSLATION

The copies of the writ and proclamation by the king for the taking of the said Cade and his fellowship.

Henry, by the grace of God, the king of England and France and lord of the whole of Ireland, at the same time with the guardians of the peace in the county of Kent and with the sheriffs of the same county and also with the mayors and bailiffs of any of the cities and towns in the same county to whom these present letters, shall extend a greeting to each one of them. I command each and every one of you to firmly impose this in the cities and villages that look to you, or where you may better see to be expediency for the aforementioned matter, the following words are thus publically announced.

For as much as one John Cade, born in Ireland, who calls himself John Mortimer and in some writings calls himself captain of Kent, who is openly known as a false traitor. John Cade, who the last year prior was dwelling in Sussex with a knight called Sir Thomas Dacre, slew there a woman with child and for that cause took control of the church, and after that incident was banished form the king's land. John Cade, who also years before this was sworn to the French kingdom and dwelled with them. Who has now, as of late, intended to enrich himself by robbing and despoiling from the king's liegemen as it is now openly known, to bring himself to a great and high estate falsely and untruly deceived many of the king's people, and under the color of holy and good intents made them to assemble with him against the king's sovereignty and his laws, and not agreeing to the king's grace and pardon granted not only to him but to all the king's subjects, who by his deceit have assembled with him. He received this with great reverence on the previous Monday and so did all those that were assembled with him. Notwithstanding all this labor now of news to assemble the king's people again, and to intend for them to have on hand the king's letters of pardon granted to him and to them are not viable nor of no effect without authority of parliament, whereas the contrary is true, as it is openly known that the king grants from time to time his charters of pardon in such a manner as he desires of all manner of crimes and offences, both general and special. The king therefore directs and commands that none of his subjects give faith nor credence to the said false information of the said false traitor, nor accompany him in any manner, nor comfort nor sustain him or his [company] with supplies nor with any other things. But whosoever of the king's subjects may take him, shall take him, and that whosoever takes him and brings him, alive or dead, to the king or to his council shall have one-thousand marks for his labor, truly paid to him without fault or delay by the provision of the king's council. And whosoever takes any of those that from this day forward accompany him shall have five marks for his reward truly to be paid in the above said manner and form. And over this commanding all constables, ministers, and officers of the said shire that none of them, on the pain of death, take upon themselves to execute any commandment by word or by writing sent or made unto them by the said Cade, calling himself Mortimer and captain, be it to incite any people or to any other intent, but to arrest and make to be arrested as such, and take it upon themselves to bring any such commandment by writing or by word.

Hereof in no way fail. Written by myself at Westminster on the tenth day of July in the twenty eighth year of my reign.

Chapter 21

Letters from Jack Cade to Sir Thomas Cook

OVERVIEW

These two documents in Middle English are included in the commonplace book of John Vale: London, British Library MS Add. 48031A; moreover, John Stow copied and printed these items into London, British Library Harley 545 and printed it in his *Annales* (1600). Thomas Cook, junior, was an alderman and mayor of London. His father-in-law was Philip Malpas, the wealthy draper and alderman of London whose house was looked during the Cade Rebellion. Thomas Cook, senior, was a draper in the city. Sutton and Visser-Fuchs, in Kekewich, observe that while both Cooks were in London during the uprising, the "elder, as one of the bridge wardens, was busy receiving hand-guns and organizing the defense of the bridge under the overall command of alderman Robert Horne," and that the younger Cook, who was "an energetic, ambitious common councilman with a ready tongue," was more likely the Cook named in these two letters, for he was "an obvious choice for his fellow citizens as a negotiator with Cade" (77). These two letters document Cook's role as an emissary between the city of London and its government and the rebel camp. The date of Cook's mission is not recorded in any of the chronicles, though it is possible that, as Sutton and Visser–Fuchs suggest in Kekewich, he may have accompanied the two archbishops, the king's negotiators, and the Duke of Buckingham around 16 June 1450 to meet with Cade and force (77). David Grummitt comments that these two documents demonstrate how, during the uprising, Cade "usurped the language and authority of royal government," and that they "were self-conscious appropriations of royal authority, mirroring the content and form of royal signet letters (even down to Cade's mock-regal sign manual), and signaled the same claim to public authority as had been made by the rebels in 1381" (111).

The first item below allows Thomas Cook safe passage so that he may travel between London and the rebel encampment at Blackheath. This item includes Vale's copy of Cade's signature, authorizing the safe conduct. The second item details how Cade and his men will be armed; it describes the role that Italian merchants within London played in providing the rebel force with horses and weapons.

MANUSCRIPTS

London, British Library MS Add. 48031A.
London, British Library MS Harley 545.

SOURCE FOR TRANSLATION

Kekewich, 206–7.

FURTHER READING

Barron, 484–85.
Griffiths, 625.
Grummitt, David. "Deconstructing Cade's Rebellion: Discourse and Politics in the Mid Fifteenth Century." In *The Fifteenth Century VI: Identity and Insurgency in the Late Middle Ages*, edited by Linda Clark, 107–22. Woodbridge: Boydell Press, 2006.
Harvey, 81.

TRANSLATION

I. Document Giving Safe Conduct to Sir Thomas Cook, Issued by Jack Cade

The safeguard and autograph signature of the captain called Jack Cade of Kent, sent to Thomas Cook of London, draper.
 By the captain of the great assembly in Kent.
 By this our sealed writing, we grant and will promise truly that Thomas Cook of London, Draper, shall come in good surety and in safeguard to our presence without any hurt of his person. And so avoid from us again at his

pleasure with all other persons assigned at his designation with him coming in likewise.[1]

II. Jack Cade's Orders to Thomas Cook

The commandment by Jack Cade, captain of Kent, sent to Thomas Cook, above said.

For your instruction, first you shall charge all of Lombardy and foreign merchants being Genovese, Venetians, Florentine, and others, this day to draw them together and do ordain for us, the captains, twelve complete harnesses of the best fashion, twenty four brigandines, twelve battle axes, twelve spears,[2] six horses with saddle and bridal completely harnesses, and one thousand marks of money. And if this, our desire, is not observed and done, we shall have the heads of as many as we can get of them.

NOTES

1. The remainder of this line contains John Vale's imitation of Jack Cade's signature. For an image of this item, see *Vale's Book*, p. 78.
2. The weapons are "gleyves" (207). See *MED*, "glaive" (n.), "(a) A weapon with a long shaft ending in a point or an attached blade; lance, spear; also, a bill, gisarme."

Chapter 22

The Pardon Roll of July 1450

OVERVIEW

In early July 1450, Henry VI granted a pardon to Jack Cade and then to men (and a few women) who wanted to have a royal pardon. As Harvey has observed, those pardoned fall into three large categories: those who did not take part in the rebellion (a low percentage), those who are representing members of their home communities who may or may not have taken part in the rebellion but may have been implicated in some way, and finally those who were indeed active participants (192). Some 3,000 names are recorded, and of these around 65 percent represent those from Kent, 12 percent from mid-Sussex, and 12 percent from eastern Surrey, close to London (Griffiths, 622). Released prisoners are found within this roll, but their numbers are small, for "only a few dozen individuals" are recoded in king's bench records to having engaged in criminal activity before 1450 (Harvey, 195). Some names appear three times, while several hundred appear with no place of origin; for the latter group, 114 are women, possibly from Greenwhich or Southwark, who may have aided the rebels by providing lodging and food. The majority of the names recorded in the general pardon, Harvey argues, do represent insurgents, as may named take part in subsequent uprisings in the southeast of England (198–99).

NOTE ON CONTENTS OF THE PARDON

For consistency and to demonstrate the uniqueness of these entries, I have chosen to maintain the spelling of the individuals' personal names and the place names in this pardon roll. With digital books, readers can search for specific names unique to this record. Abbreviations for "co." have been expanded throughout as "county." Many of the professions named in the pardon roll are archaic words. Using the *MED*, I have provided definitions for the professions.

SOURCE

Calendar of Patent Rolls. Henry VI, Vol. V, 1446–1452. London: His Majesty's Stationery Office, 1909. Pp. 328, 338–74.

FURTHER READING

Griffiths, 619–23.

Harvey, 102–30, 192–99.

Virgoe, Roger. "Some Ancient Indictments in the King's Bench Referring to Kent, 1450–1452." In *Documents Illustrative of Medieval Kentish Society*, edited by F. R. H. Du Boulay, 214–65. Kent Archaeological Society 18. Ashford: Headly Brother, 1964.

PROFESSIONS IN THE GENERAL PARDON

abbess: *MED* "abbes(se" (n.), 1. A woman superior of a convent of nuns.

armerer: *MED* "armūrēr" (n.), 1.(a) One who makes or repairs armor or weapons, an armorer.

baile: *MED* "baillif" (n.), 1.(a) An official of the English crown with delegated administrative or judicial authority; the king's officer in a county, hundred, or town; the keeper of a royal castle, gate, or forest. 2.(a) An important administrative official elected by the citizens of an English town. 3. An agent of a lord, responsible to the lord or his seneschal for the management of a manor. 4. A minor officer of justice under a sheriff or judge.

baker/bakere: *MED* "bākere" (n.), 1.(a) A baker; a member of the craft of bakers or of one of the two divisions [broun-bakeres, whit ~] of the craft.

barbour/barboure: *MED* "barbǒur" (n.) 1.(a) One who shaves beards and cuts hair; a barber, hair-dresser; also, one who combines this occupation with blood-letting, tooth-extraction, and minor surgery; hence, a barber-surgeon. 2. A member of a craft-guild or company of barbers and barber-surgeons. 3. One who trims wool fleece.

bocher: *MED* "bǫcher, bǒcher" (n.) 1. One who slaughters cattle and swine and sells the meat, a butcher.

The Pardon Roll of July 1450

boteman: *MED* "bōt" (n.) (1). 3. In cpds. and combs.: (c) ~ man, one who owns or manages a boat or ship; also, a sailor.

brasyer: *MED* "brāsier" (n.) 1. (a) A worker in copper, bronze, or brass.

brewer/bruer: *MED* "breuer(e" (n.) 1. (a) A craftsman who brews and sells ale or beer, brewer.

burgess: *MED* "burǧeis" (n.) 1. (a) A freeman of a town, a citizen with full rights and privileges; also, an inhabitant of a town; – usually used of city merchants and master craftsmen in the guilds. 2. (a) A magistrate or other official of a town; a member of the council or assembly governing a town; (b) the representative of a town in the House of Commons.

capper: *MED* "capper" (n.) 1. A maker or seller of caps.

carpenter/carpynter: *MED* "carpentēr" (n.) 1. (a) A carpenter. (c.) member of a guild or company of carpenters.

chaplain: *MED* "chapelein" (n.) 1. A priest officiating in a chapel (whether public or private). 2. (a) (a) Any clergyman who assists a cleric of higher rank in performing his administrative and religious duties.

chapman: *MED* "chap-man" (n.) 1a. (a) A merchant, trader, dealer; also, a peddler, hawker. 2. (a) A merchant's agent or factor; (b) a buyer or customer.

chaundeler: *MED* "chaundelēr" (n.) 2. (a) One who makes candles or deals in materials for making candles; a chandler. (b) the servant of a noble's household in charge of lighting.

clerk: *MED* "clerk" (n.) 1. (a) A member of the clergy (as distinguished from the laity), an ecclesiastic, cleric. 2. (a) One who is educated; a learned person, scholar, master (of some subject); (b) a man of letters, writer, author; (c) a pupil, student; esp., a university student. 3. (a) Secretary, amanuensis, recorder; also, an official in charge of records and accounts.

coke: *MED* "cōk" (n.) (6) 1. (a) One who prepares and cooks food in a household, a cook; (b) one who prepares and sells cooked articles of food.

colyer: *MED* "cōliēr" (n.) 1. (a) One who makes and sells charcoal, collier.

constable: *MED* "cŏnstāble" (n.) 2. (a) The chief officer of a ruler's household or court; major-domo, chief steward. 3. (a) A governor or warden of a royal castle, stronghold, or domain. 5. (a) An officer of the king's peace (as of a county, hundred, or town); justice of the peace, constable.

cordener/cordewaner/cordewayner: *MED* "cordewānēr" (n.) 1. (a) A worker in cordovan leather; one who makes shoes of cordwain; cordwainer, member of a cordwainers' guild.

corvescer/corveser: *MED* "corveisēr" (n.) 1. A worker in leather, a shoemaker.

coryour: *MED* "curr(e)iȝur" (n.) 1. (a) One whose trade is the currying of leather; leather-dresser, currier; a member of the guild of curriers.

coser: *MED* "cŏssēr, cōssēr" (n.) 1. A dealer; esp., a horse-dealer.

coteler: *MED* "cutelēr," (n.) 1. A craftsman who makes cutting instruments, such as knives, daggers, etc.; a cutler.

couper: *MED* "cŏuper(e" (n.) 1. (a) One whose occupation is the making and repairing of casks, tubs, etc.; a cooper.

coverlydwever: *MED* "cŏverlīte" (n.) 1. A cloth for covering a bed; bedspread, coverlet. 3. *Combs.* ~ maker, ~ wever, ~ yarn.

dobeletemaker: *MED* "dŏublet" (n.) 1. (a) A man's tight-fitting garment, covering the body from the neck to the hips or thighs, a doublet; (b) a similar garment reinforced with metal rings or plates. (d) ~ *maker*, a maker of doublets.

draper: *MED* "drāpēr" (n.) 1. (a) One who weaves and/or sells cloth; clothier.

drover: *MED* "drover(e" (n.) 1. (a) One who drives livestock to market, a dealer in livestock; drover; (b) one who drives a draft animal, driver.

diere/dyer: *MED* "deier" (n.) 1. One who dyes cloth, etc.; a dyer.

esquire: *MED* "esquiēr, esquīer" (n.) 1. A squire, ranking under a knight, in feudal military service or in landed tenure. 2. A young nobleman charged with personal attendance upon a sovereign or other high personage.

fyssher: *MED* "fisher(e" (n.) 1. (a) One who is engaged in fishing, fisherman; (b) one who sells fish, fish monger.

fleccher: *MED* "flecchēr, -iēr, -ŏur" (n.) 1. (a) A maker or seller of arrows.

freser: *MED* "friser, -are" (n.) 1. A maker of frieze cloth; one who friezes cloth.

fuller: *MED* "fullere" (n.) 1. A fuller of cloth.

fysshmonger: See "fyssher."

gentilman/gentylman: *MED* "ğentīl-man" (n.) 1a. (a) A man of noble or gentle birth, one of the gentry. 2. A member of the nobility whose behavior conforms to the ideals of chivalry and Christianity, a gentleman.

glover: *MED* "glōver" (n.) 1. (a) One who makes or sells gloves; a member of a glovers' guild.

goldsmyth: *MED* "gōld-smith" (n.) 1. (a) One who works in gold, goldsmith; also, one who works in silver or other precious metals.

graver: *MED* "grāver(e" (n.) 1. (a) A carver, sculptor, engraver; (b) a digger, miner.

grocer: *MED* "grōcer" (n.) 1. (a) A wholesale dealer in merchandise, such as wine, spices, pharmaceutic items, foods, etc.

grome: *MED* "grōm" (n.) 1. (b) a boy; (c) a youth, young man. 2. (a) A male servant, attendant; a retainer; a knight's squire; (b) an attendant or minor officer in any of the various departments in a royal, noble, or ecclesiastical household, ranking below the yeoman but higher than the page. 3. (a) A man of low station or birth; also, a worthless person; (b) a man.

haburdassher/haberdasaher: *MED* "haberdasher" (n.) 1. "A seller of various small articles of trade; also, a member of a company of such tradesmen; *haberdasher(es ware*, caps, purses, points, beads, spurs, inkhorns, thread, stationery, etc.

hadwarman: *MED* "hard-wāre" (n.) 1. Metal goods, hardware; ~ *man*, a dealer in hardware

hakeneyman: *MED* "hakenei(e" (n.) 1. (a) A small saddle-horse, often one let for hire; a hackney horse. 2. In cpds. & combs.: ~ *man*, a man who keeps hackneys for hire.

halywaterclerk: *MED* "hōlī water, hōlī-water" (n.) 1. (a) Water consecrated to be used in various religious ceremonies and observances. (b) in cpds. and combs.: ~ *clerk*, a clerk in minor orders who carries the holy water vessel.

helyare: *MED* "hēliere" (n.) 1. (a) A roofer, tiler, slater; thatcher.

hosyare: *MED* "hōsier" (n.) 1. (a) A maker or seller of hose, hosier.

husbondman: *MED* "hus-bōnd-man" (n.) 1. (a) The head of a family or a household, householder. (b) a steward; (c) a farmer, tiller of the soil, owner of a farm; also, a rustic. (d) a married man, a husband.

inholder: *MED* "in-hōlder" (n.) 1. An innkeeper.

joynour: *MED* "joinǒur" (n.) 1. (a) A maker of furniture, small boxes, handles, etc.

knight: *MED* "knīght" (n.) 1. (a) A noble warrior; a member of the land-holding ruling class, owing military service to his lord and fighting on horseback; one who had received the status of knight from the king or other important knight.

laborer: *MED* "lābǒurer(e" (n.) 1. (a) A manual worker; esp. an unskilled laborer, casual laborer; (b) an agricultural worker, plowman, digger, etc.

maltman/malteman: *MED* "malt" (n.) 1. (a) Grain, usually barley, which has undergone the malting process; malt. 2. In cpds. & combs.: ~ *man*, a maker or seller of malt.

marchaunt: *MED* "marchaunt" (n.) 1. (a) A wholesale businessman; a factor, broker; a peddler, retailer; a shopkeeper.

mariner/maryner: *MED* "marinēr" (n.) 1. (a) A seaman, sailor; navigator; boatman.

mason: *MED* "māsǒun" (n.) 1. (a) A mason, worker or builder in stone; one who dresses, lays, or carves stone.

melwryght: *MED* "milne" (n.) 1. (a) A water mill for grinding grain; (b) a wind mill; (d) any power-driven mill for grinding grain, etc.; (e) a hand mill, a quern; (f) a fulling mill. 2. In cpds. & combs.: ~ *wright*, designer or maker of mills.

mercer: *MED* "mercer" (n.) 1. (a) A merchant; a dealer in textiles, member of the Mercers' Guild; or a seller of sundry small items.

miller: *MED*, "milner(e" (n.) 1. (a) A miller; one who runs a mill.

notery: *MED* "nōtārī(e" (n.) 1. (a) A scribe authorized to draw up and authenticate documents and legal instruments, act as a witness, take depositions, etc.; notary public. (b) a secretary, an amanuensis.

parisshclerk: *MED* "parish(e" (n.) 1. (a) A parish, an ecclesiastical or civil administrative division. ~ *clerk*, q.v. See "clerk."

parker: *MED* "parker" (n.) 1. (a) A parker; an official in charge of an enclosed tract of land or forest; official charged with the management of game in a royal forest or preserve.

pedeler: *MED* "ped(e)lere" 1. A peddler, hawker.

plomer: *MED* "plumber" (n.) 1. (a) A worker in lead, plumber; an installer or repairer of lead roofs, gutters, pipes, etc.

pulter: *MED* "pultēr(e" (n.) 1. (a) A poulterer; a member of the craft of poulterers. (b) a minor officer in a great household dealing with poultry.

pynner: *MED* "pinner(e" (n.) 1. (a) A maker of various kinds of metal pins and nails.

reder: *MED* "rēder(e" (n.) (1) 1. (a) One who reads or peruses something written; (b) one who reads or recites aloud; (c) a clerk responsible for reading or expounding religious works; also, a reader at collation; (d) a cleric who reads the lessons in a church service; a cleric in the minor order of reader, lector; one who exercises similar functions in the Old Testament. "rēder(e" n. (2) 1. (a) A thatcher.

repyer/ripier/rypyer: *MED* "ripier(e" (n.) 1. (a) One who carries fish inland for sale.

roper: *MED* "rōper(e" (n.) (a) A maker of ropes, cables, cord, or string; also, a rope seller.

sawyer: *MED* "sauer(e" (n.) 1. (a) One who saws, a sawyer.

sadeler/sadler: *MED* "sādelēr(e" (n.) 1. (a) A maker or seller of saddles or saddlery.

servant/servaunt: *MED* "servaunt" (n.) 1. (a) One owing a duty of service to a master or lord; a laborer for hire; a male or female domestic servant, household servant.

sexteyn: *MED* "sextein(e" (n.) 1. (a) An officer of a church or religious house who cares for the buildings, ornaments, vestments, etc., and who attends to bell-ringing, burials, etc., a sexton.

sherman: *MED* "shēr-man" (n.) 1. (a) One who shears the nap of woolen cloth, a shearman.

shipman: *MED*, "ship-man" (n.) 1. (a) A sailor, seaman; one skilled in navigation; also, an oarsman.

skynner: *MED* "skinner(e" (n.) 1. (a) One who prepares or sells animal skins, a furrier, skinner.

smyth: *MED* "smith" (n.) 1. (a) A blacksmith, an ironworker; a farrier; also, a worker in various metals. (b) an artisan, a workman; a carpenter.

soudeer: *MED* "soudiŏur" (n.) 1. (a) One engaged in military service, a fighting man, soldier; a paid soldier. (b) a professional soldier serving in a foreign army, a mercenary.

spyser: *MED* "spīcer" (n.) 1. (a) A dealer in spices, an apothecary.

syngleman: *MED* "sengle" (adj.) 2. Single, unmarried; also, as noun: an unmarried person; ~ *womman* (*man*, etc.).

taloghchaundeler/talogh chaundeler: *MED* "talou(e" (n.) 1. (a) The fatty tissue of an animal; fatty tissue from around the kidneys or other internal organs of an animal. (b) rendered animal fat, suet, tallow; tallow used in waterproofing, soapmaking, etc., or sold as a commodity. ~ *chaundeler*, one who makes or sells tallow candles.

tanner: *MED* "tanner(e" (n.) 1. (a) One who tans hides to make leather, a tanner.

taverner: *MED* "taverner(e" (n.) 1. (a) A tavernkeeper.

tayler/tayllour/taillour: *MED* "taillŏur" (n.) 1. (a) A maker of clothes, tailor.

thaccher/theccher: *MED* "thaccher(e" (n.) 1. (a) One who covers the roof or walls of a building with thatch or other material.

tilemaker: *MED* "tīle" (n.) (2) 1. (a) A brick; a masonry tile. 2. (a) A roofing tile; a stone slate used as a roofing tile. 3. (a) A paving tile; a painted paving tile. 4. In misc. cpds. related to senses 1., 2., & 3.: ~ *formere (makere)*, one who makes or shapes bricks or tiles.

trumpet: *MED* "trompet" (n.) 2. A trumpeter.

turnour: *MED* "turnŏur" (n.) (1) 1. (a) One who fashions objects of wood, metal, etc. on a lathe;—usu. with ref. to a member of the guild of turners; also, a basketmaker.

tyler: *MED* "tīler" (n.) 1. (a) One who lays tiles on roofs, houses, floors, etc. (b) a maker of tiles.

underconstable: See "constable".

vyntner: *MED* "vintner" (n.) 1. (a) A wine merchant; a vintner.

waterberer: *MED* "wāter" (n.) 4c. In cpds. and combs. related to one or more senses of b) denoting transporters or purveyors of the commodity of water: ~ *bere (berere, fecchere, secher)*.

waterman/watirman: See "waterberer".

webbe: *MED* "webbe" (n.) 1. (a) One whose occupation is weaving, a weaver; also, a member of a weavers' guild.

wever: *MED* "wēver(e " (n.) 1. (a) One who weaves or whose occupation is weaving; a member of the weavers' guild.

wexchaundeler: *MED* "wax" (n.) (1) 2a. (a) Beeswax as used in tapers or other types of candles; also in fig. context; also, coll. beeswax candles. (b) ~

chaundeler (makere), one who makes wax candles, a wax chandler; also, a member of the guild of candle makers.

yoman: *MED* "yēman" (n.) 1. (a) A free-born male attendant in a royal or noble household holding a rank above that of groom and page but below that of squire, a household official; an attendant or assistant to someone of higher rank, a retainer. (b) a subordinate officer in a specific department of a royal or noble household, ranking below a sergeant and above a groom. (c) a subordinate military officer. (d) a hired laborer; also, a member of a ship's crew, seaman; (e) as a term of disparagement: an underling, inferior. 2. A member of the landholding class below the rank of squire; a man holding a small landed estate.

PARDONS

July 6, 1450, Westminster, Membrane 21

Pardon to John Mortymer of all murders, insurrections, treasons, Westminster, felonies, misprisions, offences, impeachments, confederacies, conspiracies, interlocutions, ignorances, negligences, plunderings, spoliations, robberies, contempts, forswearings and misdeeds and of all penalties, punishments and forfeitures incurred thereby. By King.

July 6, 1450, Westminster, Membrane 20

Pardon to John Mortymer, as above and below. By King.

July 6, 1450, Westminster, Membrane 13

General pardon to John Mortymer, at the request of the queen, though he and others in great number in divers places of the realm and specially in Kent and the places adjacent of their own presumption gathered together against the statutes of the realm to the contempt of the king's estate; and if he or any other wish for letters of pardon, the chancellor shall issue the same severally. By King.

The like to the following:—

William Tyrell the younger, esquire, Matthew Hay, esquire, John Batell, esquire, Richard Shodewell, "gentilman," Roger Wyke of Colchestre and Richard Stace the elder, in Essex and Middlesex. By King.

July 6, 1450, Westminster, Membrane 13

John Robynson, William Bygge, Simon Morley and John Swayn of Canterbury, county Kent. By King.

July 7, 1450, Westminster, Membrane 13

Richard Yonge of Westerham, county Kent, "yoman," in the hundred of Westerham. By King.

William Norden and George Colier, constables of the hundred of Tenam, county Kent, and William Aytheherst of Tenam, "yoman," and the rest of that hundred. By King.

Henry Appelton of Bukwell in Boghton Aluph, county Kent, "gentilman," Nicholas Godefelawe of Boghton Aluph, "yoman," John Lane of the same, "yoman," Thomas Sabyne of the same, "yoman," William Hely of the same, "husbondman," and Richard Les of the same, "smyth," and all men of that parish. By King.

John Miller of Holyngbourne, county Kent, "gentilman," William Spert of Halden, county Kent, "gentilman," Thomas Phelip of Ledes, county Kent, "yoman," John Norton of Stapelherst, county Kent, "yoman," John Morys of Holyngbourne, "laborer," Thomas Heron of Assheford, county Kent, "laborer," William Miller of Wrotham, county Kent, "pulter," Robert Miller of Wrotham, "pulter," William Miller of Orpyngton, county Kent, "husbondman," Richard Miller of Saint Mary Cray, county Kent, "pulter," and Thomas Miller of Orpyngton, "laborer." By King.

Laurence Miller of Lenham, county Kent, and Richard Miller of Lynstede, county Kent, "yoman." By King.

Richard Stydolf of Westerham, "mason," and John atte Welle of Westerham. By King.

John Thorpe and John Wybern, constables of Wroteham hundred, and Thomas Arcall and all others dwelling in that hundred. John Rowe of Boxle, James Burbage, John Burbage, Henry Dore, Robert Burbage, William Rowe of Aylysford, Edmund Rowe of Aylysford and Hugh Wode of Rydyng, county Kent. By King.

Richard Forthe of Strode, county Kent, "yoman," William Petur of Strode and John Northe of Strode. By King.

John Colyer of Mersham and Richard Rolf of Kynggysnoth, constables of Langebregge hundred, and Thomas Chapman and all others of that hundred. By King.

William Symon of Godmersham, county Kent, and Denys Bakke of Chilham, county Kent, constables of Felbergh hundred, and Nicholas Hylles of Godmersham and all others of that hundred and town. By King.

William Foughyll, constable of Chart hundred, and Andrew Sprotte and all others of that hundred. By King.

Thomas Grymston and Henry Crompe, constables of Molton hundred, and Stephen Waste of Stokebery and all others of that hundred and town. By King.

John Godyng, constable of Tunbrigge town, county Kent, "yoman," John Partriche of Tunbrigge, "yoman," John Tyherst the elder, "baker," John Huchyn, constable of Heldon in Tunbrigge, and John Kyppyng, constable of la South Burgh in Tunbrigge, "yoman," and all in that town. By King.

July 7, 1450, Westminster, Membrane 13
Thomas Wareham of Croydon, county Surrey, "yoman."

Laurence Mongeham of Stone, county Kent, and Henry Dobyll of Wyttersham, county Kent, and all others in Oxney hundred.

John Cheyne of Estchirche in the isle of Shephey, county Kent, knight, and John Symond of Mynstre in the said isle, "husbondman," and all others in the isle.

Goodman Durbarre and William atte Towne, constables of Langporte hundred, county Kent, and Thomas Bewefrere of Hope, county Kent, and all of that hundred.

Stephen Hogge of Frithynden, county Kent, "gentilman," and Stephen Norton of Chart by Sutton, county Kent, "gentilman," and all others of those parishes.

Henry Sonde of Dorkyng, county Surrey, "gentilman," Henry Carpenter of Dorkyng, "yoman," Richard Plome of Dorkyng, "baker," John Goodman of Dorkyng, "skynner," Richard Brigges of Dorkyng, "roper," and John Gerard of Dorkyng, "carpenter," and all others in the hundred of Wotton.

Thomas Pyke of Notehurst, county Sussex, "yoman," John Elvy of Notehurst, "yoman," William Lucas of Notehurst, "husbondman," John Bottyng of Notehust, "husbondman," Stephen Bottyng of Notehurst, "husbondman," John Monke of Notenust, "laborer," William Benke of Notehurst, "laborer," John Selede of Notehurst," laborer," Thomas Weller of Notehurst, "tayllour," Thomas Polyngton of Notehurst, "yoman," and John Croft of Notehurst, "parker."

John Goolde of Middilton, county Kent, "gentilman," Richard Grovehirst of Middilton, "gentilman," and John Buntyng of Middilton, "gentilman."

Henry Cutbussh of Bydynden, county Kent, "yoman," and Laurence Heausell of Bydynden, "yoman," and all other men in that parish.

John Browne, bailiff of Folkston, and all other men in Folkston hundred.

John Ysaake of Patrykesbourne, county Kent, esquire, and William atte Wode of Brigge, county Kent, "smyth," and all other men in Brygge hundred.

Thomas Stokynbury, constable of Lytelfeld hundred, county Kent, William Hexstall of Estpekham, county Kent, esquire, Richard Erkenbold and Richard Bake of Estpekham, "yoman," and all other men in the hundred.

Thomas Bullok of Letherhede, county Surrey, "baker," Thomas Dene of Letherhede, "husbondman," John Grofham of Letherhede, "husbondman," William Holewey of Letherhede, "mercer," Thomas Holme of Letherhede, "husbondman," and George Barde of Letherhede, "tanner," and all other men in Coppedthorn hundred, county Surrey.

John Foreby of Isfeld, county Sussex, "gentilman," Thomas atte Welle of Bukstede, county Sussex, "gentilman," William Bailly of Maghfeld, county Sussex, "gentilman," Thomas Baker of Ukfeld, county Sussex, "yoman," William Manser of Ukfeld, "yoman," and William Pont of Magfeld, "yoman," constables of Lokesfeld hundred and all other men in the hundred.

Thomas Buste of Ryngmere, county Sussex, "yoman," and Andrew Thaccher of Ryngmere, "yoman," constables of Ryngmere hundred, and all men within the hundred.

Richard Braybroke of Suthwerk, county Surrey, "sadeler."

Thomas Gymmour of Westfyrle, county Sussex, "gentilman," and John Bysshe of Westfyrle, "yoman."

Andrew Kebbyll of London, "gentilman," Thomas Grene of Melton by Gravesende, county Kent, Thomas Ballyng of Gravesende, "husbondman," Thomas Plot of Gravesende, "yoman," and John Laurence of Melton by Gravesende, "yoman."

Richard Maye of Saundryssh, county Kent, and all others in that parish.

John Mars, in Essex.

Nicholas Cumberworth of Suthwerk, "graver," and John Brettayne of Suthwerk, "brewer."

John Somer of Dorkyng, county Surrey, "husbondman," and Henry Godman of Dorkyng, "husbondman."

Gabriel Berwerd of Tysherst, county Sussex, "yoman," and John Holbeme of Tysseherst, "yoman," constables of Shoeswell hundred, county Sussex.

July 7, 1450, Westminster, Membrane 12

John Baker of Pecham in Camerwell, county Surrey, the elder, "yoman," one of the constables of Brixstone hundred, county Surrey, Richard Baker of Pecham, "yoman," John Baker of Pecham, "yoman," and John Baker of Pecham in Carnerwell, the younger, "gentilman."

Richard Fynche of Heighton, county Sussex, "husbondman," and William Herston of Bisshopeston, county Sussex, "husbondman," constables of Flexbergh hundred, and Richard Dunton of Bisshopeston, "husbondman," William Gefferay of Blachyngton, county Sussex, "husbondman," Richard Clerk of Heighton, "husbondman," and Richard atte Lay of Denton, county Sussex, "husbondman."

William Deraunt of London, "gentilman," and Alice his wife.

John Clerke of Boughton Menchonse, "yoman," Robert Meryhome, Henry Hunt and Richard Pikenden.

John Pastron, John Welles, Richard Shymyng of Boxle and all other men in that parish.

William Fynne of Erith and John Michell of Erith, county Kent.

John Michell of Erith, county Kent, "baker."

Richard Gildeford of Haukeherst, county Kent, "taillour," Henry Pelham of Haukeherst, "couper," Robert Mercer of Haukeherst, "carpenter," Simon Pode of Haukeherst, "carpenter," and John Frenshe of Haukeherst, "laborer," and all other men in that parish.

Robert Bernes of Haukeherst, "gentilman," John Tongeherst of Haukeherst, "gentilman," John Watte of Haukeherst, "yoman," Robert Stonden of Haukeherst, "husbondman, Robert Foucener of Haukeherst, "parisshclerk," and Laurence Heausell of Bydenden, county Kent, "yoman."

Guy atte Wode of Boughton Menchonse, "yoman," William Norton of the same, Thomas atte Wode, Henry Purs and Guy Ensyng of Chilham and all others in those towns.

John Roberd of Cranebroke, county Kent, the elder, "yoman," and John Roberd of Cranebroke the younger, "gentilman," and all other men in that town.

John Tothe of Chipstede the younger, Stephen Tothe of Chipstede and John Tommes of Chipstede and all other men in that parish.

Thomas Changle late of Flete, county Lincoln, chaplain, alias of Ealdyng, county Kent.

Thomas Lawe of Ealdyng, "yoman," Robert Ryng of Ealdyng, "husbondman," John Kyrbill of Ealdyng, "halywaterclerk," and Richard Kyrbill of Ealdyng, "laborer."

William Edward of Sandeherst, county Kent, "gentilman," Thomas Heausell of Haukeherst, "yoman," William Bocher of Haukeherst, "smyth," and Thomas Mercer of Haukeherst, "repyer."

Richard Sankee of Seele, county Kent, "yoman," and all others in that parish. Thomas Heth of Wolwiche, county Kent, "gentilman," and Richard Lovelace of Byngesdoun, county Kent, "gentilman."

John Haton alias Langeston of Bermondessey, county Surrey.

William Morecok, Thomas Morecok, John Morecok and Thomas Labe, in Kent.

Robert Neyte, Thomas Bedmynton, Hugh Frere and William Bedmynton, all of Harytesham, county Kent, and all other men in that parish.

John Burbage of Buxle, "husbondman," Nicholas Faram, of Buxle "husbondman," Richard Sebrid of Buxle, "mason," John Joce of Buxle, "mason," Richard Manney of Maydeston, "mason," Robert Burbage of Boxle, "laborer," John Faram, William Faram and John Bance, in Kent.

Robert Nee of Heryotesham and William Chaumber of the same and all others in that parish.

Simon Shipton of Wolwiche, county Kent, "yoman," Robert Newedegate of Wolwiche and William Pegge of Wolwiche.

William Northampton of Wolwiche, "gentilman," Thomas atte Wode of Wolwiche, "husbondman," John Edwyn of Wolwiche, "husbondman," Robert Egell of Wolwiche, "boteman," John Frost of Wolwiche, "boteman," and Nicholas atte Gore of Wolwiche, "yoman."

Richard Chyntyng of Petynghoo, county Sussex, "husbondman," constable of Holmescrowe (*sic*) hundred, county Sussex" John Walkelyn of Mechyng, county Sussex, the elder, "yoman, John Shulder of Radmylde, county Sussex," husbondman," John Theccher of Southse, county Sussex, "husbondman," John Auecok of Tecelescombe, county Sussex, "husbondman," and John Porter of Petynghoo, "laborer," with all others of the said hundred.

Laurence Engette, John Grene, John Crounber, Thomas Engette, John Grovehurst, William Colsall, George Warman, John Barker, Thomas Clement, Guy Whithors, William Lambert and John Harry, all of Ewade, county Kent, "husbondmen," and all in that parish.

Thomas Sprever, Thomas Grene, Thomas Wattys, "yoman," John Page, "yoman," John Hammes, "barbour," Robert Hall, "laborer, and John Rede, "waterman," all of Melton by Gravesende, county Kent, and William Flour, "chaundeler," Thomas Stace, "yoman," Thomas Est, "haburdassher," John Baker, "husbondman," William Shene, "waterman," and William Fill, "carpenter," all of Gravesende.

Thomas Basset, the elder, "yoman," Thomas Basset the younger, "yoman," and John Basset, "yoman," all of Cullesdon, county Surrey, and all other men in that town.

William Piert of Alveley, John Lowes of Thorrok Grey and Thomas Barker of West Thorrok and all men in Chafford hundred, county Essex.

John Merymouth late of Honyton, county Devon, "fuller."

Thomas Appuldurfeld of Feversham, county Kent, esquire.

John Clerke of Kenordyngton, county Kent, "husbondman," Thomas Benet, John Spaget, Richard Bolte, "cordewaner," Stephen atte Hill, "husbondman," John Miller, "husbondman," Richard Andrewe, "carpynter," John Lyggand, "carpynter," Richard Judde, "husbondman," Richard Miller, "cordewaner," William Whiton, "fyssher," Richard atte Rygge, "husbondman," William atte Reche, "cordewaner," and John Lucas, "husbondman."

Bernard Cavell of Chesylherst, county Kent, "husbondman," and John Cavell of the same, "husbondman."

John Stanmer alias Davy of Feversham, county Kent, "yoman," and all others of that town.

Bartholomew Bourne of Dodyngton, and John Eytherst, Richard Miller, Laurence Roger, John Cotyng, Richard Bedyll, John Dene, Adam Grenstrete, William Marlere and Thomas Best, all of Lyndestede.

Richard London late of London alias late of Westminster county Middlesex, "corcer," alias "waterberer."

William Isle of Sundrysshe, county Kent.

Richard Taillour, Stephen Saveryn, William Heggeman, Thomas Nicholl, Alan Miller and John Heggeman the younger of Orsette, county Essex, and all in that town.

John Martyn of Crassalton, county Surrey, the elder, "laborer," and all of that town.

William Mareys of Preston by Feversham, county Kent, esquire, and all of that parish.

Walter Kyng of Hunslowe, county Middlesex, "gentilman," and George Selet of Twykenam, county Middlesex, "yoman," constables of Thistilworth hundred.

Walter Waleys of Penshurst, county Kent, "yoman," William Warde of Havyr, county Kent, "yoman," constables of Somerden hundred, Thomas Wilbore of Chiddynston, John Clerk of Hevyr," yoman," John Broker of Chiddyngston, "yoman," and Roger atte Wode, "yoman," John Wodgate, "yoman," William Ware, "yoman," Richard Clerk, "yoman," and William Clerk, "yoman," all of the same, and John Coret and William Wymbyll, "yoman," both of Hevyr, and all others of those parishes and hundred.

William Edward of Sandeherst, esquire, Thomas White of Sandeherst, county Kent, "husbondman," and Robert Bernes of Haukhirst, county Kent, "gentylman," and all others of those towns.

John Horell of London, "dyer," alias of Dakenan, Richard Goldsmyth of Dakynham, county Essex, "husbondman," and Richard Wodelond, "colyer," John Plom, "husbondman," and John Sparwe, "husbondman," all of the same, and all others in Dakynham and Berkyng.

Laurence Pakke and Robert Rows and all others in Barmyage, John Tutsam, Richard Tutsam, John Reve and William Hunt and all others in Westfarlegh, Stephen Crouche and all others in Watryng, Richard Baker and all others in Pekham, and John Crompe, John Pakke the elder, John Pakke the younger John Myller, John Southland, William Gore, John Gore, William Kenelyn, John Reve, John Porter, John Clyffe, Thomas Nasshe and John Hamond and all others in Tearston.

Thomas Hunte and Philip Castell, constables of Folkeston hundred, and John Grenford, William Fyneux and Nicholas Everynge and all others in that hundred.

John Halke, constable of Pecham hundred, and Thomas Dowll and Simon Court and all others in that hundred.

John Raymes of Hadley, county Suffolk, "fuller."

Robert Pryk of Hadley, "mercer."

William Clovyer of Hadley, "wever."

John Grene, "gentylman," Richard Weller, "husbondman," John Weller," husbondman," Richard atte Lowe, husbondman, Roger Fourlonger, "husbondman," John Fourlonger, "hus bondman," Robert Offyngton, "husbondman," William Folvyle, "husbondman," Thomas Edwyn, "husbondman," Roger Joppe, "laborer," William atte Herst, "laborer," Roger Mayster, "laborer," Richard Wyker, "laborer," Roger Streter, "laborer," John Valyer, "laborer," John Mychell, "laborer," John Creps, "laborer," and Richard Pacche, "laborer," all of Sheple, co Sussex, John Dowce of Westgrensted, county Sussex, "husbondman," and Ralph Parson, "husbondman," John Apsley the younger John Broker, "husbondman," John Maunsell, "husbondman, Robert Hunt, "laborer," Richard Frensshe, "laborer," Stephen Champeneys, "husbondman," and John Colman, "laborer," all of Stenynge, and Roger Wolffe, "gentylman," John Wolffe,"gentilman," William Bouchy, "husbondman," John Cradyll, "laborer," William Chapman, "carpenter," John Waterman, "laborer," and Laurence Perys, "laborer," all of Assyngton, and Richard Pollard, "husbondman," Thomas Webbe, "laborer," John Hardyng, "laborer," Laurence Couper, "couper," John Longe the younger, Clement Cayn, William Capeleyn, "husbondman," Robert Capeleyn, "husbondman," and James Pacchyng, "carpenter," all of Wassyngton, and Thomas atte Hille, "husbondman," Richard Parker, "webbe," Thomas Waterman, "husbondman," William Heryssh, "laborer," James Turgis, "laborer," Richard Melward, "laborer," and John Bregger the younger, all of Wormyngherst.

Richard Kyng of Cowlyng, county Kent, "husbondman," constable of Shamull hundred, county Kent, Henry Spenser, chaplain of the parish church of Cowlyng, and John Pardour and Roger Smyth, "husbondman," both of Cowlyng, and all other men in that parish.

Robert Ball of Thornham, county Kent, "gentilman," and William Lorde, "bocher," Herman Pokill, "draper," and John Wenyall, "ripier," all of Berghstede, county Kent, and John Reynold, "bocher," Thomas Reynolde, "bocher,* Robert Wodegate, "husbondman," and William Everynden, "husbondman," all of Ledys, county Kent, and George Lovynden, "fuller," Richard Peny, "laborer," John Adam, "corveser," John Ayot the elder, "husbondman," John Broke, "husbondman," John Lambe, "husbondman," William Fox, "laborer," Robert Gybbys, "draper," William Breche, "draper," Robert atte Wode, "husbondman," Robert Paulyn," laborer," Gilbert Bresyng," laborer," Robert Isowede, "laborer," John Tayllour, "husbondman," Thomas Charlys, "laborer," Thomas Halk, "fuller," and Simon Halk, "carpenter," all of Holyngbourne, county Kent, and all others within those parishes.

Roger Stede of Heryettesham, county Kent, "repyer."

Thomas Childe of Witham, county Essex, "yoman." John Mason of Maydeston, county Kent, "wexchaundeler."

John Cattys, "gentylman," Thomas Chapman, "yoman," John Barbour, "yoman," John Whyte, "yoman," Stephen Wrango "yoman," Richard Benet, "yoman," John at Well, "yoman," John Sexteyn, "yoman," Thomas Wryght, "yoman," Thomas Arcell, "yoman," John Hunte, "yoman," and John Palgrave, "yoman," all of Wroteham, county Kent.

Henry Lecheford of Craweley, county Sussex, "gentilman."

Thomas Scute of Lambehithemerssh, county Surrey, "yoman," and Rose his wife and all others in that town.

William Belde of Canterbury, "gentilman."

John Penwortham of Canterbury, "gentilman."
Thomas Chapman of Lambehithemerssh, "waterman,"
Henry Wraston of Upchirche and William Wraston.
Robert Lauther. chaplain.
Thomas Andrewe, "soudeer" alias "baker" alias "newebafcer of Dertford, county Kent.
Thomas Stone of Oxford, county Oxford, "gentilman."
Thomas Stokyngbury, "smyth," Thomas Partriche, "smyth," John Roos, "husbondman," William Knokker of Estpekham, county Kent, "smyth."
Arnald Poynt, "hadwardman," Thomas Sybnam, "mercer," Hugh Johnson, "haberdasaher," Ralph Alamdam, "sherman," Dederic Goldsmyth, "goldsmyth," John Daucart, "goldsmyth," William Bullok, "goldsmyth," John Staunton, "coser," John Bruke, "servant," and Edmund Coope, "freser," all of Suthwerk, county Surrey.

July 7, 1450, Westminster, Membrane 11

John Carter, constable of Crasaalton town, county Surrey, and Thomas Leycestre, "yoman," Thomas Broker, "fuller," Thomas Barton, "draper," John Sumpter, "laborer," John Coke, "cordener," and Thomas Cok, "laborer," all of Crassalton. By King.

John Chaury of Oxstede, "husbondman," constable of that town, and John Couper the elder, "tanner," and John Couper the younger, "tanner," both of Oxstede.

Simon Hunt, "taloghchaundeler," William Porter, "yoman," and Nicholas Philpot, "yoman," all of Suthwerk, county Surrey.

John Mavsyn of Cattysfeld, county Sussex, and John Parker of Hoo, county Sussex, constables of Nenefeld hundred, county Sussex, and Henry Mavsyn of Cattysfeld.

Richard Beche of Setelescombe, county Sussex, "yoman," and Robert Morfote of Ewherst, county Sussex, "draper," constables of Staple hundred, county Sussex.

Roger Mapilton of Totenham, county Middlesex, "mason."

John Clerk, parson of the church of Halgesto in Hoo hundred, county Kent, and Stephen Nelyr and John Turner, constables of that hundred, and all of the same.

Thomas Andrewe of Laughton, county Sussex, "yoman," and Richard Melewerd of Chidyngleygh, county Sussex, "yoman," constables of Shepelake hundred, county Sussex, and Henry atte Bregge the younger, "yoman," Thomas Upton, "yoman," Richard Edewyn, "yoman," John atte Legh, "yoman," Thomas Frytour and William Snoddon, "yoman," all of Laughton, and William Lullam of Rype, county Sussex, "yoman."

Roger Cheseman of Eltham and Edmund Ryculff of Lee, constable of Blakeheth hundred, county Kent, and all others, etc.

Thomas Pympe of All Hallows parish in Hoo hundred, esquire, and John Turnour, constable of that hundred, and all others in the said town.

Thomas atte Wode, "smyth," Richard Longfeld the elder, "husbondman," Richard Somer, "fyssher," John Addys, "laborer," William Parke, "carpenter," Thomas Flucke, "husbondman," Richard Hauker, "husbondman," John Hull, "husbondman," William Edwyn, "halywaterclerk," William Ingram, "husbondman," Daniel Longfeld, "husbondman," Simon Letot, "husbondman," Richard Letot, "notery," Richard Gervays, "husbondman," William de Roy, "husbondman," William Kyng, "husbondman," John Garred, "husbondman," Thomas Gold, "husbondman," William Smyth, "husbondman," John Leveshot, "husbondman," Stephen Shadde, "husbondman," Henry Dyker, "laborer," Richard Goldger, "laborer," Richard Tyler, "tyler," Richard Longvyle the younger, "husbondman," John Harlowe, "husbondman," Robert Harlowe, "husbondman," John Dyve, "husbondman," John Pers, "husbondman," and John Wright "husbondman," all of Northflet, county Kent.

John Martyn of Dertford, county Kent, "gentilman," alias late of Quaplod, county Lincoln, and William Rotheley, "yoman," Roger Rotheley, "yoman," Robert Aleyn, "gentilman," and Walter Groveherst, "gentilman," all of Dertford.

John Reynold, "yoman," Peter Dynot, "glover," Thomas White, "husbondman," William Strode, "yoman," Richard Lye, "pedeler," and Nicholas Cowper, "bocher," all of Flecchyng, county Sussex.

Robert Pepisden, "husbondman," and Robert Braban, "husbondman," both of Saleherst, county Sussex, constable of Henherst hundred, county Sussex.

John Rowe of Boxle, "gentilman," and Robert Rowe, William Rowe and Edmund Rowe, "gentilmen," of Aillesford, and Henry Dore, James Burbage, John Burbage and Robert Burbage, "yoman," all of Boxle, and Hugh Wode of Ealdymre, "gentilman."

Thomas Fynhawe of Westifeld and Christopher Halle of Croweherst, constables of Baldeslowe hundred, county Sussex.

Richard Oxenbrigge of Pesemerssh, constables (*sic*) of Colspore hundred.

William Kirketon of Suthwerk, county Surrey, "gentilman."

William Howlette of Brede, county Sussex, "husbondman," and William Hunte of Oldemere, county Sussex, "husbondman," constables of Gostrowe hundred, county Sussex.

Robert atte Mille of Wartlyng, county Sussex, "yoman," and Robert atte Wode of Warbylton, county Sussex, "husbondman," constables of Foxherle hundred, county Sussex.

Robert Somerey, "gentilman," Stephen Hernden, "husbondman," John Exherst, "husbondman," Thomas Engherst, "barbour," John Berman, "husbondman," Thomas—"laborer," Thomas Beuryng, "husbondman," and Richard Moys, "husbondman," all of Stapulherst, and all others in Stapulhirste.

William Lovelace alias Lovelas of Merton, county Surrey, alias late of Betrysden, county Kent, "gentilman."

Robert Clyffton of Clyffton, "gentilman," and John Bocher, "yoman," Richard Martyndale, "yoman," and Richard Broun, "yoman," all of Barmesey.

John Chaloner, "yoman," and Roger Russell, "yoman," both of Lynfeld, county Sussex, and all others in the said hundred.

John Burwessh of Enysford, county Kent, "yoman."

William Morant, William Milton, John Wodesdon and Thomas Turnour, all of Wolkestede, county Surrey, and Thomas Bysshe, John Holman, Stephen Body, John Carnarthur, William Derby, William Brymstede, Edward Harlyng and Robert Bele.

John Elys, "gentilman," William Colyn, "yoman," and Thomas ate Hache, "bocher," all of Ottham, county Kent, and Walter Lovell of Langle, "yoman," county Kent.

John Cook and John Bekquyth, constables of Lewes, county Sussex, and the burgesses thereof.

William Hokeby of Haylesham, county Sussex, and Richard Heggyngworth of Walderne, county Sussex, constables of Thille hundred, county Sussex, and Thomas Waunemer, Richard Turnor, Stephen Maynard and John Sander, all of Haylesham.

Thomas Rasshford, citizen and "osteler" of London, and John Hole, citizen and "taylour" of London.

John Calcote of Lambehith and John Baker of Pecham with others of Bryxton hundred, county Surrey. Henry Goodman and others of Wotton hundred, county Surrey.

John Calcote, Roger Stable, Andrew Burell and William Baker all of Lambehith.

Roger Yong of Westram hundred, county Kent.

Thomas Holme, Thomas atte Done and Thomas Bullok of Coppythorn hundred, county Surrey.

Robert Deneham of Horsham, county Sussex, "yoman."

Richard Sabyn, constable of Madeston hundred, and John Colney and William Bele of the same.

William Symond and Denys Bak, constables of Felbergh hundred, county Kent, and all others within the same.

William Kayem alias Roule, Henry Crumpe, Philip Sayer, Ellis Bocher, William Frensh, Thomas Breggeham, Ellis Breggeham Thomas Drury, Robert Drury, William Grenehell, Ellis Grenehell, John Couper, John Castell,

William Heneger, Richard Canon, William Lather and Peter Premer, all of Bradgare, eo. Kent.

William Taverne of Totyng, county Surrey.

Adam Crofte of Stretham, county Surrey.

William Rydon, Robert Rydon and Nicholas Rydon with others in Batricheley (sic), county Surrey.

Richard Yonge of Westerham, county Kent.

Roger Twysden and John Gybbes, "gentilmen" of Great Chart, county Kent.

William Chaundeller and Richard Carter, constables of Coteshethe hundred, and all men thereof.

Denys Buttur and John Simons, constables of Felbarogh hundred, county Kent, William Petet, Bartholomew Dryland, Robert Godebarn, Nicholas Hylles and all others of that hundred.

William Fyssher, "carpenter," Gilbert Skynner, "husbondman," John Bury, "draper," John Crotehole, "husbondman," and Thomas Kyngewode, "tanner," all of Wadeherst, county Sussex, and John Fyssher of Maydeston, county Kent, "carpenter."

John, lord of Clynton, James Hope and John Oxenden, "gentilmen" of Wyngham, and James Shiterynden and Richard Pury, constables of Wyngham hundred, and all other men in that hundred.

William Haute, esquire, Richard Mynot, John Denne and all other men in Kynghanford hundred.

Walter Waleys and William Warde, constables of Somerden hundred, county Kent, and Thomas Wilbore, "yoman," John Broker, "yoman," Roger atte Wode, "yoman," John Wodgate, "yoman," William Ware, "yoman," Richard Clerk, "yoman," William Clerk, "yoman," and William Hunt, "yoman," all of Chiddyngston, and John Clerk, "yoman," John Coret, "yoman," and William Wymbyll, "yoman," all of Hebyr (sic), and all others in that hundred.

William Bowman of Stratfordlangthorn, county Essex, "gentilman." Robert Mylle.

Simon Benet and Thomas Mantell, constables of Boughton atte Blenne hundred, and Thomas Burgeys and Robert Drylond and all men of that hundred.

John Cobbe, "yoman," Thomas Henfeld, "yoman," and Richard atte Wode, "yoman," all of Perpoundeshirst, county Sussex.

Richard Walshe and Be[r]nard Cavell, constables of Rokesle hundred, county Kent, and John Mager, Philip atte Welle, Richard Maynard, John Bertlotte and William Rowe and the rest of that hundred.

Robert Darcy, esquire, William Comyn, "husbondman," William Wykston, "husbondman," Thomas Fuller, John Raven, John Hunt, "coke,"

John Hunt, "hakeneyman," Geoffrey Pava, John Goos, John Aleyn, John Porter, John Benet alias Godeknape, "sherman," John Maksey, "coverlydwever," William Groce, Thomas Trotte, "talough chaundeler," John Gate the younger, William Bocher, John Smyth, John Beudeley, John Jacob the younger, John Bailly, John Peverell, William Burgh, Thomas Estwode, John Wynsley, Thomas Parkyn, John Helman and Robert Relegh, all of Maldon, county Essex.

John Mortymer, and William Foule, "husbondman," Thomas Wodeward, "husbondman," William Aleyn, "husbondman," and Thomas Stone, "husbondman," all of Westwykham, county Kent.

Hugh Chedyngston, John Style, Thomas Baker, "clerk," and all others in Sundrysshe, county Kent.

Thomas Heuere, Robert Seylyard, John Seylyerd, John Josewey, Thomas Chaunceler, John Bardog, William Colman, John Slyghtre, Richard Oughtrede, Roger Wodewarde, Richard Swon, John Swon his son, John Fychet, Richard Fychet, Richard Ware, John Chepstede the younger, Thomas Chelscombe, William Twyford, John Rouland, John Ganyll and all others of the same county (sic).

William West, Richard Aleyn, John Yam and Robert Abram of Robertysbryg, county Sussex, and all others in that town.

William Merihome, John Whitlok, John Levenoth of Boughton Menchonse, John Herynden and John Tempulmarche and all others of that town.

Thomas Childe of Branketre, county Essex, "draper."

Thomas Saundre the elder, "yoman," and William Saundre, "gentilman," both of Charlewode, county Surrey.

Thomas Reme of Renham, county Kent, "gentilman."

Peter Pedynden of Borden, county Kent, "husbondman," and Richard Capron of the same, "husbondman."

John Richynggood of Kyngesloue in the isle of Thanete, county Kent, and all men within that borough.

Arnald van Osenbrug alias de Osenbrygge of London, "goldsmyth."

July 7, 1450, Westminster, Membrane 10

Thomas Welde, constable of Brastede, and Lucate de Tunbrigge, Robert Parker, Thomas Crowe, John Harry, Nicholas Bore, Richard Harry, Robert Harry, George Jurdayn, William atte Meer, Thomas Lake, John Brightrede, John Swan, "drover," and Richard Pakke of Kent and all others in the said town.

Robert Clyffton of Clyffton, "gentilman," John Bocheres, "bocher" of Barmesey, "yoman" (sic), Richard Martyndale, "yoman," and Richard Broun of the same, "yoman."

John Nassh, "yoman," and John Rolf, "yoman," and all others of Merden, county Kent.

William Norton of Sheldwych, county Kent, "gentilman," and all in that parish.

John Fraunceys, underconstable of Estgate in the parish of Saint Nicholas in the suburb of Rouchestre, and all in that parish.

John Gerold of the parish of Saint Margaret in the suburb of Rouchestre, "husbondman," and all in that parish.

John Bornman, John his son, Richard Bornman, Stephen Bornman and James Bornman of Boughton Menchonse, county Kent, and all others in that parish.

John Lovell, "yoman," and John Porter, "brewer," both of Suthwerk, county Surrey.

Robert Mertyn of Wye, John Rose, William London, Thomas Wyllok and John Curle of Wye, county Kent, and all others in that town.

John Godyng, "yoman," John Esthawe, "yoman," Robert Colyn, "smyth," and William Godyng, "yoman," all of Estpekham, county Kent, constables of Lyttelfeld hundred, and all other men of that hundred.

Ridhard Forde of Penseherst, county Kent, "gentilman," and all in that parish.

Thomas Whyte of Charlewode, county Surrey, one of the constables of Reygate hundred, county Surrey, "yoman," John Jurdon, constable of Charlewode, "yoman," and John Saundre, "yoman," Richard Saundre, "yoman," William Manne, "husbondman," John Knyght, "husbondman," Thomas Mauncell, "husbondman," Thomas atte Wode, "laborer," Simon Knyght, "laborer," Henry Mantell, "laborer," William Motte, "laborer," Richard Wheler, "laborer," Henry Tony alias Carpenter, "carpenter," John Squyer, "husbondman," Thomas Macche, "laborer," William Whyte, "carpenter," William atte Wode, "laborer," Simon atte Wode, "laborer," Thomas atte Hyde, "husbondman," Stephen Elys, "laborer," John atte Porte, "laborer," Thomas Tekerygge, "husbondman," John Peers, "taillour," and William Broker, all of Charlewode, county Surrey.

John Byrkewode, Richard Byrdemere and John Tysedale of Kent.

Thomas Waller of Fokyngton, county Sussex, "yoman," John Drewe of Jevyngton, in county Sussex, "yoman," Thomas Hendyman of Wannok in Fokyngton, "yoman," Thomas Drewe of Otham, county Sussex, "yoman," Walter Reynold of Fokyngton, "husbondman," John Fotour of Wotton, county Sussex, "husbondman," Roger Fotour of Wannok, "yoman," and John Eyr, "yoman," Robert Frenssh, "yoman," William Raynold, "husbondman," Geoffrey Russell, "yoman," Geoffrey Russell, "husbondman," all of Fokyngton, Geoffrey Hendyman of Wannok, "husbondman," William Renne of Jevyngton, "husbondman," Laurence Renne of Jevyngton, "husbondman,"

Thomas atte Welle of Fokyngton, "husbondman," Henry Raynold of Fokyngton, "husbondman," and Thomas Phylpot of Fokyngton, "husbondman."

John Gulby, Robert Barbour, John Herde, John Freman, John de Dene and Henry Serman, all of Dertford, county Kent, and all other men of Stoneham, Mersshstrete, Stoneheld and Dertford.

William Oldbury of Westminster, county Middlesex, "hosyare."

Nicholas Champeneys, Richard Edlyn, John atte Novyn, Thomas Gylbe, John Mason, John Stokke, John Sandyr, Richard Frere, Simon Boydon, Richard Alcote, John Coryour, Thomas Hencote the elder, Thomas Hencote the younger, Thomas atte Novyn, John Alcote, John North, John Ely, William Copedyll, Henry Tenaker, Thomas Couper the elder, John Adam, Thomas Kyng, John Capell, John Archer, John Thomson, William Yonge, Richard Auncell, John Clerk, Richard Harbard, Gilbert Harbard, William Harbard, William Carpynter, John Abbotte, Richard Jordan, Roger Couper, Gerard Wangystell, John Neuman, John Herte, William Palmer and Thomas Pesok of Strode, county Kent, and all others in that parish.

Richard Holford of Flecchyng, county Sussex, "husbondman," constable of Denhille hundred, county Sussex, and William Strode, "bocher," Thomas Auecok, "carpenter," and Philip Cavill, "husbondman," all of Flecchyng.

William Rose, "husbondman," Edward Dene, "husbondman," Robert Lovell, "gentilman," and Thomas Compton, "husbondman," all of Cheyham, county Surrey.

Thomas Butte, "husbondman," John Atkyn, "baker," Henry, Atkyn, "laborer," Simon Doy, "husbondman," all of Suthwerk county Surrey, and William Lake of Newenton, county Surrey, "husbondman."

Thomas atte Merssh, "husbondman," constable of Nutfeld town, county Surrey, and others of the hundred of Reygate.

John Sevayn and Richard Hardy, constables of Westgate hundred, county Kent, and all others in that hundred.

John, prior of the priory of Saint Pancras, Lewes, and the convent of that place, and all their men and servants.

Thomas Deynold of Canterbury, John Garwynton, William Bele, Roger Toly, Richard Carpenter, Richard Upton, John Bate and John Beke and" all others of Canterbury.

Thomas Halyday, "yoman," and John Hill, "capper," both of Suthwerk.

Robert Saman, "yoman," John Todymere, William Shipherde, "husbondman," John Gardyner the elder, "husbondman," William Folke, Richard Gubyon, "gentilman," William Havelok, "smyth," all of Estham, county Essex.

William Lorde, "bocher," Herman Pokell, "draper," Simon Meller, "mason," Robert Heynes, "husbondman," Philip Joce, "carpenter," John Coker, "husbondman," Roger Edward, "husbondman," William Carter, "yoman," Henry Brewer, "mason, Andrew Gardener, "mason," Simon Coker, "mason," Robert Style, "mason," Thomas Rokesacre, "mason," Richard Clerk "barbour," John William, "webbe," and John Hopkyn, "husbondman," all of Berstede, county Kent, and all others in that parish.

William Reynold the elder, William Reynold the younger, "tanner," Richard Reynold, "tanner," William Edwyn the younger, "husbondman," John Whepyll, "smyth," and John Camp the elder, "husbondman," all of Stondon, county Essex, and all others of that town.

Herbert Brewes, "smyth," William Kyng, "brewer," William Shirlonde, "baker," John Barboure, "yoman," Thomas Cardyff, "brewer," Henry Gilford, "brewer," Oliver Nelot, "yoman, Richard Gloucetre, "pynner," John Knyght, "barboure," John Redon, "barboure," John Rotelond, "yoman," Thomas Haggley, "yoman," William Mounford, "brewer," Richard atte George, John Wheler, Henry Carnyssh, "yoman," Thomas Saweser, "glover," and William Wyrdrawer, all of Southwerk, and all others in that borough.

John Chamberleyn alias Smethcote of Estfarle, county Kent, "gentilman."

John Boteler, clerk, William Clerk the elder, "husbondman," William Clerk the younger, "husbondman," Henry Swerenden, Thomas Wylkyns, "laborer," John Aleyn, "husbondman," John Hooker, "husbondman," John Coveney, "laborer," John Tyler, "tyler," Henry Cook, "wever," Geoffrey Brodewey, "laborer," John Sednour, "husbondman," William Stonehous, "husbondman," John Stonehous, "husbondman," John Stonehous, "sexteyn," John Hasylwode, "husbondman," and John Rogger, "husbondman," all of Boghtoh Malherbe, county Kent, and all others within that parish.

Richard Coyff, "husbondman," John Crudde, "yoman," both of Speldehurst, county Kent, and Richard Crudde, "yoman," and Nicholas Crundewell, "yoman," both of Penshurst, county Kent.

Walter Waleys, "yoman," Thomas Berkele, "yoman," both of Penshurst, William Peyntour, "husbondman," John Basset, "yoman," both of Chidyngston, county Kent, and William Harlakenden, "yoman," William Clerk, "yoman," and Alan Engeham, "yoman," all of Wodechirche, county Kent.

Walter Langley of Estry hundred, county Kent, "gentilman," and all of that hundred.

Alice, late the wife of William Broun, John Broun, William Assheby, John Meyre, Henry William and William Watyngham, all of Suthwerk, county Surrey.

Joan, late the wife of John Kent, William Hubard, Joan, wife of Edmund Marchall, and Nicholas Stapulton, all of Suthwerk.

William Wynterbourne of Esshetisford, county Kent, alias of Wy, county Kent, "gentilman," and Richard Dodyston of Westwelle.

John Holmiton of Homilacy, county Hereford, "gentilman."

John Gerveys of Zele, county Kent, and all in that parish.

John Stone the younger, "gentilman."

Thomas Swyft of Sandwich, county Kent, "yoman," and Thomas Stokes [of the same], "yoman."

Henry Fraunces, "yoman," and John Glover, "bocher," both of Baburham, county Cambridge.

John Cosyn of Canterbury, "grocer."

Thomas Chelscombe of Sundrysshe, county Kent.

Membrane 9

Thomas Reculver, constable of half the hundred of Chateham, county Kent, William Couler, John Couler, Hamo Couler, Richard Couler, Thomas Friday, William Thorp the elder, John Thorp the elder, John Thorp the younger, John Smyth, Thomas Smyth, Roger atte Wode, William Warner, Thomas Warner, John Symcok, Richard Lorkyn, Richard Cristyan, Roger Roper, Stephen Cok, John Cok, Simon Couper, Robert Wodear, Richard Bedmynton, William Short, William Neel the younger, John Pylcher, William Pylcher, John Chapman, Richard Marchall, John Wolf, William Neel the elder, John Tomme, Thomas Pery the elder, Thomas Pery the younger, John Pery, "bocher," Hamo Long, William Long, John Pylcher, Robert Chelfeld, Richard Long, Thomas Long, Robert Godfray, constable of half the hundred of Gyllyngham, John Broun, Thomas Pery, John Mylle, William Mylle, John Dygon, John Keneworth, Michael Gybbe, John Harry, Thomas Davy, Thomas Acton, John Ram, William Grenehill the elder, Richard Rogger William Grenehill the younger, Richard Bery, Stephen Heyward, "bocher," and all of the parishes of Chateham, Gyllyngham and Grean and the said half hundreds.

William Pery of Gyllyngham and all of that parish.

Thomas Edolff of Westmallyng, county Kent, "yoman," and all of that town.

William Taverne, "husbondman," and Thomas Cokfeld, "husbondman," both of Totynggravenyng, county Surrey, and all of that town.

William Longe and William Haccher, "husbondmen" of the same.

John Porter of Suthwerk, "husbondman," and Margaret his wife and all of that town.

Nicholas Preest, "husbondman," and Katharine his wife of the same.

Richard Stone, "carpenter," and John Bele, "husbondman," both of Miccham, county Surrey, and all others of that town.

William atte Hylle and John atte Hylle, "husbondmen," of Bansted, county Surrey, and all others of that town.

Laurence de Doune, "gentilman," John atte Lye, "gentilman," Otto North, "yoman," Thomas Wheler, "husbondman," John North, "husbondman," all of Effyngham, county Surrey, Richard Baker of Little Bokeham, county

Surrey, "laborer," Stephen Stylewell, "husbondman," Bartholomew atte Style, "smyth," and Nicholas Bowet, "husbondman," all of Great Bokeham, county Surrey, and all of those towns.

Thomas Stevene, "yoman," John Hogge, "laborer," John Lambe, "yoman," Thomas Hunte, "yoman," William Taillour, clerk, Adam Wodesill, "yoman," William Sterlynge, "laborer," Stephen Alfryge, "laborer," Simon Rook, "yoman, Simon Croucher, "laborer," all of Dalyngton, county Sussex, and all of that town.

Thomas de Dene, "yoman," John Martyn, "laborer," Richard Cok, "laborer," Laurence Cok, "laborer," Thomas Posyngworde, "laborer," Thomas Russell, "yoman," Simon Russell, "laborer," John Prior, "laborer," all of Dalyngton, and all etc.

John Shepherd and William Shepherd," husbondmen," of Bromley, county Kent, and all others of the hundred of Bromley and Bekenam.

Thomas Besewyk of the parish of Saint Katharine Colmans, London, "wever."

William Piele, John Piele his brother and John Piele his son, all of Croydon, county Surrey.

John Hotespore, John Skele, both of Cbipsted, and all in that parish.

Philip Gyllot, Thomas Gyllot, John Comber, all of Lymnesfeld, county Surrey, and all in that parish.

John Richynggood, John Adam of Silvestre Hithe, Richard Cosyngton, Robert Tele, John Pete, John Sandre, Thomas Hethe, John Butte and Richard Clerk alias Reynham.

William Harry of Est Gate in the parish of Saint Nicholas, in the suburb of Rouchestre, "bruer."

John Drury of Sandwich, county Kent, esquire.

John Fyneux [of the same], esquire.

William Symond and Denys Bak, constables of Felbergh hundred, county Kent, and all others in that hundred.

John Duke, James atte Forde, John Smytheot the elder, John Rolf, John Bechyng, Robert Kent, John Badisden, Richard Bechyng and Stephen Capell of Haukeherst, county Kent, and all others in that town.

John Paston of Sandwich, county Kent, "bocher."

Henry Sonde, Henry Carpenter, Henry Goode, John Somer, Richard Brygges, John Gerard, William Godynowe and all others in Wutton hundred, county Surrey.

William Monde and Richard Mace of Bromfeld and all others in that parish.

Philip Aleysaunder, Robert Dame, Robert Rose, Thomas Fytyll, William Caweston, Richard Pykenote, John Dawe, John Umfrey, Robert Langley, Richard Langley, Thomas Dawe, John Halston, John Kyng. John Beton,

William Plege, John Aylemer, John Whode, Ralph Mason and John Johnservantelangge of Bekynham, county Kent.

Simon Batys, "gentilman," John Erle, "laborer," John Martyn, "laborer," Thomas Twyford, "laborer," Nicholas Jolyf, "laborer," William Meryfeld, "yoman," John Meryfeld, "yoman," John Bele, "laborer," John Pouke, "laborer," all of Britlyng, county Sussex, and all of that town.

William Burford of Britlyng, "yoman," and Richard Wyker of Bataill, county Sussex," yoman," constables of Nederfeld hundred, county Sussex, and John Snayleham, "laborer," Thomas Hert, "laborer," Richard Bayly, "laborer," John Wodeman, "laborer," Thomas Godesole, "yoman," Stephen Crotehole, "laborer," Walter Martyn, "laborer," William Smalefeld, "laborer," John Kenne, "laborer," William Haylok, "laborer," John Adam, "laborer," John Godehyve, "laborer," all of Britlyng, and all of the said hundred.

John Bacheler, "husbondman," William Baynard, "yoman," William Longlond, "yoman," Richard Foxley, "yoman," John Salyng, "yoman," John Malard, "yoman," William atte Wode, "yoman," William Goly, "yoman," all of Merton, county Surrey, Simon Yong, "yoman," John Shipman, "yoman," Geoffrey Yong, "smyth," all of Myccham, county Surrey, and Henry Gode of Dorkyng, county Surrey, "yoman," and all of those towns.

Thomas Hamlyn of Pullokeshill, county Bedford, "husbondman."

Robert Wolcy of Croydon, county Surrey, and Robert Glover of the same.

Thomas Thornton, "hakeneyman," and William Fyll, "carpenter," both of Gravesend, county Kent.

Robert Derlond, "yoman," Richard Revell, "husbondman," John Chaunterell, "husbondman," Stephen Aymer, "husbondman," John Symond, "husbondman," John Walware, "husbondman," William Cristian, "husbondman," and William Whitle, "husbondman," all of Reynham, county Kent.

Robert Cheseman and Thomas Cheseman of Estgrenewiche, county Kent, and all other men of that town.

Simon Vaghen, "gentilman," Richard Plotte, "shipman," John Mersshe, "maryner," John Plotte, "maryner," Thomas Hardy, "maryner," Thomas Plotte the younger, "maryner," William Hardy, "maryner," William Wodestoke, "maryner," John Feryer, "bargeman," and Thomas Gwyn, "maryner," all of Gravesende, and all other men in that town.

John Russell of Suthampton, "maryner."

John Bokynfold of Upcherch, county Kent, "yoman," John Clement of Newenton, county Kent, "husbondman," and Thomas Longe of Newynton, "husbondman."

William Selowe, "mercer," and John Fernyngham, "bocher," both of Canterbury, county Kent.

Stephen Wyt the elder, "yoman," Stephen Wyt the younger, "yoman," William Westbourne, "laborer," John Norman, "laborer," Richard atte Wode, "yoman," John Kempe, "laborer," William Cropwode, "yoman," William Crecy, "laborer," James Cropwode, "yoman," Thomas Smyth, "yoman," John Smyth, "yoman," Richard Riche, "laborer," John Horsman, "laborer," John Hukstepe the elder, "yoman," John Hukstepe the younger, "laborer," Robert Loke, "yoman," all of Mundfeld, county Sussex, and all of that parish.

Thomas Beaufitz, "gentilman," Robert Beaufitz, "gentilman," Richard Robyns, "yoman," William Robyns, "yoman," and all men in Stratford atte Bowe, county Middlesex.

Robert Smalwode, "fuller," Robert Overton, "fuller," and Christopher Shawe, "fuller," all of Suthwerk, and all of that town.

Stephen Rychert of Broke, county Kent.

John Cambrey, Roger Walter, Laurence Byx, John Byx, John Walter, all of Lyndestede, county Kent, Thomas Wolgate, Thomas Walter, Robert Brewer of Tenham and John Frende and Richard Catelete of the same, county Kent.

John Rose of Ewell, county Surrey, "yoman," and all of that town.

William Snawedon late of York, "marchaunt."

John Chamberleyn alias Smethecote, "husbondman," John Stace, "husbondman," Thomas Rayme, "husbondman," all of Est Farle, county Kent, Thomas Barmyng, "smyth," Thomas Tryps, "turnour," John Glover, "carpenter," Henry Glover, "carpenter," Robert Smyth, "smyth," William Gylys, "laborer," Alan Andrewe, "melwryght," all of Lose, and all others in those towns.

John Forger of the parish of All Saints, Lewes, county Sussex," yoman," and all of that parish.

John Wryther, "marchaunt," John Chamberlayn, "yoman," John Lardener, "yoman," Thomas Podey the elder, "yoman," Andrew Somer, "glover," William Cheseman, "yoman," Richard Cole, "chapman," William Bourehunte, "smyth," Richard Benet, "sherman," Thomas Cheseman," "chapman," and John Worthe, "yoman," all of Clive by Lewes, county Sussex, and all men of that town.

Edward Fitz Symund late of Little Shobury, county Essex, esquire, and John Frank of the same, the younger, "yoman."

James Burbage, "husbondman," Richard Culter, "husbondman," John Polehell the elder, "husbondman," John Polehell the younger, "husbondman," Thomas Webbe, "husbondman," Thomas Bacheler, "husbondman," William Bacheler, "husbondman," John Stretend, "husbondman," and Andrew Parker, "husbondman," all of Detlyng, county Kent, and all in that parish.

William Trussell of Aylemesthorp, county Leicester, knight.

Peter Wydon, Thomas Steward and John Vyell, "husbondmen" of Sutton, county Surrey.

158   *Chapter 22*

John Baker of Maydeston, county Kent, "yoman."

John Ildergate of Sandewich, county Kent, esquire.

Edmund Chertesey of Rouchestre, county Kent, "gentilman," and Richard Culpepyr late of Estfarlegh, county Kent, "gentilman."

Thomas Cardon, "gentilman," John Cardon, "gentilman," Laurence Mundyn, "shipman," Richard Mepham, "chaundeler," and Thomas Mepham, "husbondman," all of Clyve, county Kent.

Walter Crepegge of Denton, county Kent, "husbondman," and John Martyn of Chalk, county Kent, "husbondman."

John Potkyn the elder and John Potkyn the younger, "husbondmen," of Chalke.

Katharine de la Pole, abbess of the monastery of Saint Mary, Berkyng, and her men, tenants and servants in Berkyng and elsewhere in Essex.

John Rande of Berkyng in Bekyngtre hundred, esquire, and Richard Crampe, "yoman," John Crampe the elder, John Crampe the younger and Robert Crampe, all of Brendwode in Chafford hundred, Richard Wroxham, "gentilman," John Squyrell, "yoman," Henry Cheseman, "yoman," and John Yong, "yoman," all of Berkyng, and all others in the said hundreds.

John Parker of Terlyng, "gentilman," William Chartesey, esquire, Richard Wroxham, "gentilman," Nicholas Preston, esquire, William Harlyston, "yoman," Thomas Congreve the younger, "gentilman," Thomas Frost, "yoman," John Waller, "yoman," Richard Carre, "yoman," and all others in Bekyngtre hundred.

Thomas Hakkere late of Maydenhithe, county Berks, "yoman."

John Cokke of Borstall in Plumstede, county Kent, "yoman," and Thomas Pycard of Erehithe, county Kent, "yoman," constables of the hundred of Lytle and Leson, county Kent, and all other men in that hundred.

William Colyn and John Potman, constables of Tottenore hundred, Richard Ballard and Thomas Eton, both of Westfyrlez, and all of that hundred.

Bartholomew Bolney of Westfyrle, county Sussex, "gentilman," and all his men and servants.

William Hampton, bailiff of Pevensee, county Sussex, "yoman," and John Morley, "gentilman," Richard Porter, "yoman," and Richard Motard, "yoman," all of Westham, county Sussex, and all other men in those towns.

Richard Selewyn of Selmyston, county Sussex, "gentilman," John Hereward, "gentilman," William Grent the elder, "yoman," both of Erlyngton, county Sussex, Richard Delve of Michelham, county Sussex, "yoman," Richard Fotur of Wilmyngton, county Sussex, "yoman," Richard de Milton of Milton, county Sussex, "yoman," Richard Roper of Lolyngton, county Sussex, "husbondman," John Wyngeton of Erlyngton, "taillour," John Warener of Milton, "laborer," Robert Smyth of Wyngeton, "husbondman," Thomas Smyth of Wyngeton," husbondman," John Lencote of Alfriston, county

Sussex," laborer," and Simon Lencote of Alfriston, "laborer," and all other men in those towns.

Stephen Colney of Maydeston, county Kent, "goldsmyth."

John Creke of Suthwerk, "bocher," and all of that town.

William Fynche of Maydeston, "taillour."

John Clerk of Stretham, county Surrey, "tilemaker."

William Ederiche and Alice his wife, Roger Cokke, Henry Newerk and Margaret his wife, John Brambill and Alice his wife, all of Estgrenewiche, county Kent, and all others of that town.

Richard Snelgorre of Boxley, county Kent, "yoman."

Membrane 8

Henry Carpenter, "yoman." and William Godenowe, "mercer," both of Dorkyng, county Surrey, and all of that town.

Thomas Seton," yoman," John Rose, "yoman," Thomas Codyngton, "yoman," Peter Patyn, "husbondman," Thomas Lucas, "husbondman," Thomas atte Feld, "husbondman," John Cole, "husbondman," John Aglond the younger, "husbondman," John Aglond the elder, "husbondman," Edmund Hermode, "husbondman," Robert Sutton, "husbondman," and William Sutton, "yoman," all of Ewell, county Surrey, and all of that town.

John Staunford, "yoman," Thomas Dexter, "fuller," John a Bury, "fuller," Henry Wodecok, "fuller," Robert Medewe, "cordener," William Plavier, "wever," John Ive, "wever," John Raymes "fuller," Thomas Giles," laborer," John Hawe," brasyer," and William Skynner, "ekynner," all of Hadley, county Suffolk.

Robert Pryk of Hadley, "marchaunt," and Emma (Enma) his wife.

John Newenham of Strode, county Kent, "yoman," and Richard Broke of Rouchestre, county Kent, "yoman."

Thomas Lemman, "yoman," constable of Walyngton, county Surrey, Robert Fresill, "gentilman," John Ivy, "fuller," John Palle, "husbondman," John Lewer, "taylour," Adam Taylour," yoman," Reynold Weden, "yoman," John Huntyngdon, "smyth," John Whyte," yoman," Robert Snell, "laborer," John Smyth," yoman," John Gardener, "laborer," and Richard Hewet, "laborer," all of Walyngton, and all of that town.

Robert Chamberleyn of Merworth, county Kent, and John Chamberleyn of Lose.

Robert Est of Maydeston, "gentilman."

William Trussell of Aylemesthorp, county Leicester, knight.

Thomas Cheteman, "gentilman," John Seke, "husbondman," and John Braknale, "wever," all of Ebbesham, county Surrey.

Robert Myrfyn the younger, "gentilman."

Thomas Vusty, "gentilman," John Sherman, "corveser," Robert Bystrete, "tanner," Thomas Dobbys, "taillour," Michael Haryot, "corveser," John Knyght, "laborer," Andrew Page, "yoman," John Grent, "tanner," Robert Gilderygge, "yoman," William Osbern, "bocher," Walter Osbern, "yoman," John Osbern, "bocher," and John Toby, "tanner," all of Haylesham, county Sussex.

John Soneman and Agnes his wife, John Soneman, Thomas Forge and Joan his wife, Robert Richer and Joan his wife, Joan Stayn, Richard Swette and Joan his wife, Thomas Swette, Richard Richer and Emma his wife, John Neve and Emma his wife, Michael Mellere and Alice his wife, Thomas Mellere, Thomas Bradmede, Laurence Gille, John Gille, John Halle the elder, John Halle the younger, Henry Tastyn and Agnes his wife, John Wilkyn, Stephen Tunten and Anne his wife, Stephen Herry and Alice his wife, Richard Herry, John Richere the elder and Isabel his wife, John Richere the younger, Richard Richere, William Richere, John Carewe and Agnes his wife, John Cartere and Joan his wife, Richard Cartere, Stephen Fluk and Agnes his wife, Robert Fluk, John Fluk, John Bocher and Joan his wife, Richard Gandre and Joan his wife, John Gandre, Adam Periot and Joan his wife, John Periot, Robert Periot, William Periot, Thomas Tribler and Idonea his wife, Richard Tatter, Richard Richere and Isabel his wife, John Richere, Thomas Gille and Agnes his wife, Richard Gille, John Dunston and Christiana his wife, Joan Triblere, Richard Periot and Joan his wife, William Richer and Christiana his wife, Michael Richer, John Newman and Avice his wife, William Newman, Richard Newman, Richard Noven, Richard Marchaunt, Thomas Walkelyn and Joan his wife, William Cornhill and Alice his wife, Richard Cornhill, Thomas Cornhill, Nicholas Morys and Agnes his wife, John Crips and Cecily his wife, Stephen Crips, Thomas Crips, John Doke and Agnes his wife, Gregory Sandre and Idonea his wife, John Wade and Christiana his wife, John Wade, Richard Patwyn, Robert at Noven, Thomas Reynold, Thomas Morpath and Margery his wife, John Poleyn and Agnes his wife, Agnes Poleyn, John Boteler, John Dawe and Alice his wife, John Petir and Agnes his wife, Richard Permantre and Margery his wife, Alice Permantre, John Hern, William Dixy and Joan his wife, John Dixy, William Hern and Christiana his wife, John Sompnour and Joan his wife, Thomas Sompnour, Thomas Smyth the elder and Margaret his wife, Thomas Smyth the younger, John Reynold and Agnes his wife, Richard Elis and Isabel his wife, William Elis, John Elis, John Oldhauk, Stephen Richer, Christopher Standyssh and Joan his wife, William Lenegreve and Joan his wife, Philip Short and Alice his wife, Thomas Short, Adam Munde and Joan his wife, John Carter and Joan his wife, William Carter, Thomas Serke and Joan his wife, John Serke, Laurence Serke, Thomas Pastour the younger and Margery his wife, John Saye the elder and Joan his wife, John Saye the younger, John Terry and Emmote his wife, John Sompnour the elder and Joan his wife, Robert Sompnour, Richard Sompnour, John Bek, John Triblere, Thomas Smyth, William Sompnour, Thomas Pastour the elder and Alice his wife, William Cartere and Isabel his wife, Robert Gyell, William Rye, Thomas Aleyn, John Sompnour, "shipman," and Margery his wife, John Sompnour, William Plume and Joan his wife, Henry Chapman and Agnes his wife, William Chapman, William Dawe, John at Noven the elder and Idonea his wife, John at Noven the younger, Stephen Broun and Alice his wife, John Erpyngham and Agnes his wife, John Chirch, Anne Cherch, Thomas Chirch the younger, John Cherch, John Herry the younger and Joan his wife, Thomas Dawe and Alice his wife, William Berton and Joan his wife, John Berton, Richard Berton, John Frowen and Joan his wife, Thomas Marchaunt and Joan his wife, John Marchaunt, John Sharp and Idonea his wife, John Herry the elder and Joan his wife, John Herry the younger, Robert Mannyng and Katharine his wife, John Mannyng, Thomas Cruste the elder and Joan his wife, William Cruste, Thomas Cruste the younger, Richard Cruste, Laurence Soneman and Agnes his wife, Robert Soneman, Stephen Welle and Marion his wife, John Welle, William Brevell, Adam Broun and Margery his wife, John Broun, John Bet and Joan his wife, John Hiklot the elder and Joan his wife, John Hiklot the younger, John Soneman the younger and Margaret his wife, John Smyth the elder and Agnes his wife, John Smyth the younger, Salamon Herry and Joan his wife, Thomas Lieston, John Frere and Joan his wife, Robert Brademede and Margery his wife, John Brademede, Thomas Bradmede, Richard Brademede, Thomas Dulle and Joan his wife, John Portewyn, John London and Joan his wife, Thomas Sprake and Joan his wife, John Martyn and Alice his wife, Joan Smyth, John Smyth, Thomas Smyth, Robert Smyth, William Sprake and Marion his wife, Richard Coke, John Dulle, John Swett and Agnes his wife, Thomas Swet, Gosselin Smyth and Idonea his wife, John Smyth, John Webbe and Alice his wife, Joan Webbe, John Cok and Margaret his wife, John Cok, Thomas Cok, William Rye and Katharine his wife, Katharine Rye, Thomas Broun and Idonea his wife, William London and Joan his wife, Thomas London, Thomas Draper and Joan his wife, John Umbrey, John Lamb, John Bewels and Alice his wife, John Bewels, Thomas Bewels, William Ballard and Agnes his wife, William Ballard, John Reyson and Margaret his wife, John Reyson, Thomas Reyson, William Miklot and Agnes his wife, Agnes Southlond, Thomas Southlond, John Cheros and Rose his wife, John Cheros, Richard Cheros, Thomas Cheros, William Cheros, Robert Whatman and Agnes his wife, Goselin Hewet and Alice his wife, John Hewet, Thomas Hewet, John Sandre and Joan his wife, John Sandre, John Periot and Joan his wife, John Periot, Thomas Periot, Richard Periot, William Periot and Alice his wife, Thomas Periot, John Rolff and Joan his wife, John Rolff, Nicholas Fraunceys and Margery his wife, John Fraunceys, John at Rede and Joan his wife, John Usbarn, John Felde, Richard Heth and John Lambe.

William Beane and Thomas Gilberd, constables of Lonynbergh hundred, and Hamo Beele, Robert Woghelete, Andrew Wodehill, Stephen Courthope and all others in that hundred.

William Fylopot and Hamo Genor, constables of Stowtyngge hundred, and Robert Holynden, Thomas Smyth and all others in that hundred.

James Scheterynden and John Perye, constables of Wyngham hundred, and John Oxenden and William Bovyngton and all others in that hundred.

William Wodhell, constable of Preston hundred, and John Halle, John Rekedon and all others in that hundred.

Richard Hervy and John Downe, constables of Estry hundred, and John Chamberleyn, Thomas Roger and all others in that hundred.

John Bury of Hadley, county Suffolk, "yoman."

William Wodden of Warlyngham, John Wodden of Chelsham, John Planesfeld of Warlyngham, and Thomas Thor[n]don. John Thorndon, Richard Fythyan, John Blakbourne and John Virgely, all of Chelsham, and John Volantyne, Laurence Wanegate, William Maye and Thomas Knot, all of Warlyngham.co.. Surrey.

John Cokke, "yoman," John Crabbe, "yoman," and Ralph Yonge, "yoman," all of Borstall in Plumstede, county Kent, Robert Ricard of Plumstede, "maryner," Edmund atte Wode of Erehithe, county Kent, "yoman," Thomas Jonson, Richard Jonson, Roger Rodley, John Forger, John Hychecok, John Bolton of Erehithe, Robert Drynker of Plumstede and Geoffrey Herte of Creyford, county Kent, "yoman."

John Crouche and William Bull, "husbondmen" of Milton, county Kent.

Richard Adam of Little Charte, county Kent, "yoman."

William Crauford of Higham, county Derby, "mason."

John Legh the elder, "gentilman," John his son, "gentilman," Robert Legh, John Nykelot, John Broke, William Croucher, Michael atte Hethe, Thomas Brunger, John Isak, William Hayward, John Brice, John Wodeman, William Talmache, and John Dawe, all of Adyngton, county Surrey, John Legh of Ewell and Richard Thorndon of Croydon and all of those towns.

William Savage of Bristol, "chapman."

John Hereford, late of Kilkenny, "yoman," Robert Hereford late of London and Peter Hereford late of Bristol.

Thomas Colbrond, "gentilman," Richard de Lay, "draper," both of Wrotlyng, county Sussex, John Barward, "yoman," William Peggan, "yoman," John Jamyn, "husbondman," Richard Wellys, "carpenter," all of Warbulton, county Sussex, Richard Brette, "yoman," Richard Ladde, "husbondman," both of Eshpernham, county Sussex. William Write, "yoman," Thomas Briksnode, "yoman," Thomas Austyn, "clerk," John Pynfowle, "mercer," all of Nortlyng, county Sussex, John Brounfeld, "husbondman," Peter Elys, "carpenter," John Hamonde, "fuller," John Lande, "corveser," William at Stokke, "turnour,"

John Prat, "laborer," all of Herst, county Sussex, Alan Tysherst,"carpenter," Thomas Bole, "carpenter," John Russell, all of Ashburneham, John Lampam the younger, "bocher" Thomas Burgeys, "husbondman," and John Whyte, "hushondman," all of Wratlyng.

Thomas Ballard, esquire, John Shamele, William More, John Sharpe, William Hanford, Robert Ayton, Robert Turnour and John Pyers, all of Estgrenewyche, county Kent, Richard Hunte, Thomas Andrewe, Thomas Lynsey, all of Charteham, county Kent, Thomas Osmere of Est Sutton, Philip Joce of Melton and Adam Boke of Pecham, county Kent.

James Grandon and Thomas Boorne of Hithe, county Kent. William Serle, "yoman," and William Sharp, "yoman," both of Chevenyng of Chepstede (sic), county Kent.

John Notyngham and John att Chirch alias Cherch, "yomen," of Herne, county Kent.

Membrane 7

Robert Payn of Bekenam, county Kent, "husbondman," and Andrew Wodecok of Bromley, county Kent, "husbondman," constables of the hundred of Bromley and Bekenam.

John Bolt, John Hert, John Grombrigge, Thomas Godeyere, Walter Beche the elder, Nicholas Crondewell, John Roger, John Holt, Nicholas Holt and Walter Beche, "husbondmen," Walter Waleys, "yoman," Richard Hamond, "bocher," John Bulman, "gentilman," Thomas Fuller, "husbondman," and Richard Fuller, "husbondman," all of Pensherst, county Kent, and John Wodegate the elder, John Wodgate the younger, John Sleyghter and John Basset, "husbondmen," of Chedyngstone or Chedynstone, county Kent, and John Crudde, "husbondman," William Crudde, "husbondman," and William Sakery, all of Speldherst, and all others of Pensherst.

Richard Carpenter, bailiff of Seford, county Sussex, "yoman," John Walkelyn the younger, "yoman," Thomas Man, "yoman," John Crowelynke, "yoman," Simon Bernevale, "yoman," John Chukke, "yoman," Robert Sampson, "yoman," William Frenshe, "yoman," Thomas Barbour, "barbour," John Tanner, "husbondman," and John Bocher, "bocher," all of Seford, county Sussex, and all others of that town.

John Rakle of Willyngdon, county Sussex, "gentilman," John Bray the elder, "gentilman," and William Bray, "gentilman," both of Westden, county Sussex, John Parker of Willyngdon, "gentilman," and Simon Potteman of Fryston, county Sussex, "yoman."

Thomas Hasilwode of Alfriston, county Sussex, "yoman," constable of Alfton hundred, county Sussex, Richard Seger late of Alfriston, "yoman," alias of Marsfeld, county Sussex, Thomas Chapman, "chapman," John

Coptrowe," yoman," Roger Frenshse," yoman," Richard Chukke, "baker," Thomas Colyn, "yoman," John Irland, "yoman," John Haweden, "carpenter," John Ray the younger, "husbondman," John Smyth, "chapman," William atte Dene, "smyth," Edward atte Broke, "husbondman," Roger Smyth, "smyth," Thomas Man, "husbondman," Thomas Pekham, "corveser," John Hiches, "smyth," John Colvile the younger, "laborer," John Benet, "laborer," and John Crop, "corveser," all of Alfriston, and Richard Profot, "yoman," John Profot, "husbondman," Peter Profot, "husbondman," Robert Profot, "husbondman," and Edward Newe, "laborer," all of Milton, county Sussex, and all others of the said hundred and towns.

John Porter of Southwark, county Surrey, "brewer," and Richard Pykeman, "yoman," William Carter, "yoman," William Pele, "yoman," John Pele, "yoman," and William Prynce, "yoman," all of Croydon in the hundred of Walyngton and Bristone, county Surrey.

John Norton, Thomas Scodyere, John Grangeman, Thomas Godwat, William Peny, Peter Breggeham, Richard Tomlyn, Thomas Daue, William Dylot, Richard Storey, William Storey, Ellis Ladde, William Louce, Henry Storey, Robert Strangbowe the elder, Walter Coke, Ellis Locsmyth, William Catelot, Robert Locsmyth, John Locsmyth the elder, William Strangbowe, William Barlyng, Benedict Geley, John Holman the elder, John Coke, John Tomlyn, Henry Rere, Richard Caperon, Robert Strangbowe the younger, John Strangbowe, John Lowe, Robert Lowe, John Locsmyth the younger, Henry Kyryell, Richard Roger, Thomas Tomlyn, John Bedell, Peter Petynden, William Mowere, William Jan, John Lydsyng, Thomas Clenche, Bartholomew Plotte, John Lovedere, Thomas Heystede, Robert Knyght, John Gygman and Stephen Daue, all of Borden, county Kent, and all others in that parish.

Robert Rogger, "yoman," John Colyare, "yoman," John Bysshopp, "taillour," John Bakere, "bakere," William Gybbe, "tanner," John Gybbe, "tanner," and Safir (Safirus) Couper, "couper," all of Lenham, county Kent, and all others in that parish.

Richard Kelshale, "husbondman," John Tylare, "taillour," and William Filcote, "husbondman," all of Holyngbourne, county Kent.

Robert Perry, "trumpet."

Richard Goldyng of Shrewsbury, county Salop, "yoman," and all of that town.

Thomas Tragosse of Boughley, county Kent, "gentylman," and all others of that town.

Thomas Childe of Branketre, county Essex.

William Odyerne, "gentilman," James Glover, "yoman," Laurence Taillour, "yoman," William Budde, "yoman," Augustine Potyn, "yoman," William Aas, "yoman," William Austyn, "yoman," John Jolyf, "husbondman," John Mapysden, "yoman," James Mapysden, "yoman," William Browenyng, "husbondman," James Huberd, "yoman," Thomas Godfrey, "yoman," John Warner, "husbondman," John Potyn, "yoman," John Glover, "yoman," William Morleyn, "husbondman," William Potyn, "husbondman," John Chyboll, "husbondman," Stephen Boydon, "husbondman," Stephen Sexteyn, "husbondman," all of Wittresham, county Kent, and all in that town.

Nicholas Trendeherst of Lyde, county Kent, "yoman."

Thomas Harry of Halden, county Kent, "draper," William Fox of Mersham, county Kent, "yoman."

John Roser and all men in Estlyng hundred, county Sussex.

John Tameworth, "gentilman," and John Horton alias Langston, "yoman," both of Bermonsey, county Surrey, and all other men in the abbey of Bermonsey.

John Hughlyn of Ivechyrche, county Kent, "yoman," John Kempe of Romaney, county Kent, "yoman," Richard Heed, "yoman," Thomas Heed, both of Snergate, county Kent, and John Adam of Brokelond, county Kent, "wever."

William Mason, "mason," William Wytton, "dyer," John Bychet, "carpenter," John Mayhowe, "yoman," Richard Hughson, "yoman," James Lok, "helyare," John Adam, "syngleman," Robert Knyght, "taillour," John Clypsam, "carpenter, Osbert Watte, "husbondman," and Edmund Letherland, "yoman," all of Hastynges, county Sussex.

John Osbern, "yoman," Richard Chaunceler, "husbondman," John Tenecre, "husbondman," Robert Symcok, "husbondman," Richard Rous, "husbondman," John Cheseman, "taillour," Thomas Osbern, "laborer," and John William, "husbondman," all of Trottesclyf, county Kent, and all others in that parish.

Henry Cutbusshe of Bedynden, county Kent, "yoman."

John Baker of Maydeston, county Kent, "yoman."

Thomas Smyth, John Goldsmyth, "yomen" of Ealdyng, county Kent, and William Goldsmyth of Hunton, county Kent, "yoman," and all other men in those towns.

John Burgoyne.

John Pepysham of Goodherst, county Kent, "laborer," Robert Rye of Coumbewell, county Kent, "laborer," John Iregge, "husbondman," John Courthope, "husbondman," both of Flemynwell, county Kent, Robert Jurdan of Haugherst, county Kent, "husbondman," Thomas Jurdan, husbondman," William Mugge, "rypyer," Thomas Mugge, "rypyer," John Norton, "corveser," Roger Smyth, "laborer," Stephen Berworth, "laborer," and Thomas Berworth, "yoman," all of Goodherst.

John Mullyng, John Wynter, Thomas Proude, William Sellowe, "mercer," John Harnhill, Ralph Sutton, Richard Barnes, "brasyer," and William Bryan, all of Canterbury, and all others of that town.

Roger Ridlee, "gentilman," John Newerk, Richard Pargate, Richard Munden and Richard Newerk, all of the same, as above.

Laurence Stonestrete, Nicholas Bulbroke, John Cotyng, William Sprynget, John Polyner, Robert Wykern, Laurence Gerad, Nicholas Bokyngham, John Urderdowne, Thomas Baskevyle, Laurence Lovell, Robert Taillour, John Myles of Sydyngburn, Simon Sylk, Thomas Pers, John Beche, John Baker, William Denwey, Nicholas Graungeman and John Loksmyth.

William Ayot of Holyngburn, county Kent, "yoman."

John Buttet alias Jevyn Buttet of Brounley, county Kent, "husbondman."

Walter Culpepyr, esquire, John his son, Richard Culpepyr, William Foule, Thomas Sancok, Thomas Wychynden, and Richard Moys, all of Gouteherst, county Kent.

Adam Lytle of Cheyham, county Surrey.

John Culpepyr, "gentilman," William Mugge, John Love, John Base, Stephen Love, John Benke, John Baldok, Thomas Dorley, Thomas Wayte, John Patyndon, John Baker and Richard Streter, all of Gouteherst, county Kent, and all other men of that parish.

John Yorke alias Kelyng the elder, "husbondman," John de Yorke alias Kelyng, "husbondman," John Middey, "husbondman," and William Midday, "husbondman," all of Bekenam, county Kent, in the hundred of Bromeley and Bekenam.

John Clyfford of Dollyng, county Kent, "gentilman."

John atte Water, Geoffrey Breknok, Thomas Stranbowe, Thomas Hogyn, of Bobbyng, county Kent, and all others of that parish.

William Sprynget, "yoman," Laurence Lovell, John Quynte, John Norden and John Mylys, all of Sedyngburn, county Kent, and all others in that town.

John Wyke, Thomas Wyke, Robert Wyke, Richard Tornour, John at Well, John Gerard, Roger Drewe and John Kempe, "husbondmen" of Hedle, county Surrey, and all others, of that town.

John Mounford, Richard Godard, "husbondman," Richard Willyam, "husbondman," John Petle, "husbondman," John Smyth, "husbondman," William Mathewe, "husbondman," John Erle, "yoman," William Walleys, "gentilman," all of Doun, county Kent, John Maynell and John Rowehed, both of Codham, county Kent, and all others of those towns.

Membrane 6

John Blowere, "draper," Robert Bonham, "skryvener," John Frauncheys, "laborer," Nicholas Picard, "smyth," Peter Bierles, "bocher," Thomas Fuller, "bruer," John Blakburn, "bruer," all of Rouchestre.

Edmund Chymbham, "gentilman," William Edmond, "yoman," Richard Jurdon, "yoman," John Shirwode, "yoman," all of Southflete.

John Frere, "shipman," Robert Frere, "shipman," Robert Worme, "barbour," John Cheseman, "corveser," Thomas Hencote, "mason," Simon Hert, "shipman," John Hert, "shipman," all of Strode.

Roger Appelton the elder, "gentilman," Margery his wife, Roger his son, "gentilman," Thomas Herry, "yoman," all of Derteford, county Kent, and all other men and servants of Roger, Margery and Roger.

William Blosme of Southbenflete, county Essex, "gentilman," Thomas Halle of Hadley, county Essex, "laborer," and Peter Geffrey, "yoman." and John Sawold the younger, "husbondman," both of Southbenflete.

Thomas Undirdowne, "watirman," John his son, "watirman," and John Webbe, "waterman," all of Dertford, county Kent.

William Worthe, "inholder," Walter atte Heath, "ferrour," Richard atte Heathe, his son, "laborer," Richard Holte, "sadler," John Page, "plomer," John Gubby, "ehaurideler," Thomas Gubby, "laborer," Thomas Revet, "couper," all of Dorteford.

Henry Ruste alias Rous of Crayford, county Kent, Stephen Large, "yoman," William Herry, "barbour," Thomas Smyth, "yoman," John Baker, "inholder," all of Derteford, William Fuller of Stone, county Kent, "yoman," Roger Loundyssh of Southflete, county Kent, "husbondman," John Turnour of Derteford, "couper," and Thomas Marchaunte, "yoman," and Thomas Capell, "laborer," both of Southbenflete, county Essex.

Stephen Rogger, "bocher," Richard Norton, John Melle, "husbondman," William Marlare, "taillour," Thomas Elys, "husbondman," Laurence Marlare, "taillour," Nicholas Engeherst, "husbondman." John Hogge, "chapman," John Holstrete, "husbondman," Thomas Pell, "husbondman," Thomas Cook, "husbondman," Richard Scot, "clothmaker," Thomas Heyman, "clothmaker," Robert Heyman, "chothmaker," (sic), Robert Whithed, "laborer," Oliver Dowele, "tyler," John Dowele, "tyler," John Materas, "bocher," William Materas, "smyth," William Habynden, "laborer," Thomas Stace, "husbondman," Thomas Sharp, "taillour," William Melle the elder, "husbondman," Robert Tuysnoth, "husbondman," Thomas Tuysnoth, "laborer," John Philpot, "fleccher," John Blechynden, "carpenter," William Blechynden, "carpenter," Thomas Kene, "fuller," Henry Burwassh, "carpenter," Richard Thaccher, "carpenter," Nicholas Philip, "corveser," Thomas Burwassh, "carpenter," Richard Romynden, "bocher," John Hooke, "corveser," John Clerk, "baker," Thomas Clerk, "corveser," Robert Clerk, "baker," Alexander Sawyer, "barbour," John Jaffrey, "taillour," John Hamond, "husbondman," William Bromley, "husbondman," William Swyft, "husbondman," Thomas Fuller, "sawyer," Henry atte Dene, "husbondman," John Colyn, "thaccher," John Hunt, "wever," Robert Cheseman, "laborer," William Philpot, "colyer," Richard Burney, "draper," Stephen Omynden, "clothemaker," Robert Dowenyng, "turnour," Peter Hoope, "laborer," Richard Blacche, "laborer," William Hamond, "sawyer," John Tobyll, "laborer," William Tobyll, "turnour," Laurence Whytherynden, "bocher," John Asshcombe, "coryour," John Bocher, "laborer," Richard Bocher, "carpenter," William atte Heye, "laborer," Henry Cloke, "laborer," Richard Comber, "laborer," Henry Baker, "sawyer," Simon Melle, "laborer," Henry Colyn, "taillour," Philip Baker, "laborer," Richard Baker, "corveser," Stephen Baker, "thaccher," John Glover, "bocher," Richard Glover, "glover," Robert Butterford, "chapman," William Engeherst, "laborer," Robert Couper, "wever," Richard Couper, "laborer," Thomas Bresynden, "fuller," William Bresynden, "thaccher," Laurence Bresynden, "sawyer," Henry Gervays, "laborer," John Rede, "laborer," John Tyernden, "wever," Thomas atte Hoo, "tanner," John atte Wode, "husbondman," John atte Wode, "tanner," William Hamme, "smyth," James Bresynden, "smyth," John Symond, "laborer," Thomas Bailly, "clothmaker," William Bailly, "wever," Thomas Bailly, "wever," John Yve, "wever," William Newenden, "laborer," John Cheseman, "wever," Thomas Treton, "turnour," Robert Smyth, "laborer," Henry Petyte, "taillour," John Stone, "laborer," Laurence Pope, "bocher," Richard Bailly, "wever," and Nicholas Stykker, "skynner," all of Smerden, county Kent.

Thomas Burgeys of Gravene, county Kent, esquire, and John Thornbury of Feversham, county Kent, esquire.

Thomas Ussher, "husbondman," John Hassok, "carpenter," Thomas Bradford, "husbondman," and Thomas Brabon, "carpenter," all of the parish of Saint Margaret by Rochester, county Kent.

Robert Tuk, "carpenter," Thomas Petsmyth, "mason," and Walter Prebyll, "husbondman," all of Esterfarlegh, county Kent.

Edmund Chertesey, "gentilman," Thomas Burden, "husbondman," Thomas Baker, "draper," Michael Burden, "husbondman," Robert Lyslesden, "husbondman," Henry Brice, "bocher," and Thomas Edenden, "bocher," all of Hedecrone or Edecrone, county Kent.

John Ferry of Gyllyngham, county Kent, "yoman," William Wynter and John Floure, "husbondmen" of Pepybury, county Kent.

Richard Cokset, "yoman," William Dunston, "yoman," William Wyse, "yoman," John Rogger, "cordewayner," Richard Yate, "yoman," Thomas Maunfeld, "taillour," and John Baker, "yoman," all of Rouchestre.

John Rede the elder, "yoman," John Rede the younger, "yoman," William Herry, "bruer," Laurence Holbroke, "joynour," Nicholas Wever, "wever," all of Rouchestre, and Robert atte Wode of Asshe by Frenyngham, county Kent, "yoman."

Thomas Tebbe of Brynchesle, county Kent, "yoman," and Thomas Brok of Mardem, county Kent, "yoman."

William Hereward, "talloughehaundeler," William Wollys, "husbondman," John Malet, "chapman," John Botswayne, "laborer," John Couper, "servaunt," Robert Quyllok, William Godfrey, Nicholas Truley, Richard Godfrey, Peter Carpenter and William Coke, all of Rouchestre. William Estmere, John Gybbe, Nicholas Sarles, John Crukkys, John Cok, Henry Polan, John Heremyte, William Wrothton, Henry Waryn, William Osbarn, John Hamelet the younger, John Wadde, John Hamelet the elder, John Bokenfold, John atte Heeche, William atte Wode, Thomas Pollard, John May, John Spuddell, Simon Canon, William Crippys, John Frende, Thomas Gillot, John Symond, John Colyn, Henry Bedell, Richard Poland, William Grene, Thomas Robyn, John Gilbe, Richard Pollard, William Pore, Thomas Upton, William Wade, Simon Estleffe, James Gedewyn, Henry John, Thomas Page, John Slikdod, John Ware, Hamand Basset, Robert Cokman, William Grantham. William Brodeville, John Cosyn, John Parys, Thomas Trill, Thomas Clerk of Upchirche, county Kent, "husbondman."

John Dygges, Richard Dygges, Robert Barford, Thomas Herry, John Herry, William Herry, John Thomas, William Woddard, John Clement, William Geffray, Thomas Long, and John Geffrey, all of Newynton in Milton hundred, county Kent.

John Tredaunt, "yoman," John Wattes, "yoman," William Egerynden, "bocher," all of Asshford, county Kent, and Peter Kynet of Wyvelesbergh, county Kent, "bocher."

John Ferry of Gyllyngham, county Kent, "yoman," William Wynter ot Pepynbury, county Kent, "husbondman," and John Floure of the same, "husbondman."

William Brownyng of Herietisham, county Kent, "yoman."

David Wylkyn of Middelton, county Kent, "shipman."

William Penyngton, of Osprynge, county Kent, "chaplain."

Robert Shayle and Richard Wode of Maydeston, county Kent.

Thomas Osbarn of Stratford Longthorn, county Essex, "tanner."

Robert Bettenham, "gentilman," Ralph Welde, "yoman," William Gyles, "yoman," Richard Tylgheman, "yoman," Henry Hert, "yoman," William Hoke, "yoman," Richard Duoll, "draper," Thomas Tylgheman, "smyth," Richard Pekenham, "draper," Thomas Wauden, "draper," Thomas Pix, "carpenter," William atte Forde, "husbondman," Stephen Piryfeld, "couper," Richard Child, "carpenter," Valentine Child, "carpenter," John Godard, "wever," William Godard, "wever," John Hert, "husbondman," Thomas Hert, "husbondman," John Beste, "husbondman," Roger Peteman," "husbondman," Roger Bever, "husbondman," William Monde, "husbondman," James Bocher, Richard Kyngessnoth, "husbondman," William Kyngessnoth, "husbondman," John Brounsmyth, "husbondman," John Baker, "tyler," Thomas Elys, "husbondman," Robert Monde, "husbondman," Thomas Denys, "husbondman," Geoffrey Spyce, "taillour," William Materas, "husbondman," John Gybon, "husbondman," Thomas Philpot, "husbondman," Thomas

Scot, "husbondman," John Rukke, "laborer," Robert Sawyere. "laborer," John Sawyere," laborer," John Kyngessnoth," laborer," John Hasilherssh," laborer," John Hoget," laborer," John Bocher, "fuller," Denys Rychard, "taillour," William Bocher, "laborer," William Doull, "fuller," Thomas Kyngessnoth, "fuller," Thomas Gybon, "laborer," George Baker, "laborer," and Richard Grenstrete, "laborer," all of Plukley, county Kent, and all other men in that parish.

Richard Dyve of Maydeston, county Kent, "gentilman."

John Gouell, Henry Asshby, Roger Man, Robert Man, Thomas Gulley and John Clynton," yomen" of Boxle, county Kent.

John Knyght of Charryng, county Kent, "yoman."

James Janyn of Croydon, county Surrey, "yoman," and Richard Rokenam of Collesdon, county Surrey, "yoman," constables of Walyngton hundred, and all in that hundred.

Robert Chertesey, "draper," and Alice his wife, William Coventre, "yoman," and Cornelius John, "servaunt."

William Chilton, "cordener," William Heryngman, "husbondman," Richard Dyssher, "husbondman," all of Miccham, county Surrey, John Sanger of Moredon, "husbondman," and Richard atte Stone of Miccham, "carpenter."

Thomas Boll late of Temysford, clerk.

John Hornhey, clerk, John Broun, "gentilman," William Rotheley, Thomas Fryth, John Gulby, Henry Trewer, John Taillour, Richard Holte and William Hebbegood.

Thomas Heed of Plukle, county Kent, "yoman."

Thomas Codyngton, "gentilman," John Philpot, John Ismonger, John Lyghtfoot, William Stonyng, Robert Techesey, Thomas Carleton, John Semer, John Palmer, Ralph Carleton, John Carleton, John Salyng and John Bacheler, all of Merton, county Surrey.

John Thrope of Ightham, "baker," Richard Thrope, John Mercer, William Godewyn, William Sawyer and John Smyth, of Ightham, and all others, etc.

John Sencler, esquire, William Barbour the elder, "gentilman," Simon Orwell, "bruer," John Ulf, "fysshmonger," Richard Brayton, "bruer," Richard Croft, "gentilman," Robert Wastell, "bocher," John Orwell, "bruer," John London, "yoman," John Poland, "glover," William Welles, "bocher," Stephen White, "tanner," and Thomas Stede, "yoman," all of Feversham, county Kent.

Roger Heth, "husbondman," Thomas Heth, "laborer," and Robert Heth, "laborer," all of Ore, county Kent.

John Steveneson of Suthwerk, county Surrey, "yoman," and Isabel his wife.

John Selle the elder, "maltman," John Selle the younger, "malteman," John Selle, "theccher," all of Enfeld, county Middlesex.

Richard Lynde, "gentilman," John his son, William Lynde, William Ounestede, John Whyte and Robert Brook, all of Sanderstede, county Surrey.

William Foughill of Great Chart, county Kent, "diere," constable of Chart hundred, John Fogge, esquire, of the same, Roger Twysden, William Goldwell, William Assherst, "husbondman," Richard Sprot, "yoman," John Watte, "yoman," and John Foughill and all other men in the said hundred.

William Egerynden, constable of Longebrygge hundred within the liberty of the dean and canons of the free chapel within Westminster palace in Asshetesford, county Kent, and William Brokman, "gentilman," John Brokman, "gentilman," John Werde, "mercer," Alexander Harry, "sherman," John Tredaunt, "tayllour," Mark Salman," "fleccher," and Richard Burman, "chapman," all of the same liberty, and all others therein.

John Crips of Lenham, county Kent, "yoman."

Richard Bowle of Banbury, county Oxford, "yoman."

John Salmon, Richard Aleyn, John Roger, Thomas of Hoo, William Stevyn, "shipman," John Stephyn, John Carew, John Northwode, John Stevyn of Brokestrode, William Whithayles, John Edward, John Balsyr, Hamond Pers, John Baker, Richard Baker, Thomas Baker, Henry Northwode, John Wygyn, Thomas Porker, Henry Baker, Henry Colyn, Salmon Ryche, Gilbert Bocher, William Stephyn, John Stephynson, Thomas Colyn, John Rose, William Whytthalys the elder, John Hopkyn, Richard Copyn, John Crame, Henry Hamond, Henry Bochier, William Knepe, Thomas Rogerre, Robert Martyn, Adam Balsyre, John Porker, Richard Shypwassh, Henry Parker, Peter Thomson, William Godfray, John Elmere, William Brodstrete, Richard Brodstrete, Richard Frensshe, William Osey, Thomas Osey, Thomas Martyn, Richard Balsyre, John Dyrward, Robert Sarys, John Shepper, William Jonson, John Coole, Thomas Levyng, Thomas Janyn, Thomas Osey the younger, Thomas Rogere the elder, John Boll, John Hopkyn, Thomas Pax, John Brede, William Balsyre, Thomas Boll, Henry Gylmyn, John Janyn, Thomas Derett, John Rogere the younger, Thomas Barbur, John Pax, John Strode, John Luuse, William Luse, John Brede the elder, Salmon Elmere, Thomas Elmere, Peter Smyth, Robert Brede, John Brede the younger, Thomas Merssh, John Smelt, John Moys, Thomas Taillour, Thomas Brede, William Coke, Christopher Boll, John Brede, Adam Edward, William Aleyn, John German, John Taylour, Robert Bellard, William German, William Shyppwassh, William Olyf, Richard Elnore, John Pottere, John Symond and all others of the parish and hundred of Whytstaple.

Richard Bowle of Banbery, county Oxford, "yoman."

Membrane 5

William Wodegate and John Wodegate of Edyngbrygge, county Kent.

William Canon and Richard Reyson, "maryners" of Tenham, county Kent.

John Lounsford, "gentilman," Richard de Nore, "laborer" William atte Feld, "laborer," John Ideyn, "laborer," John Fermesham, "laborer," all of Batayle, county Sussex, Simon Martyn, "laborer," William Martyn, "laborer," Thomas Colyn, "laborer," all of Assheburnham, county Sussex, and William Byrchet, "laborer," and John Byrchet, "laborer," both of Cattesfeld, county Sussex.

Thomas Elys of Maydeston, county Kent, the elder, "husbondman," Thomas Elys the younger of the same, "husbondman," John Reder, "husbondman," Thomas Mayster, "husbondman," Thomas Luk, "husbondman," William Joce, "husbondman," Thomas Ippymbury of Merden, "husbondman," John Harry of Lynton, "husbondman," Thomas Tylden of Merden, "husbondman," and John Stercought of Lynton, "husbondman."

Richard Dene, "dobeletemaker," Alan Gerad, "smyth," Robert Fordman, "corvyser," Ralph Long, "spyser," John Long, "wexchaundeler," Richard Long, "barbour," John Crompe, "barbour," Richard Maynard, "corvyser," Nicholas Celkys, "laborer," John Chapman and Peter Park, "yoman," all of Maydeston.

James Hyllys of Horsmonden, county Kent, John Baker, Henry Hykmot and Richard Bygland.

Stephen Carder of Cranebroke, county Kent, and Thomas Carder his son.

Thomas Cotyng, "yoman," Lewis John, "husbondman," Thomas Messenger, "husbondman," Laurence Dauber, "husbondman," Richard Bromfeld, "husbodman" (sic), John Messenger the elder, "husbondman," John Messenger the younger, "husbondman," Adam Messenger, "husbondman," Nicholas Newenton, "husbondman," Robert Crewese, "husbondman," Roger Stampyke, "husbondman," Nicholas Clove, "husbondman," John Wayman, "husbondman," William Wayman, "husbondman," Robert Wylson, "husbondman," John Metar, "husbondman," Benedict Metar, "husbondman," William Russell, "husbondman," William Steker, "husbondman," Henry atte Wode, "husbondman." Stephen Peere, "husbondman," all of Bakchyld, county Kent, and all others in that parish.

John Hylder of Kyngeston by Lewes, county Sussex, "yoman," and Richard Elyot of Smythwyke, county Sussex, "husbondman," constables of Swambergh hundred, county Sussex, Thomas Holybon the elder, "yoman," John Holybon, "husbondman," both of Iford, county Sussex, William Holybon of Clive by Lewes, "yoman," John Machyn, "husbondman," Thomas Holybon the younger, "laborer," Simon Holybon, "laborer," all of Iford, Richard Sowedan, "webbe," Thomas Hyches, "carpenter," and William Merston, "taillour," all of Westoute or Westou by Lewes.

William Forger of Westfyrlle, county Sussex, "yoman."

Thomas Styler, "gentilman," Walter Styler, "gentilman," Thomas Styler the younger, "gentilman," Thomas Bartelot, "gentilman," Thomas Horle, "yoman," John Frensham, "husbondman," Thomas Mose, "husbondman," John Tylth, "husbondman," Richard Gardyner, "husbondman," John Man, "husbondman," William Frenshe, "husbondman," William Gerad, "husbondman," Thomas Brode, "husbondman," Richard Hasty, "laborer," John Mose, "husbondman," and Richard Mose, "husbondman," all of Rowesparre, county Sussex.

William Benet, "taillour," John Wylby, "husbondman," Peter Pryour, "husbondman," Thomas Hall, "laborer," William More, "husbondman," William Clyfford, "husbondman," John atte Water, "laborer," John Clerk, "laborer," Philip Palmer," laborer," Richard atte More, "husbondman," John Morgan, "husbondman," John Knovesall, "laborer," John Wellis, "laborer," John Byrtfeld, "laborer," Adam Craft, "yoman," Richard Noble, "laborer," Nicholas Baudry, "laborer," John Gerard, "husbondman," Thomas Hert, "husbondman," John Roweley, "husbondman," John Roger, "husbondman," John Eton, "laborer," John Craft, son of Adam Craft, and Richard Godeherte, "laborer," all of Streteham, county Surrey, and all others in that parish.

Richard Smyth of Shorne, John Smyth, William Hamme, John Davy, John Hauke, Peter Hauke, Peter Page, Thomas Bedill, Richard Yong, Thomas Coke and Richard Neweman.

Adam Daue, Roger Rolff, William Gildewyne, John Kemmysle, John Fylle, Thomas Sayyere, Thomas Costedyll, "huabondmen," of Bredherst, county Kent, Thomas Flete, John Stretys the elder," husbondmen," Thomas Stretys the younger," yoman," all of Boxle, county Kent, John Jelyffe, William Bratyll, "husbondmen," John Well, "laborer," all of Gelyngham, county Kent, Adam Stretys of Bredherst, "husbondman," and Peter Page of Stokebury, county Kent, "laborer."

Bernard Kawyll of Chesylherst, constable of Rokysley hundred, county Kent, Philip atte Well of Orpyngton, William Miller of Orpyngton, Thomas Stabyll of Saint Mary Cray, John Peteley of Downe, John Jeter of Chelsfeld, Robert Mabelote of Orpyngton, Vincent Broke of Orpyngton, and Richard Walsshe of Saint Mary Cray, and all others of that hundred.

John Gate, "bocher," and Margery his wife, Richard Henham, "carpenter," and Margery his wife, Richard Gate, "reder," and Margaret his wife, Richard Fox, "laborer," and Pernell his wife, John Berde, "couper," and Margaret his wife, Simon Nele, "pulter," and Pernell his wife, Nicholas Astyng, "taillour," and Margery his wife, Ralph Denys, "baker," and Alice his wife, John Lavender, "bocher," and Robert Hervy, "barbour," all of Estgrenewiche, county Kent, and all men of that town.

Thomas Elbrigge, "taverner," and Joan his wife, William Thurston, "yoman," Thomas Maunsell, "taillour," and Richard Nicoll, "tynker," all of Rouchestre.

Hugh Godewyn and Richard Culpeper, "gentilmen," and all their men, tenants and servants in Kent.

Willirtm Croycher, "husbondman," John Isak, "laborer," Robert Legh, "gentilman," John Dawe, "laborer," Michael atte Heth, "laborer," Thomas Brungore, "laborer," John Bryse, "laborer," John Brook," carpenter," John Wodeman, "laborer," and William Hayward, "laborer," all of Adyngton, county Surrey, and all others of that town.

John atte Wychye of Lamporte, county Sussex, "hnsbondman," and Thomas Underwode of Newyke, county Sussex, "yoman," constables of Bercompe hundred, county Sussex, and Richard Profyt, "gentilman," John Marquyk, "yoman," Richard Marquyk, "yoman," Richard Blome, "yoman," Richard Hawekyn, "laborer," Thomas Truslove, "laborer," all of Hammessay, county Sussex, and Henry Perys, "yoman," and Thomas Sandere, "laborer," both of Bercompe.

John Payne, "gentilman," Robert Chaumberleyn, "gentilman," and John Taillour, "husbondman," all of Merworth, county Kent, and all others in that parish.

Roger Passelewe, "yoman," William Parker, "husbondman, John Quyk, "smyth," all of Angre at the Castle, county Essex, and William Tyng, "yoman," and Andrew Fynche, "pulter," both of Stanford Ryvers, county Essex.

John Bygge, "baker," Robert Hauter, "laborer," Robert Rotyng, "laborer," and William Landesdale, "laborer," all of Estwell, county Kent.

John Couper the elder and John Couper the younger of Okestede, county Surrey.

Thomas Sport, "smyth," Henry Malls, "shipman," William Maas, "shipman," Richard Shipman, "husbondman," William Cok, "shipman," John Tresbon, "husbondman," John Bragh, "fuller," Alan Baron, "cordwayner," William Bole, "tanner," Sampson atte Style, "barbour," Thomas Saire, "shipman," John Stepemham, "shipman," Gerard Bus, "bereman," Thomas Stevyn, "shipman," John Cok, "shipman," Henry Wythlok, "shipman," John Synmet, "shipman," William Synmet, "shipman," William Synmet," shipman," Nicholas Gate, "roper," John Noke," bocher," William Bugge, "husbondman," John Bugge, "husbondman," and Thomas Echet," husbondman," all of Middelton, county Kent.

William Grene and Thomasia his wife. Reynold Tutyng, constable of Birstowe, county Surrey, and all men in that town.

Richard Cosynton, John Joce, John Wylkyn, John Hoskyn, William Whytelok, John Short, Edmund Danyell, John Plumsted, William Blower, Philip Cornhyll, Hamo Pyte, James Colet, John Wether, Adam Geffery, William Rygman, Richard Gefferey, Henry Damyon, Thomas Wodegate, William Joce, William Mershe, Ralph Jurdon, Gilbert Hylle, John Hylle,

William Corveser, John Heyward, John Bote, John Fletesby, William Broke, John Salman, Henry Crowed, Nicholas Cultour, William Wytelef, John Elys, Richard Pecok, Henry Taillour, Richard Rifeld, John Chaunterell, Thomas Coventre, Rober, Dirlond, Robert Walwern, John Walwern, Stephen Hyet William Wylkyn, William Pantery, Stephen Aymer, John Malteman, William Walwern, Stephen Hoke, John Danyell, John Merdale, John Marchant, John Coyne, Henry Nasshe, John Daue, William Cristyan, Robert Joce, Thomas Stonard, Nicholas Stonard, Richard Herbelon, Michael Stonard, Adam Smyth, Thomas London, Thomas Robert John Butte the younger, William Butte, John Hoke and John Pyper, of Renham, county Kent.

Richard Johonson, of Croydon, county Surrey, "tyler."

Laurence Levyngdall of Kent.

John Rotlond of Suthwerke, county Surrey, "yoman."

John atte Wode the younger, Nicholas Cotys, John Cotys and John atte Wode the elder, "yomen" of Wodemersthorne, county Surrey.

Robert Walkyngham and Peter Flemyng, "husbondmen," of Bykysle, county Kent, and all others of that parish.

Richard Thorn, Henry Lityljohn, William Slyghter and Simon Clerk of Kent.

William Hayward of Suthwerk, county Surrey, "yoman," and Alice his wife.

Thomas atte Wode of Holyngborn in Heyhorn hundred, county Kent, "husbondman," and all others in that parish.

William Bainton late of Burne, county Cornwall, "yoman," alias of Flexbure, county Cornwall, "baile," and John Bainton of Flexbure, "gentilman," and all other men of Cornwall.

Roger Mapilton of Totenham, county Middlesex, "mason."

James Cheynwe of Westerham, county Kent, "gentilman."

John Mayster of Chesthunt, county Hertford, "miller."

John Aston of Maydeston, county Kent, "yoman," and Bartholomew Everden and Richard Aston of Gowteherst, county Kent, "yoman."

John Rychefeld, Thomas Tyrry, constable of Ryngyslowe hundred, William Manston, Thomas Saynt Nicholas, John Sandeway and John Malyn.

Thomas Cornyssh, Thomas Wayte, Robert Bernard, Thomas Wodam the elder, Richard at Hille, John Stonache, John Hawkyn, Thomas Cowlande, John Cornyssh, William Bekener, John Baddekokke, John Ramme, William Blacche, John Barbour, John Chylde, John Fordom, John Tanner, Thomas Bekener, Thomas Wodam the younger, Richard Fawse, John Grove, Barnabas Fawse. John Whitlokke, John Wronggey, Robert Blacche, John Gyne, John Artour, John Turnour, John Wryght, William Turnour, John Davenyssh, Thomas Turnour, William Turnour, John Swetyng, William Bykener the younger, John Brede, Thomas Wyllynghale, John Creuch, William Everard,

Thomas Smyth, John Colop, "clerk," John Colop, "tayler," John Deve, John Davenyssh the younger, John Arwaker, John Lewgor, John Goodyeve, John Meller, John Warenger, Adam Blacche, John Brewer, John Newmaa Simon Curlewe, Thomas Bedell, John Wagge, William Ramme, John Edeward, William Blacche the younger, John Roper, John Hille and Nicholas Thomasservantcornyssh, all of Great Waltham, county Essex.

John Bokyngham and Margaret his wife.

Richard Chalkhill of Maydeston.

Thomas Godyng of Yeldyng, county Kent, "yoman," and John Snode of Hunton, county Kent, "husbondman," and all others in those towns.

John Clyfford of Bobbyng, county Kent, esquire, and William Norton of Sheldwych, county Kent, esquire.

William Downe, "gentilman," Robert Langley, "gentilman," and William Gunne, "yoman," all of Westmallyng, county Kent.

Membrane 4

William Robert, John Heuer, Richard Shot, Richard Aleyn, Alan Nasshe, John Aleyn, Hugh Kechill, William Frensshe and Simon Kechill, "husbondmen," of Hese, county Kent.

Richard Nether, Robert Payn, Henry Payn and Thomas Thornton "yomen" of the hundred of Beknam and Bromeley, county Kent.

William Agas of London, "grocer."

John Parker of Hoo, county Sussex, "yoman," constable of Hoo hundred, John de Wellys, Thomas de Broke, John Kneller, William Scotte and John Broke, of the said hundred.

Hugh atte Wode, "gentilman," John Orger, "yoman," William Water, "yoman," and Richard Coveney, "chapman," constable of Twyford hundred, all of Ealdyng, county Kent.

Roger Lacche, "gentilman," Henry atte Fenell, "yoman," John atte Fenell, "husbondman," Laurence atte Fenell, "husbondman," John Lyon. "husbondman," John Cheseman, "husbondman," and Robert Parker, "husbondman," all of Litlyngton, county Sussex.

John Elphy, Richard Welcok and William Broune, "carpenters" of Birlyng, county Kent, and all of that parish.

Richard Bolt, John Bolt, Richard Veisy, Richard Osbern and John Bisshop, "husbondmen" of Denton, county Kent, Andrew Wilby of Chalk, county Kent, "husbondman," Thomas Kebbyll late of Shorne, county Kent, "grome," and John Kebbyll of the same, "grome."

Thomas Huchon, John Godfrey the elder, John Godfrey the younger, John Aleyn, Richard atte Crowche, Robert Prall, Thomas Dyve, Nicholas Bosyne, Robert Rolf, Clement Rolf, Thomas atte Strete, Robert Godfrey, Roger

Murstok, Robert Halstok and William Poynant, of Stone in Oxney hundred, county Kent, "husbondmen," Henry Northland, William Moseden and William Kynet of Ebney in the same hundred, "husbondmen."

Richard Toly, "vynter," and John Grene, "yoman."

Hugh Caxton, "mercer," Richard Halk, "chapman," William Nede, "spycer," Thomas Davy, "harbour," Thomas Bromer, "chapman," Henry Chadilwode, "chapman," John Pette, "bruer," and Nicholas Saunder, "taloughchaimdeler," all of Sandwich, county Kent.

Richard Joskyn the elder, "husbondman," John Joskyn, "yoman," John Sprever, "bocher," William Sprever the elder, "yoman," William Sprever the younger, "yoman," Walter Chippe, "yoman," Henry Stace, "husbondman," Thomas Wright, "yoman," and Walter Stace the elder, "yoman," all of Cobham, county Kent, and all others in that parish.

Thomas Profot, "gentilman," Richard Burton, "yoman," and Thomas Motard, "yoman," all of Estbourne, county Sussex.

Gilbert Homewode of Cokefeld, county Sussex, "yoman," and John Homewode of Plumpton, county Sussex, "yoman," constables of Strete hundred, county Sussex, John Wyldegoos of Holdelegh, county Sussex, "yoman," John atte Roe of Wyvelysfeld, county Sussex, "yoman," and Thomas Esthanfeld of Wyvelysfe (sic), "yoman."

Thomas Kelsham, "gentilman," Richard Burden, Michael Burden, Thomas Burden, Peter Widynbroke, Thomas Bakere, Thomas Homersham, Thomas Widynbroke, Thomas Edynden, Simon Whitsperok, Henry atte Well, John Homersham, Walter Turnour, Richard Haspere, Thomas Turnour, John Frary, John Fullere, John Bowdon the younger, Thomas Thornherst, Henry Hamond, Thomas Fullere, Robert Lellisden, Peter Hoigge the elder, William Grigge, John Fox, William Manne, Stephen Manne, Simon Hoigge, Ralph Blechynden, Thomas Blechynden, Roger Bakere, Ralph Bayman, John Gateman the younger, Ralph Blechynden, Stephen Rede, John Bachelere, Roger Turnour, John Turnour, William Sandir, William Hamme, Roger Edynden, Geoffrey atte Wode, Ralph Baily, John atte Crowche, Thomas Baily, Ralph atte Crowche, Robert Burghaissh, Richard at Chambir, John Thornherst, Thomas Prat, Stephen Symme, John Ropere, Henry Burden, Thomas Birthet, John Hovynden, Peter atte. Brigge, John atte Brigge the younger, John Bishop, Henry Bisshop, William Bysshop, Peter Hoigge the younger, Stephen Boycote, Stephen Adam, Thomas Bakere, John atte Tonge, Roger Hamond, Robert Marketman, John Burdon, John Southlond, John Grigge, Henry Grigge, Stephen Elcok, Henry Brice, John Boicote, John Gateman the elder, Thomas Boicote, Robert Whithede, William Gunne, John Swyneham, John Whitsperehauke, Henry Whitsperehawke, Thomas Pix, John Blachynden, Walter Gaunt, of Hedecron, county Kent.

Walter Brencheley, "gentilman," and John Sharp, John Wylert, Robert Wolf, Thomas Stays and William Keppyng, "yomen," all of Benynden, county Kent.

John Stempe, constable of Suthuover by Lewes, county Sussex, and William Delve, Thomas Best, Richard Dymmok, Peter Bromfeld, "yomen," William Reymys, "husbondman," and Richard Codnore, "couper," all of Suthuover by Lewes.

Richard, abbot of Saint Martin's, Battle, county Sussex, and the convent of that place and all their men and servants.

William Kamme, "wever," William Skynner, "capper," William Stuward, "brewer," John de Cave, "taillour," and Henry Emery, "tanner," all of Bermondesey, county Surrey.

Edward Blakburn of Middlesex, "gentilman."

John Golle the elder, "yoman," John Britexwater and Thomas Hacher, "husbondmen," Robert Hacher and William Cok, "laborers," and Adam Kyng, "husbondman," all of Croydon, county Surrey.

William Sandhirste of Lamberhirste, county Kent, "yoman," and John Martyn of Brynchesle, county Kent, "yoman."

Richard Coife of Spelhurst, county Kent, "yoman," and William Knyght of Pepynbiry, county Kent, "yoman."

John Elinebrugge, "gentilman," of Blecchynglye, county Surrey, and John Kyllyk, constable of Blecchynglye and all others in that parish.

Thomas Burton, "gentilman," William Halyday, chaplain, and William Shelton, "mercer," all of Suthwerk, and all of that town.

Thomas Carter, "draper," William Brok, "barbour," William Smyth, "mason," Thomas Claveryng, "grocer," Richard Carter, "draper," William Colyn, "wexchaundeler," Hamo Clerk, "harbour," all of Maideston, John Brok, "wever," Richard Piers, "draper," and Richard Maunfeld, "barbour," all of Caldyng (sic).

John Baker, "husbondman," Stephen Baker, "coteler," Richard Bakere, "glover," Laurence Baker, "laborer," William Olyver, "servant," Richard Joce, "husbondman," William Cloute, "carpenter," Stephen Cloute, "carpenter," and James Hulles, "husbondman," all of Horsmonden or Horsmoden, county Kent, and all others of that town.

Thomas Harry and John Rychevile, constables of the hundred of Ryngsloue, and William Manston and John Septvans and all others in that hundred.

John Hancok of Suthwerk, county Surrey, "armerer."

John Blundell, "yoman," Henry Metewey, "yoman," William Plawe, "ferrour," and John Alfrey, "yoman," all of Lyngefeld, county Surrey.

Thomas Balster, John Balster, "yoman," and Walter Duke, "husbondman," all of Totynggravenyng, county Surrey.

Robert Puttok of Newynton, county Middlesex, "gentilman."

John Leef, "yoman," and Roger Poynt, "husbondman," both of Newynton, county Surrey.

John Prat, "carpenter," Thomas Dousynd, "husbondman," Thomas Swyft, "smyth," Richard Plotte, "carpenter," Thomas Russell, "yoman," John Clobyer, "corvescer," William Humfrey, "smyth," Thomas Lott, "laborer," Robert Fyssher, "taillour," and Richard Beanden, "laborer," all of Maideston.

Richard Leiard, Richard Poynte, Robert Waker, Nicholas Glover, Nicholas Waker and Thomas Holeon, "husbondmen" of Bedyngton, county Surrey.

Robert Rose, Thomas Cownde, constables of Dounhamforth hundred, Robert Lovelas and William Barton.

Roger Warangere, "taillour," George Cordewayner, "cordewayner," John Hoo, "yoman," Francis at Bury, "yoman," Robert Miller, "yoman," Thomas Colford, "yoman," John Hollewell, "laborer," John Baker, "laborer," John Clerke, "yoman," Richard Lyncolne, "smyth," and William Gippe, "yoman," all of Navestoke, county Essex.

John Cokeram, mayor of Queneburgh, county Kent, "marchaunt," and John Swalman, "yoman," William Baker, "baker," William Britte, "mariner," John Britte, "mariner," John Masyn, "maryner," William Canon, "maryner," Alan Jacob, "maryner," Geoffrey Benet, "maryner," Robert Somter, "maryner," and John Willys, "mariner," all of Queneburgh.

Richard Smyth, "yoman," Thomas Stacy, "tanner," and John Man, William Chawry and Thomas Gillot, "husbondmen," all of Westram, county Kent.

John Cok and Thomas Pycard, constables of the hundred of Litle and Lesyn, and all other men in that hundred.

John Leef, "yoman," Richard Wode, "husbondman," and William Morgan, "yoman," all of Totynggravenyng, county Surrey.

Thomas Weston and Thomas ———, chaplain, both of Mafeld, county Sussex.

Robert Langley, William Appes and William Bodyll, of Fernth.

John Harnes, John Hoke, John atte Forde and John Nevyll, all of Mafeld, county Sussex.

Richard Berbet, William Serles the elder, Thomas Serles, Stephen Mathewe, "husbondmen" of Hastynglye, county Kent, and William Serles and Thomas Bette, "husbondmen" of Wy, county Kent.

Laurence Edward, "husbondman," Walter Cokerell, "laborer," James Waterman, "husbondman," John Hanham, "husbondman," all of Walarn, county Essex, and John Pres of Hadstoke, county Essex, "husbondman."

Thomas Palmer, "parker," Robert Taillour, "husbondman," Thomas Absolon, "corveser," all of Hallyng, county Kent, and John Moref, John Chambre and Richard Absolon, "husbondmen" of Cokston, county Kent.

Robert Chirche, "mason," John Wanhell, "husbondman," William Lord, "bocher," Herman Pokyll, "drapere," Simon Meller, "mason," all of Berstede, and Robert North, "husbondman," James Plot, "laborer," both of Stokbury, Henry Bedill of Thornham, "husbondman," and John Smyth of Boxle, "husbondman."

Henry Pakeman, John Never and John Malyt, "husbondmen" of Hoo, county Kent, and all others of that town.

John Clerke, parson of the church of Halgesto in Hoo hundred, county Kent, and Simon Dalam and John Neweman, "husbondmen" of Halgesto, and all others of that town.

Chapter 23

From *The Antient Kalendars and Inventories of the Treasury of His Majesty's Exchequer*

OVERVIEW

The money and goods that Cade and his followers stole was substantial. On 21 July 1450, the exchequer received an indenture (written in both Middle English and Latin) that listed all that was taken in Kent from Cade and his followers as they made their retreat. A number of the items listed below belonged to Philip Malpas, the alderman of London. Those persons who wanted their possessions back were required to buy it back from the exchequer at a slightly reduced rate.

SOURCE FOR TRANSLATION

Palgrave, Francis, ed. *The Antient Kalendars and Inventories of the Treasury of His Majesty's Exchequer.* Vol. 2. London: Eyre and Spottiswoode, 1836. Pp. 219–20.

FURTHER READING

Harvey, 100–101.

TRANSLATION

Firstly, in money counted £105 pounds and 15*s*.

Also, in a round box of leather: six parish cups of silver; nine spoons of silver; one purse made with a band with seventeen counters of silver; one stone of beryl; one girdle of purple, not harnessed; a bicorn[1] claw, harnessed; one musk ball;[2] one stone of beryl, harnessed; two laces of silk.

Also, in two travelling chests: one salt dish of silver and in the style of a gilded castle, with three small salt dishes of silver in three corners and the fourth lacking; one chalice of gold garnished with pearls and one platter also; two large serving plates and twelve little dishes of silver; two bowls of silver; one nut container; three embossed cups; a necklace of silver; one pair of knives; two purses; a clock of silver; three salt dishes of silver, with a lid of a cup; one chalice of gold with a cover; one horn harnessed with silver and gilded; one covered dish of gold, garnished with sapphires and pearls; one water pitcher of silver; two gold, half-gallon pots; one spice plate of silver and gold; two standing cups[3] of one suit, covered, with an ornamental boarder and embossed; one standing bowl vessel, covered with gilding; one pair of table knives; three [knives] in a sheath with gilded handles; one water pitcher of silver without a knob; one drinking vessel; one cruet;[4] one pax-board of silver and gilded;[5] one socket of a candlestick of silver; one girdle in the old fashion, harnessed with silver;[6] one scallop of silver;[7] one little piece of red fabric; one purse made with a band; one gallon pot of silver without a lid; one gilded, half-gallon pot; one quart pot of silver; one goblet in the old fashion; one statue of silver and gilded; one covered standing cup, gilded, without a knob; one flat, covered cup, gilded; one salt dish, covered, of silver; one little goblet of silver, covered; one saucepan of silver; one black remnant of velvet cloth; one old vestment; one primer with claps of silver; one pair of sheets; five small pieces of fur; nine pieces and remnants of silk cloth threaded with gold; one standing cup, covered, and gilded; one flat cup of silver, covered.

The same jewels and parcels, by virtue of the writ of the Lord the King, under his great seal to the Treasurer and Chamberlains of the Exchequer directed remaining among the mandates of the Easter term, in the twentieth-year of the said Lord the King, were sold by Thomas Rothewell, Clerk of the Treasurer of England, in the stead and names of the said Treasurer and Chamberlains to diverse persons for the sum.

Of which, it is answered to the King in the Office of the Exchequer for Easter Term, in the same twenty eighth year, on the twenty-ninth day of August, as more fully there appears in form the following: from Philip Malpas, for goods of the said John Cade, £114 pounds, 9s, 4d. From Richard Joynour, for goods of the said John Cade, £20. From Thomas Rothewell, for goods of the said John Cade, £131, 9s, and 3d. From Thomas Stokdale, for goods of the said John Cade, £8, 9s, and 10d.

And it remained, in a certain box of wood, in a green chest, under the sign, "Cade, otherwise known as Mortimer."

From The Antient Kalendars and Inventories of the Treasury

NOTES

1. A bicorn is a mythological creature that has the face of a human, and a body that is part-cow and part-panther. This "claw" must be an ornamental object of art.

2. This would be an ornamental container that would contain musk perfume from a deer.

3. These standing cups were often present at guild meetings, ceremonies, and dinners, were the master of the guild drank first from the cup (usually ale) and then all members of the guild took turns drinking.

4. A cruet is a small vessel, often with a stopper, that is used to keep liquid inside. Cruets are used in the home and often kept on the table; these frequently contain vinegar or oil. Cruets are also used in church services in the celebration of the Eucharist, and on these occasions they contain either holy water or sacramental wine.

5. A pax-board is a plaque, made of wood, glass, or metal, that is decorated with the image of Christ's passion or other religious imagery. This religious object is used during Mass, for after the priest gives it the kiss of peace, he then passes it around to members of the congregation.

6. This girdle more than likely refers to the belt that one would wear around the waist to which was fashioned a sword or purse.

7. This scallop could be one of a number of items: a vessel (used for keeping food or household items) shaped like a scallop; a decorative heraldic scallop charge; or a souvenir token that a pilgrim would have received when visiting the shrine of Saint James of Compostella.

Chapter 24

From the Parliament Rolls of England

OVERVIEW

The rolls of parliament were the records of England's parliamentary meetings from the reign of Edward I (1272–1307) to Henry VII (1485–1509). The clerks who recorded the records wrote in Latin, Middle English, and Anglo-Norman. For over two centuries, the edition that scholars relied on for these records was the *Rotuli Parliamentorum; utet Petitiones, et Placita in Parliamento* published in 1767 under the general editorship of John Strachey. In 2005, under the general editorship of Chris Given–Wilson, the original rolls were reedited into sixteen volumes, with new material added, and new translations written; a CD-Rom and an online, searchable edition is also available. Four items related to the Cade rebellion from parliament are included below, which I have translated into Present Day English.

Item I is from the parliament that began on 6 November 1450 and was dissolved in May 1451. It is a common petition of attaint against Jack Cade for his treasonous actions and comes from the third session of this parliament, which began on 5 May 1451 and lasted until the end of that month. Given–Wilson notes that while Cade was captured and killed, he never stood trial, and that this formal attaint "was a useful re-statement of royal authority as well, perhaps, as a way of bringing to mind again what Cade and his followers had been demanding" (170).

Items II and III are common petitions from either the first or second sessions of parliament of March 1453. Item II asks for Jack Cade to be formally declared a traitor. Item III in the rolls immediately follows it and is a common petition asking that Sir William Oldhall also be considered a traitor and outlawed for his actions in the rebellion as a counselor to Cade. Given–Wilson observes how "the wording of the two petitions was intended as an indirect but obvious attack by Somerset and his associates on the duke of York," and it is "given further credence by the reminder in the petition concerning Cade that he also called himself Mortimer" (218).

Item IV comes from the parliament of 1453, which began on 6 March 1453 and ended on 17 April 1454. This common petition is from the last session of this parliament, which began on 14 February 1454. Robert Poynings was an esquire from Twineham and Sutton, Sussex, and was commissioned by Henry VI to arrest soldiers returning from France who engaged in robbery in Edenbridge, near Sevenoaks. Poynings failed his mission and soon joined Cade's retinue, where he served as the leader's carver and sword bearer. After Cade's rebellion, he gathered together a number of former Cade associates and continued to riot in the south–east of England from 1453 to 1454.

SOURCE FOR TRANSLATION

Given-Wilson, Chris, gen. ed. *The Parliament Rolls of Medieval England, 1275–1504*. Vol. 12. Henry VI, 1447–1460. London: The Boydell Press and The National Archives, 2005. Item I: Pp. 202–3. Item II: Pp. 306–7. Item III: Pp. 307–8. Item IV: Pp. 271–72.

TRANSLATIONS

Item I: The Attainder of Jack Cade

John Cade. Your commons of this present parliament pray, where the false traitor, naming himself John Mortimer, lately called the captain of Kent, on the eighth day of July, the twenty-eighth year of your reign, at Southwark in the shire of Surrey, and on the ninth day of July in the aforesaid year, at Dartford and Rochester in the shire of Kent, also at Rochester aforesaid and elsewhere, the tenth and eleventh day of July the next ensuing, within your noble realm of England, falsely and traitorously imagined your death, destruction, and subversion of this, your said realm, by gathering and raising a great number of your people, and directing them to rise against you falsely and traitorously in the places aforesaid, and at aforesaid times mentioned, against your royalty, crown, and dignity, and there and then made and raised war falsely and traitorously against you and your highness. And how be it, though he is dead and perished, yet by the law of your said land not punished, to consider the aforesaid statements, and to put such traitors in doubt to do [such action] in the time coming, and for the salvation of yourself and your said realm, by advice of your lords spiritual and temporal in this your present parliament assembled, to ordain by authority of the said parliament, that he be attainted of these treasons, and by the authority aforesaid forfeit to you all his goods, lands, tenements, rents, and possessions, which he had on the said eighth day of July or after, and his blood corrupted and disabled forever, and to be called within your said realm a false traitor for evermore.

Reply: The king consents.

Item II: Jack Cade's Attainder

John Cade's attainder. Your commons pray in this your present parliament assembled: That where the most abominable tyrant, horrible, odious, and errant false traitor, John Cade, calling and naming himself sometime Mortimer, sometime Captain of Kent, which name, fame, acts and deeds, are to be put out of every true Christian man's language and memory forever, falsely and traitorously proposing and imagining the uttermost destruction of your most royal person, and final subversion of this your noble realm, taking upon him royal power, and gathering to him your people in great number, by false, subtle, and imaginative language, and seditiously made commotion, rebellion, and insurrection under color of justice and reformation of your laws, robbing, slaying, and despoiling a great part of your true people, purposing also by diverse subtle, false, and untrue imaginations to make variances and commotion between you, our sovereign lord, and your true people, and to remove diverse and many of your full true liege lords, and your other servants and liegemen, some of them putting away and removing from your said person, some of them falsely and feloniously slain, and some of them falsely indicted of treason and felonies, under color of justice, before certain commissioners by his tyranny thereto condemn and besiege, and more would if he might have attained to his false, traitorous purpose, the which God in his endless mercy, through the victorious knighthood of you, our sovereign lord, destroyed and annulled forever. And also false and untrue articles and petitions falsely and traitorously imagined and forged against your royal person, estate, and prerogative.

Please, your highness, these premises, with more that were too great and odious to put in remembrance, graciously to consider, and thereupon to ordain and establish by the advice and the assent of your lords, spiritual and temporal, in this your present parliament assembled, and by the authority of the same, that the said John Cade be taken, had, named, and declared a false traitor to you our most gracious sovereign lord and that all of his tyranny, acts, deeds, and false opinions be voiced, quashed, annulled, destroyed, and put out of remembrance forever. And all such indictments and the dependents thereof, had and made under the power of his tyranny, also be voided, emptied, annulled, quashed, repelled, and taken for naught. And that no man's blood be thereby defiled nor corrupted, but by authority of this your present parliament cleared and declared forever. And all indictments in time to come in a sensible manner, under power of tyranny, rebellion, and commotion, be of no record nor effect, but voided in law. And all the petitions put to your highness in your last parliament held at Westminster on the sixth day of November, the twenty-ninth year of your most noble reign, against your intent, not agreed to by you, be taken and put in oblivion, out of remembrance, quashed, voided, annulled, and destroyed forever, as a thing proposed against God and conscience, against your sovereignty, estate, and preeminence, and also worshipful and unreasonable.

[Reply:] The king consents.

Item III: The Attainder and Outlawing of William Oldhall

The attainder of William Oldhall, knight. The commons pray in this your present parliament assembled. That is please your highness, by the advice and assent of your lords spiritual and temporal in this present parliament assembled, and by authority of the same, in consideration of the false, cursed, and traitorous disposition of William Oldhall, knight, who unnaturally and against the duty and faith of his allegiance has for a long time labored by subtle, false, and untrue schemes and traitorous means, against your most royal person and estate, the welfare of you and of your realm, by all that was in him, and by his false, untrue counsel and aid given as well to those persons in the field at Dartford in your county of Kent, against your said most royal person lately assembled, as at several times toward the great traitors John Cade, John Wilkins, and now lately one John Halton, and this daily [he] continues in his said cursed and traitorous purpose, which God forbid if it should in any manner [be] accomplished. And how that he of diverse treasons stands indicted and attainted by outlawry, according to the course of your law, for which his good and chattels, lands and tenements, ought to be unto you forfeited and seized to ordain and establish that the said William Oldhall, by what name or names whatever he be called, named or known in any such indictments, be taken, deemed, reputed, and held as a traitor, and a person attainted of high treason done and committed against your most royal person. And moreover, by the said authority to ordain and establish that all manner of good, chattels, lands, tenements, rents, reversions,[1] fees, advowsons,[2] franchises, liberties, and all other inheritances and possessions, whatsoever they be, which were of the said William Oldhall at the time if any treason supposed to be done by him in any indictment, or at any time since, or that any other person or persons of any estate, degree, or condition they be, [who] at the time of any treason by any of the said indictments by the said William Oldhall supposed to be done, or since, to use or benefit from in any manner [since they were] seized or possessed, be forfeited to your highness. And that you, by the authority aforesaid, have the forfeiture of all the aforesaid matters, notwithstanding any grant or grants made by you or the said William Oldhall, or by any other, of the said goods, chattels, lands, tenements, or possessions, or of any portion of them, to any man made or held.

Provided always that the heirs of the said William, who claim by force or any record commenced and taking effect before any treason supposed by him to [have] been done, or any person or persons claiming by virtue of any reversion or remainder of the aforesaid matters, by force of any grant made by the said William, or by any other seized for his use, before any treason supposed by him to [have] been done, that those gifts and grants were not to the use or need of the said William Oldhall, be not after the death of the said William hurt or prejudiced by this present act or ordinance.

Provided also that this present act not be prejudicial to any lord or lords of any franchises lawfully entitled to have and enjoy any of the said lands and tenements, goods and chattels, by way of forfeiture by reason of their franchise and that this present act or ordinance extend not by way of forfeiture to any lands or tenements, goods or chattels, in which the said William stood enfeffen[3] or possessed, jointly or separately, to any other man's use. And furthermore, that those persons or person having any title, right, or possession in any of the said lands, tenements, goods, or chattels before any title, right, or possession was derived, taken, or held by the same Sir William, not to the use of him, by this act be not hurt, prejudiced, nor barred from their lawful action, claim, title, or entry.

Provided also that this present act or ordinance, or any other in this present parliament made, be not prejudicial or damaging to Edmund, Earl of Richmond, or to Jasper, Earl of Pembroke, of, to, or touching anything given, granted, or confirmed, or to be given, granted, or confirmed to the said Edmund or Jasper, or either of them, before the next Feast of the Nativity of Our Lord,[4] by what name or names the said Edmund and Jasper or either of them be named or called, or shall be named or called, in any of the said gifts, grants, or confirmations. And also provided that this present act or ordinance be not prejudicial to the prior of Walsingham, or to his successors, regarding any grant made to them of these aforesaid matters, or any portion thereof.

Provided also that this present act or ordinance shall not be prejudicial to Edmund, Duke of Somerset, nor to his heirs, regarding any grant made to him or them of the manor and lordship of Hunsden, with their appurtenances.[5]

The king wills that it be initiated and done in the manner and form as it is desired. Provided always that this present act of parliament [will] not extend nor be prejudicial to Sir Thomas Tyrell, knight; Master Thomas Green, clerk; Robert Tanfield and John Hewett, esquires; nor to their heirs or assigns of any right, title, claim, possession, or interest that the said Thomas, Thomas,

Robert, and John have in and of three tenements in Muswell Street in London, which their appurtenances, nor in any portion of them, in which said three tenements John Fastolf, knight; Henry Inglose, knight; Richard Waller, esquire; and Robert Norwich once stood feoffed to the use and need of Sir William Oldhall, knight.

Provided also that this present act or ordinance be not prejudicial to the prior and convent of the monastery of Saint Mary of Walsingham, nor to their successors, regarding any grant made to them of any of these aforementioned matters or of any matter of them before this twenty-second day of June in the thirty-first year of his sovereign reign.

Provided also that this ordinance and act be not prejudicial to the prior and convent of monks of Saint Mary of Thetford, nor to their successors, of and for the manor of Bodney and one hundred acres of land with the appurtenances in Bodney, nor of no part thereof, of which the said William Oldhall, long before the time of the said treasons are supposed to [have] been done, enfeoffed Wichard Waller, esquire; Robert Boerley, esquire; John Bertram, gentilman; and William Norwich, the younger; and which manor and land with the appurtenances we have licensed by our letters patent the said prior and convent to purchase, and to hold onto them and onto their successors forever, as in the same letters patent more clearly contained.

Also provided that this said act not extend nor be in any manner prejudicial or [cause] hurt to any grant made by our said sovereign lord, by any of his letters patent to Walter Bourgh, esquire, of any goods, chattels, or debts that that of late were appertained to the said William Oldhall by whatever name the said Walter is called in the said letters patent.

ITEM IV: THE PETITION OF ROBERT POYNINGS

For as much as one Robert Poynings, late of Southwark in our county of Surrey, esquire, who accompanied and [was] an adherent to the most horrible, wicked, and heinous traitor and tyrant John Cade in the time of his insurrection, and was carver and sword bearer to the said most heinous traitor, at such time as he did his robbery and tyranny in the city of London, and many other places, the which Robert . . . and stirred the great part of such as were adherents and accompanied to the said traitor, to rise against our highness, our laws and peace. This Robert yet at this day is persevering, continuing, and abiding in his said wicked, malicious disposition and intent, laboring daily as far as it is in him, to all as will be moved and stirred by him, to make assemblies and congregations of people to riot against our highness, our laws and peace, having and holding daily in his fellowship such persons who are indicted of felony and treason, as such as none other of our liege people will have in their service, and since our general pardon granted to him by us, the same Robert found certitude unto us to keep our peace, and of his good bearing against us and our liege people, as it appears in our Chancery of Record, by recognizance by him and by others made. The same Robert since that agreement found that he has done many riots, for which he has of late taken the sanctuary and liberty of the Church of Westminster for his protection. And since then, he has also gone out of the same sanctuary at many diverse times, and done many great and diverse riots and offenses, and after returning when he would, and departing when he would, not considering nor reconciling the grace to him granted by us, nor the agreement to us by him and others found to keep our peace, and of his good bearing, in the condition as it is above rehearsed. Now of late, the same Robert has assembled and intensified unto him many persons unknown to us and of evil disposition in great number, that is to say, the fifteenth, sixteenth, and seventeenth day of the month of May, in the thirty-second year of our reign, at North Cray and Farningham, in the shire of Kent, and other places rode in a riotous manner, and arrayed in a manner of war, that is to say, with jacks,[6] salets,[7] and with other array of war, against the condition of our statutes in such case provided. Wherefore, we, by the assent of our spiritual and temporal Lord, and of the Commons in this present parliament, ordain and establish, that the said Robert, and those persons that are his protection and burden as it is above rehearsed, and as it appears in the record in our chancery as it is said above, forfeit to us and pay the sums in the same record and recognizance in the said chancery contained, and leave to be made thereof by a writ of execution, or in such a manner as it can be thought reasonable by our Treasurer of England, and by our barons of the Exchequer, and by the same authority we direct and ordain, that a transcript of this same act, in all excellence has been sent and delivered unto our said treasurer, and unto our said barons, to the intent that leave may be made thereof, as truth and reason wills [it]. The half of all that that is forfeited above contained in the same recognizance [is] to be employed upon the keeping of the sea. The half of the other half [will be sent] toward our great wardrobe, and that other half of the same half to our stable.

NOTES

1. A reversion is when an estate is returned to the grantor or his heir when the grant has expired.

2. An advowson is the right to recommend a person, usually a member of the clergy, to a vacant benefice.

3. See *MED* "enfeffen" v. 1. To grant (land, an estate, an office, rights, revenue, etc.) under the feudal system;—three constructions occur: (a) to enfeoff (a person);

(b) to enfeoff (someone in, on, of something); (c) to enfeoff (something to someone). [The terms of the grants vary widely. The enfeoffment could be hereditary or for a specified period. If hereditary, it could be unrestricted or subject to various conditions.]

4. Christmas.

5. See *MED* "ap(p)urtenaunce" n. 1. A right, privilege, or possession subsidiary or incidental to a principal one (such as lordship, a manor, etc.); the totality of such rights, etc.

6. A jack is a woven tunic, which often had armor plating in the interior.

7. A salet is a light helmet.

Chapter 25

From the Paston Letters

OVERVIEW

The correspondences between members of the Paston family and their acquaintances provide us with a window into the lives of individuals in the late fifteenth and early sixteenth centuries. All told, more than one-thousand documents survive from 1422 to 1509. The Pastons were a landed gentry family whose surname comes from the Norfolk village in Norwich. The fifteenth century was a time of social change, political upheaval, and increased literacy, all of which are reflected in the letters. The two letters below correspond to the life of John Paston I (1421–1466), a lawyer who, upon his father William Paston's death in 1444, inherited the large family estate. Land was a source of income but also a symbol of power, influence, and prestige. The 1440s was a challenging time for the family as they were caught in a power struggle involving William de la Pole, the Duke of Suffolk. John Paston lost his manor of East Beckham in 1445 and nearly lost their Gresham estate in 1448, reclaiming it in 1451 after the death of Suffolk. Suffolk was a dominant, influential, and polarizing figure in the 1440s and his death was widely recorded and celebrated by many, especially those in East Anglia. During this period, Paston befriends Sir John Fastolf, hero of the Hundred Years' War and wealthy landowner, who is related to John's wife, Margaret. Paston becomes an important friend to Fastolf, for as a lawyer he aids him in a number of land disputes. When Fastolf dies in 1459, his will, of which Paston is named executor, is disputed for a number of years. Paston Letter 450 (Item I, below) is written by William Lomnor (a friend and agent of the Paston family) to John Paston and describes the events surrounding Suffolk's death. As the Gies observe, while Paston "doubtless shared the general revulsion of the murder, he must have realized the favorable effect the duke's fall from power would have on the Pastons' land wars" (70–71). Paston Letter 692 (Item II, below) is a first-hand account of Cade and the uprising. Written by J[ohn] Payn, one of Sir John Fastolf's servants, his letter recounts how his master sent him and another man to into Cade's camp to ascertain their plans. It does not go well for Payn, who is recognized as a Fastolf servant, seized, and nearly executed. The letter documents how Payn was swept into the battle on London Bridge, arrested as a traitor, thrown into Marshalsea Prison, and eventually pardoned. Payn's letter to Paston is written fifteen years after these events; as such, we must question Payn's motivation for writing to John Paston.

MANUSCRIPTS

Item I: Paston Letter 450. From William Lomnor. London, British Library MS Additional 43488

Item II: Paston Letter 692. From J[ohn] Payn. London, British Library MS Additional 43491

SOURCES FOR TRANSLATION

Item I: Davis, 35–36.
Item II: Davis, 313–15.

FURTHER READING

Gies, Joseph, and Frances Gies. *A Medieval Family: The Pastons of Fifteenth-Century England*. New York: Harper Perennial, 1999.

Kaufman, 131–48.

Richmond, Colin. *The Paston Family in the Fifteenth Century: Endings*. Manchester: Manchester University Press, 2000.

———. *The Paston Family in the Fifteenth Century: Fastolf's Will*. Cambridge: Cambridge University Press, 1996.

———. *The Paston Family in the Fifteenth Century: The First Phase*. Cambridge: Cambridge University Press, 1990.

TRANSLATIONS

Item I: Paston Letter 450. From William Lomnor to John Paston

1450, 5 May

Right worshipful sir, I entrust my services to you, and I am very sorry of what I shall say, and have so washed this little bill with sorrowful tears that you shall hardly read it.

As on Monday the next after May Day[1] there came tidings to London that on Thursday before the Duke of Suffolk came into the coasts of Kent very near Dover with his two ships and a little ship, the which small ship he sent with certain letters by certain trusted men of his toward Calais, to know how he should be rescued. And with him met a ship called *Nicholas of the Tower*, with other ships waiting on him, and from those who were on the small ship the master of the *Nicholas* had knowledge of the Duke's coming. And when he discovered the Duke's ships, he sent forth his boat to know what they were, and the Duke himself spoke to them and said he was, by the king's commandment, sent to Calais. And they said he must speak with their master. And so he, with two or three of his men, went forth with them in their boat to the *Nicholas*. And when he came, the master bade him, "Welcome, traitor," as men say. And further, the master desired to know if the shipmen would stay with the Duke, and they sent word that they would not in no manner. And so he was in the *Nicholas* until the next Saturday.

Some say he wrote many things to be delivered to the king, but that is not verily known. He had his confessor with him. And some say he was arraigned in the ship in their manner regarding the impeachment, and found guilty.

Also, he asked the name of the ship, and when he knew it he remembered Stacy, who said if he might escape the danger of the *Tower* he should be safe. And then his heart failed him, for he thought he was deceived. And in the sight of all his men he was drawn out of the great ship into the boat, and there was an axe and a block, and one of the lowest [men] of the ship bade him to lay down his head, and he should be fairly treated and die by a sword. And [he] took a rusty sword and smote off his head with half a dozen strokes, and took away his gown of russet and his doublet of mailed velvet and laid his body on the sands of Dover. And some say his head was set on a pole by it, and his men [were] set on the land by great circumstance and prayer. And the sheriff of Kent does watch the body, and sent his undersheriff to the judges to know what to do, and also to the king. What shall be done further, I know not, but thus far it is: if the process be erroneous, let his council reverse it.

As for all your other matters, they are neglected, and the friars, also.

Sir Thomas Kiriel is taken prisoner, and all the leg harnesses, and about three-thousand Englishmen slain, Matthew Gough with fifteen [men] fled and saved himself and them. And Piers de Brezé was chief captain, and had ten-thousand Frenchmen and more.

I pray you let my mistress, your mother, know these tidings, and God have you all in His keep. I pray you this bill may entrust myself to my mistresses, your mother and wife. James Gresham[2] has written to John of Dam[3] and entrusted him. Written in great haste at London, the 5th day of May.

Your [servant], W[illiam] Lomnor

Item II: Paston Letter 692. From J[ohn] Payn to John Paston

[1465]

Right honorable and my right entirely beloved master, I entrust myself to you with all manner of due reverence in the most lowly manner as I ought to so, evermore desiring to hear of your worshipful state, prosperity, and welfare, which I beseech God of his abundant grace increase and maintain to His great satisfaction and to your heart's desire.

It pleases your good and gracious mastership tenderly to consider the great losses and hurts that your poor petitioner has had ever since the commons of Kent came to Blackbeath, and that is [now] fifteen years passed, where, as my master Sir John Fastolf, Knight, who is your testator,[4] commanded your beseecher [i.e., Payn] to take a man and two of the best horses that were in his stable with him to ride to the commons of Kent to greet the articles that they came for. And so I did, and as soon as I came to Blackheath the captain made the commons to take me, and for the salvation of my master's horse I made my fellow ride away with the two horses. And I was brought forthwith before the captain of Kent, and the captain demanded of me what was my cause for coming thither, and why I made my fellow to steal away with the horses. And I said that I had come thither to visit with my wife's brethren and others that were my allies and friends of mine that were present there. And then there was one there [who] said to the captain that I was one of Sir John Fastolf's men, and the two horses were Sir John Fastolf's. And then the captain let cry treason upon me throughout all the field, and brought me at four parts of the field with an agent of the Duke of Exeter before me in the Duke's coat of arms, making four proclamations at four parts of the field, proclaiming openly by the said agent that I was sent thither to spy their strength and their military equipment by the greatest traitor that was in England or France, as the said captain made proclamation at that time, for one Sir John Fastolf, knight, who had diminished all the garrisons of Normandy and Le Mans and Maine, which was the cause of losing all of the king's title and right of inheritance that he had overseas. And moreover, he said that the said Sir John Fastolf had furnished his place with the old soldiers of Normandy and military equipment to destroy the commons of Kent when they came to Southwark, and therefore, he said plainly, that I should lose my head. And so forthwith I was taken and led to the captain's tent, and an axe and a block was brought forth to smite off my head. And then my master Poynings,[5] your brother, with other friends of mine, came and hindered the captain and said plainly that there should die one- or two-hundred[6] [persons] in case that I died, and so in that manner my life was saved at that time.

And then I was sworn to the captain and to the commons that I should go to Southwark and array me in the best manner that I could, and come again to them to help them. And so I obtained the articles and brought them to my master, and that cost me more among the commons that day than 27 shillings.[7] Whereupon, I came to my master Fastolf and brought him the articles and informed him of the entire matter, and counselled him to put away all of his military equipment and the old soldiers, and so he did and went himself to the Tower and all his company with him but Bettes and Matthew Brayn.[8] And had I not been there, the commons would have burned his place and his properties, such that it cost me of my own possession goods at that time more than six marks in food and drink. And not withstanding the captain that same time permitted them to seize me at the White Hart in Southwark, and there commanded Lovelase[9] to despoil me out of my array, and so he did. And there he took a fine gown of musterdevillers[10] furred with fine beaver and a pair of brigandines coverer with blue velvet and gilded nails, with leg harnesses, the value of the gown and the brigandines £8.[11]

Moreover, the captain sent certain [persons] of his company to my chamber in your property, and there broke open my chest and took away an obligation[12] of mine that was due to me of £36 by a priest of Saint Paul's; and another obligation of a knight of £10; and my purse with five rings of gold, and 17*s*. and 6*d*. of gold and silver; and a harness stamped with the official stamp of Milan; and a gown of fine purplish-blue cloth furred with martens; and two gowns, one furred with sheepskin, and another lined with coarse wool. And there [they] would have smote off my head when they had despoiled me at the White Hart. And there my master Poynings and my friends saved me, and so I was put up until night when the battle was at London Bridge, and then at night the captain put me out into the battle at the bridge and there I was wounded and hurt nearly to death, and I was there six hours in the battle and might never have come out of it. And four times before that time I was carried about through Kent and Sussex, and there they would have smote off my head.

And in Kent, as my wife dwelled there, they took away all our moveable goods that we had, and would have hanged my wife there and five of my children, and left her no more goods but her kirtle and her smock. And soon after that rioting, the Bishop of Ross[13] charged me on behalf of the queen, and so I was arrested by the queen's commandment into Marshalsea, and there was in very great duress and in fear of my life, and was threatened to have been hanged, drawn, and quartered, and so [they] would have made me to accuse my master Fastolf of treason. And because that I would not [do], they brought be up to Westminster and there would have sent me to the coal house at Windsor. But my wife[14] and a cousin of my own, that were yeomen of the crown, they went to the king and received grace and a charter of pardon.

Yours, Payn J[ohn].

NOTES

1. 4 May 1450.
2. Gresham was at times a clerk to William Paston I.
3. John Dam (also spelled "Damme") was a freeman of Norwich and executor of William Paston I.
4. A "testator" is a person responsible for the drawing up of a will on the behalf of another person.
5. Robert Poynings (Ponynggys), the first husband of Elizabeth Paston, and thus John Paston I's brother-in-law.
6. The text reads here "þat þer shulde dye a c or ij in case be þat I dyed (Davis, 314.37–38), which seems to suggest a hundred or two [hundred].
7. In the fifteenth century, twenty-seven shillings would be about a month's wages for a skilled tradesperson.
8. Little is known of these two individuals. Another Bettes, quite possibly the same person, is featured in Paston Letter 473, dated 1 March 1451, written by pastor James Gloys to John Paston I. For this letter, see Davis, 64–67.
9. Nothing is known of this Cade supporter apart from this mention of him.
10. See *MED*, "muster-de-vilers" (n.), "(a) A kind of woolen cloth, originally from Montivilliers in Normandy, usually of a mixed gray color."
11. The gown and armor were extremely valuable. £8 from 1450 would be worth approximately £5,000.00 in 2017. Or, perhaps in greater perspective, 266 days of wages for a skilled tradesman in 1450. See Currency Converter: 1270-2017, The National Archives, http://www.nationalarchives.gov.uk/currency-converter/, 6 August 2018.
12. This "obligation" is a formal, legal document that describes money or services owed to an individual.
13. Robert Clerk, Bishop of Ross (co. Cork).

14. The text here reads "wyves" (Davis, 315.80). Payn, as noted earlier in the letter, only has one wife, so there are two possible reading of this passage. The first is that it was a scribal error, and Payn intended to write "wif." The other reading, which is also possible, is that "wyves" in the text does not refer to Payn's spouse but instead to females (in his family, or possibly working in his household) who go to the king to seek a pardon on behalf of Payn.

Part III

POLITICAL POEMS OF THE FIFTEENTH CENTURY

Chapter 26

"On the Arrest of the Duke of Suffolk"

OVERVIEW

This political poem dates to ca. 1450 and is one of a number of verses highly critical of William de la Pole, the Duke of Suffolk. The poem is one that explores, among other literary techniques, zoomorphism, where human figures resemble and act like animals. Suffolk is personified both as a fox as well as Jack Napes, which is a popular name for a monkey. Two of Henry VI's henchmen who are present in the poem (John Talbot and John Beaumont) are both personified as dogs who drive the fox into the hole. Once the fox/Suffolk has been captured, suddenly he is transformed into the Jack Napes, more monstrous and inhuman. As noted in the introduction to the volume, by the late 1440s, public support turned against Suffolk, who was seen as responsible for the losses in France, a poor economy, the marriage of Henry VI to Margaret of Anjou, and the murder of the Duke of Gloucester in 1447. He was indicted initially by parliament on seventh February 1450, primarily for losing Maine, and again in March 1450 on charges of illegal patronage and embezzlement.

MANUSCRIPT

London, British Library MS Cotton Roll II 23

SOURCE FOR TRANSCRIPTION AND TRANSLATION

Wright, 224–25.

NOTE ON TRANSCRIPTION

For this transcription, I have eliminated all double initial consonants and regularized capitalization. I have provided Present Day English glosses for challenging Middle English words and phrases.

FURTHER READING

Robbins, xxix–xxx; 186–87.
Scattergood, V. J. *Politics and Poetry in the Fifteenth Century*. London: Blandford Press, 1971. Pp. 162–63.
Yamamoto, Dorothy. *The Boundaries of the Human in Medieval English Literature*. Oxford: Oxford University Press, 2000. Pp. 89–90.

TRANSCRIPTION

	Now is the fox drevin to hole; hoo to him, hoo! hoo!	*Driven*
	For and he crepe out, he wille yow alle undo.	*Creep*
	Now ye han founde partite, love welle your game;	*have found perfection*
	For and ye renne countre[1] thenne be ye to blame.	
5	Sum of yow holdith with the fox, and rennythe hare;	*you hold; run with the*
	But he that tiede Talbot[2] oure doge, evylle mot he fare!	*tethered; may he be unlucky*
	For now we myse the black doge withe the wide mouthe;	*Miss*
	For he wolde have ronnen welle at the fox of the southe.	*Ran*
	And alle gooth bacwarde, and donne is in the myre;[3]	*go backward*
10	As they han deservede, so pay they there hire.	
	Now is tyme of Lent, the fox is in the Towre;	
	Therefore send hym Salesbury[4] to be his confessoure.	*confessor*
	Many mo ther bene, and we kowde hem knowe;[5]	
	But wonne most begynne the daunce, and all come arowe.	*one; arrow*
15	Loke that your hunte blowe welle the chase;	
	But he do welle is pat, I beshrew is face!	*his; curse*
	This fox at Bury slowe oure grete gandere;[6]	*slew; gander*
	Therefore at Tyborne mony monne one hym wondere.	*Tyburn; many men*
	Jack Napys, with his clogge,[7]	
20	Hath tiede Talbot oure gentille dogge	*Tied*
	Wherfore Beamownt,[8] that gentille rache,[9]	
	Hath brought Jack Napis in an eville cache.	*Cage*
	Be ware, al menne, of that blame,	*Beware; men*
	And namely ye of grete fame,	
25	Spiritualle and temperalle, be ware of this,	*Spiritual; temporal*

	Or els hit wille not be welle, iwis.	*it; surely*
	Gave save¹⁰ the kynge, and God forbade	*Forbid*
	That he suche apes any mo fede.	*More*
	And of the perille that may befalle	
30	Be ware, dukes, erles, and barons alle.	*earls*
	Gens erit australis rectoe regni generalis,	
	*Et regit injustice, periet quoque postea just.*¹¹	
	He is wise that is wode, he is riche the has no goode;	*insane; goods*
	He is blynde that may se, he is riche that shalle never ithe;	*see; prosper*
35	He is fledde that is not ferde, and he abideth that make the alle your berdes.¹²	*departed; fearful; abides*

NOTES

1. See *MED* "rennen" (v.) 1. 1b(c): (c) *hunt.~ (in) countre*, follow a scent the wrong way.

2. John Talbot, Lord Lisle.

3. See *MED* "dŏn" (n.) 1(a): (a) A name for a dun horse; *don is in the mire*, the horse and cart are mired; *fig.* things are at a standstill.

4. Richard Neville, Earl of Salisbury, and a political opponent of Suffolk.

5. Many more have there been, and we could know of them.

6. This "gander" here is Humphrey, Duke of Gloucester.

7. See *MED* "clog(ge" (n.) 1. (b) a block or chunk of wood, esp. one tied to an animal or person to impede movement, or to a key to prevent loss. Suffolk's heraldic badge, as Michael Powell Siddons notes, is an "ape-clog Argent, corded Or," (231). An ape-clog is a heavy block of wood with a chain to secure and animal (such as a pet monkey), and the pet can perch on top of it. John Marshall observes how it was "probably political prudence" rather than his mother's heritage that led William's son John to change the ape-clog to a lion (43–4).

8. John Beaumont, Constable of England, who arrested Suffolk.

9. See *MED* "racch(e" (n.) 1. (a) A dog that hunts by scent, rach; *kenel of racches*, a pack of hunting dogs; ~ *mouth*, a rach's mouth; (b) as an epithet for John, Lord Beaumont (died 1460).

10. The phrase "Gave save" here is problematic to translate. On the one hand, it could be a scribal error for "God save," which would parallel the content of the rest of the line, "God forbede." Additionally, "Save'" here could also mean "salve," see *MED* "sāve" (n.)(1), that is, to "Give salve (i.e., "aid" or "remedy"] to the king . . ." Still yet another possible reading of this phrase could mean to "Give words to the king" or "Give an oath to the king"; for this see *MED* "sau(e" (n.)(2) 1. (a) What is said, talk, words; something said, an utterance; a speech, discourse. 2. (d) a promise, word; an oath; also, an agreement, a covenant.

11. "The Southern people will be the common leader of the kingdom. / And he rules unjustly, and afterward he will also die justly." Many thanks to Molly A. Martin for translating these two lines.

12. The phrase "makethealle your berdes" is a colloquialism that means "to outwit" or "to make a fool out of someone." See *MED* "bērd" (n.) (1) 4a.(b).

Chapter 27

"A Warning to King Henry"

OVERVIEW

As the title of this ca. 1450 Middle English political poem makes known, this poem presents a warning to King Henry VI and is highly critical of the courtiers who surrounded the monarch and favors Yorkist ideals. A number of personages who are major players in the Cade Rebellion, such as Lord Saye and Thomas Daniel, are mentioned in the opening stanza. The courtiers, according to this author, have taken advantage of the king, and a number of them are condemned, including William de la Pole, the Duke of Suffolk.

MANUSCRIPT

London, British Library MS Cotton Roll II 23

SOURCES FOR TRANSCRIPTION

Wright, 229–30.

NOTE ON TRANSCRIPTION

I consulted Wright's edition of this poem for the below transcription. Robbins' edition of the poem titles it "Advice to the Court, II." I have provided glosses for difficult Middle English words and phrases. Middle English double initial consonants have been made singular.

FURTHER READING

Lin, Chiu-Yen. "Innocent and Simple: The Making of Henry VI's Kingship in Fifteenth-Century England." In *Perceiving Power in Early Modern Europe*, edited by Francis K. H. So, 103–20. New York: Palgrave Macmillan, 2017.
Robbins, xxix–xxx, 203–5.
Wright, 2: lviii–lix, 229–31.

TRANSCRIPTION

	Ye that have the king to demene,	*demean*
	And frauncheses gif theyme ageyne,	*freedoms; give; again*
	Or els I rede ye fle	*else; advise; flee*
	For ye have made the kyng so pore,	
5	That now he beggeth fro dore to dore;	*from*
	Alas, hit shuld so be.	*it*
	Tome of Say[1] and Danielle[2] bothe,	*Time*
	To begyn be not to lothe;	*too angry*
	Then shalle ye have no shame.	
10	Who wille not he shall not chese,	*choose*
	And his life he shalle lese,	*lose*
	No resoun will us blame.	*reason*
	Trowthe and pore men ben appressede	*Truthful; are; oppressed*
	And myscheff is nothing redressede;	*mischief; redressed*
15	The kyng knowith not alle.	*knows*
	Throwout alle Englonde,	
	On tho that holdene the fals bonde	*those; hold*
	Vengeaunce will cry and calle.	*Vengeance*
	The traytours wene they bene so sly,	*believe*
20	That no mane can hem aspy	*man; them observe*
	We cane do theme no griffe.	*can; hardship*
	We swere by hyme that hairwede hell[3]	*swear; harrowed*
	They shalle no lenger in eresy dwelle,	*longer; heresy*
	Ne in ther fals beleve.	*Nor; belief*
25	So pore a kyng was never seene,	
	Nor richere lordes alle bydene;	*begging*
	The communes may no more.	*commons*
	The lorde Say biddeth holde hem downe,	*asks; them*
	That worthy dastarde of renowne,	*wretch*
30	He techithes a fals loore.	*teaches; tale*
	Sufolk Normandy hath swolde,	*sold/betrayed*
	To gete hyt agayne he is bolde,	
	How acordeth these to in one;	*two*
	And he wenythe, withouten drede,	*believes*
35	To make the kyng to avowe his dede,	

	And calle hit no tresoun.	
	We trow the kyng be to leere,	*believe; empty-handed*
	To selle bothe menne and lond in feere;	*good condition*
	Hit is agayne resoun.	*against*
40	But yef the commyns of Englonde	*if; commons*
	Helpe the kynge in his fonde,	*trial*
	Suffolk wolle bere the crowne.	*will bear*
	Be ware, kynge Henré, how thou doos;	*how you proceed*
	Let no lenger thy traitours go loos;	
45	They wille never be trewe.	
	The traytors are sworne all togedere	*together*
	To hold fast as they were brether;	*brothers*
	Let hem drynk as they hanne brewe.	*have brewed*
	The chaunselere that last was hath staffes take,	
50	Blanke charters, to done us wrake,	*blank; do us revenge*
	No nombre of them, hit is ferd.	*number; feared*
	He wolle not suffre the clerkes preche;	*clerks' sermon*
	Trowthe is no wise he wille not teche;	*Truth; condition*
	He is the devels sheparde.	*devil's*
55	This bille is trewe; who wille say nay,	*bill*
	In Smythfeld synge he a day,	
	And the helpe of the rode;	*The Cross*
	That traitours shalle provide;	
	More resoun can not be mevide;	*counseled*
60	Ther shalle hit be made goode.	

O rex, si rex es, rege te, vel eris sine re rex;
Nomen habes sine re, nisi recte regas.[4]

NOTES

1. James Fiennes, Lord Saye and Sele, Treasurer of England.

2. Thomas Daniel, esquire of the body.

3. This is a reference to "The Harrowing of Hell," which was a popular and important part of Christian theology, especially in the Middle Ages, and found first in the (now apocryphal) *Gospel of Nicodemus* (ca. 450 CE).

4. Latin translation: "Oh king, if you are the king, you be king, or we will be without a king; the name you have is of no matter, unless you deliberate properly."

Chapter 28

"Verses Against the Duke of Suffolk"

OVERVIEW

This verse dates to ca. 1450 and is a harsh attack on William de la Pole, the Duke of Suffolk. Line 2 of the poem is integral to its aim, for the verse implores the advisors of the king to love the commons. Wright notes in this poem that "those who support Suffolk are warned that if they did not abandon him and seek popular favour, punishment would overtake them within three months" (lix). Significantly, in the manuscript in which this poem is found, this verse immediately follows the third version of the rebels' bill of complaint, which is included in this volume.

MANUSCRIPT

London, British Library MS Cotton II 23

EDITION FOR TRANSCRIPTION AND TRANSLATION

Wright, 231.

NOTE ON TRANSCRIPTION AND TRANSLATION

I have omitted all double initial consonants from Wright's edition of the Middle English and regularized the capitalization of proper nouns and the first word in each line. Robbins titles this poem "Advice to the Court, I" in his edition of the poem. I have provided Present Day English glosses of challenging Middle English words and phrases.

FURTHER READING

Robbins, 203.

TRANSCRIPTION AND TRANSLATION

	For feer or for favour of ony fals mane,	*fear; any; false man*
	Loose not the love of all the commynalté;	*commons*
	Be ware and sey, by Seint Juliane,[1]	
	Duke, jwge, baroun, archebisshope and he be,	*judge*
5	He wolle repent it within this monthes thre.	*will; these three months*
	Let folke accused excuse theym selff, and they cane;	*the folk; themselves; do*
	Reseyve no goode, let soche bribery be;	*Receive; such*
	Support not theyme this wo bygane,	*them; woe began*
	And let theym such clothis as they spane,	*allow; clothes; spin*
10	And take from theym ther wages and ther fee,[2]	
	Or, by God and Seint Anne![3]	
	Some must go hens, hit may none other weys be,	*hence*
	And els is lost alle this lond and we;	*Or else; land*
	Hong up suche menne to oure soverayne lorde	*Hang; men*
15	That ever counseldehym with false men to be acorde.	*counseled; settled*
	Anno milleno Domini centumque quaterno	
	L. simplex pleno caveat omnis homo.[4]	

NOTES

1. This is more than likely Saint Julian the Hospitaller, born in the first quarter of the first century, CE.

2. "Fee" here could mean a number of things, including one's (inherited) lands, livestock, or heritable right.

3. Though not part of the canonical tradition, Saint Anne is commonly known as the mother of the Virgin Mary.

4. Latin translation: "In the year of our Lord, 1450, simply be wary of every man."

Chapter 29

"For Jake Napes Sowle, Placebo and Dirige"

Latin Translations by Molly A. Martin

OVERVIEW

This popular poem can be read as both a satire on the politics of the fifteenth-century and also a parody of the prayer the Office of the Dead. "Placebo and dirige" refer, respectively, to the vespers and matins for the dead, and most of the Latin phrases used in the poem come from scriptural or antiphonal/response material in the Office of the Dead. Griffiths, in studying the names of those present and those not included in the verse, argues that the poem originated not in Kent (as hated extortioners such as Crowmer and Isle are not in the poem) but rather has its origins in London and was popular there. Robbins observes how the poem "must have been written between May 3, [1450] the date of the murder of Suffolk, and June 29, the date of the murder of the Bishop of Salisbury (352). The poem can be read as pro-Yorkist, one that is critical of the members of the clergy, of Henry VI's retainers and allies, and especially of the Duke of Suffolk, for his mourners form, in Harvey's words, "a catalogue of those most despised men in his circle" (76). The form of this poem replicates and parodies the Office of the Dead, where clerics and lay individuals are each assigned parts within the prayer. As with the poem "On the Arrest of the Duke of Suffolk," included in this volume, this verse also characterizes Suffolk as a Jake Napes/Jack-a-Napes, someone who is an upstart but also a monkey.

214   *Chapter 29*

MANUSCRIPTS AND NOTES ON TRANSCRIPTION AND TRANSLATION

The poem exists in three different manuscripts and dates to ca. 1450: London, Lambeth Palace MS Lambeth 306; London, British Library MS Cotton Vespasian B.XVI; and Dublin, Trinity College MS 516. Gairdner's edition, which forms the basis for this selection, does not provide a title. Frederick Furnivall also edited the poem, and my title follows his. Robbins' edition of the poem is based on the Vespasian manuscript, and he titles the verse "The Death of the Duke of Suffolk." For the selection below, I have regularized capitalization of proper nouns, added modern punctuation, and translated Early Modern scribal "Y^e" as "the." We have kept the Latin in the poem proper (and in italics) so as to not disrupt the meter and rhyme, and Molly A. Martin has supplied, in the footnotes, the Present Day English translation and scriptural references. I have provided glosses for words and phrases that present readers may find to be challenging to understand. The poem has numerous references to individuals, and I have attempted to identify all of them in notes.

EDITION USED FOR TRANSCRIPTION AND TRANSLATION

Gairdner, James, ed. *Three Fifteenth-Century English Chronicles*. Camden Society, ns, 28. Westminster: Camden Society, 1880. Pp. 99–103.

FURTHER READING

Furnivall, Frederick J., ed. *Political, Religious, and Love Poems*. EETS, os 15. London: Trübner & Co., 1866. Pp. 6–11.
Griffiths, 639–40.
Harvey, 76–77.
Robbins, 187–86; 349–51.

TRANSCRIPTION AND TRANSLATION

Here folowythe a dyrge made by the comons of Kent in the tyme of ther rysyng, when Jake Cade was theyr cappitayn.

"For Jake Napes Sowle, Placebo and Dirige"   215

	In the moneth of May whan gres growes grene,	month; grass
	Fragrans in there floures with a swet savor,	Fragrant; flowers; sweet
	Jake Napis in the see a maryner for to bene,	sea; mariner to be
	With his clogge and his cheyne to sell more tresowr.	piece of wood; treasure
5	Suche a thynge prykkyd hym, he axid a confessour.	asked for confession
	Nycolas of the Towre[1] seyd "I am redy here to se";	see
	He was holde so hard, he passyd the same houre.	passed; hour
	For Jake Napes sowle *placebo* and *dirige*.	soul
	Who shall execute the fest of solempnite	solemnity
10	Bysshoppis and lords as gret reson is,	Bishops
	Monkes, chanons, and prestis, with all the clergy,	canons; priests
	Prayeth for hym that he may com to blys,	
	And that nevar such anothar come aftar this.	
	His interfectures blessid mot they be,	Blessed be his killers
15	And graunt them to reygne with aungellis,	angels
	For Jake Napys sowle *placebo* and *dirige*.	
	"*Placebo*,"[2] begynneth the Bishop of Hereforthe.[3]	
	"*Dilexi*,"[4] quod the Bisshop of Chester,[5] "for my avaunse."	said; benefit
	"*Hew michi*,"[6] sayd Salysbury,[7] "this game gothe ferforthe."	goes forward
20	"*Ad Dominum cum tribularer*,"[8] seyth the Abbot of Glocester.[9]	
	"*Dominus custodit*,"[10] thus seyth the Bisshoppe of Rowchestre.	
	"*Levavi oculos meos*,"[11] seyth Frere Stanbery.[12]	
	"*Si iniquitates*,"[13] seyth the Bysshope of Worcestre.[14]	
	For Jake Napis sowle, "*de profundis clamavi*."[15]	
25	"*Opera manium tuarum*,"[16] seyth the cardinall[17] wysely.	
	"Hath wronge *confitebor*,"[18] for all Jack Napis wisdome.	
	"*Audivi vocem*,"[19] seyd Jhesus on hye.	Jesus
	"*Magnificat anima mea Dominum*."[20]	
	Now to this *dyryge* most we nedys come.	need to come
30	This joyfull tyme to sey brevely,	bravely
	Nine spalmes, nine lessons to sey all and sum.	psalms
	For Jake Napys sowlle *placebo* and *dirige*.	
	Executor of this office dirge for to synge,	
	Shall begin the Bisshope of Seynt As.[21]	
35	"*Varba mea auribus*,"[22] seyth the Abbot of Redynge,[23]	
	For all our hope and joy is come to allas.	
	"*Convertere Domine*,"[24] for us wantyth grace,	wanting
	Thow Abbot of Seynt Albonys[25] full sorely synge ye.	with much sorrow sing you

	The Abbot of Towre Hyll, with his fate face,	fat
40	Tremelyth and quakyth, for "*Domine ne in furore.*"[26]	Trembles and quakes
	Master Watyr Lyard[27] schall sey "*ne quando.*"[28]	
	The Abbess of Seynt Alborghe,[29] "*Domine Deus meus, in te speravi.*"[30]	
	"*Requiem eternam,*"[31] God grawnt hem to,	grant to them
	To sey a patar nostar,"[32] [seyth] the Bysshop of Seynt Davi,[33]	
45	For the sowles of thes wyse and wurthy,	worthy
	Adam Molens,[34] Suffolke,[35] Sir Robert Ros,[36] thes thre.	these three
	And specyally for Jake Napis sowlle that evar was sly,	especially
	For his sowle *placebo* and *dirige*.	
	Rys up, Lord Say,[37] and read "*Parce michi, Domine,*	
50	*Nichil enim sunt dies mei,*"[38] that shalt thow singe.	
	The Bysshope of Carlyll[39] seyth "*credo videre*"[40]	
	All fals traytors to come to evyll endynge,	
	Dwelle thow shalt withe grete mornynge,	mourning
	Rede "*Tedet aniam meam vite mee,*"[41]	
55	"*Manus tue,*"[42] Danyell,[43] thow shall synge	
	For Jake Napis sowle *placebo* and *dirige*.	
	"*Qui Lazarum resussistasti,*"[44] Treyvilyan[45] shall singe;	
	Hungerford,[46] "*manus tue fecerunt me,*"[47]	
	Uby me abscondam,[48] for dred this day."	
60	John Say[49] synge, "*Dominus regit me.*"	
	"*Nichyll michi deerit*"[50] for owt that I can see.	doubtless
	"*Ad te Domine levavi,*"[51] Master Somerset[52] shall rede.	
	John Penycoke,[53] "*Delycta juventutis mee,*"[54]	
	Allas, whythar may I fle for dred?	whither
65	"*Dominus illuminacio,*[55] help, for now is ned."	the need
	Seyth maystar Wyll Say,[56] "I trow it wyll not be."	trust
	"*Credo videre,*"[57] Sir Thomas Stanle,[58] take hede.	heed
	For Jake Napis sowle *placebo* and *dirige*.	
	"*In memoria eterna,*"[59] seyth Mayster Thomas Kent.[60]	
70	"Now schall owre treson be cornicled for evar."	chronicled forever
	"*Patar nostar,*"[61] seyd Mayster Gerveyse,[62] "we be all shent,	are all ruined
	For so fals a company in Englond was nevar."	never
	The Abbot of Barmundsey,[63] full of lechery,	
	"*Quantas habeo iniquitatys,*"[64] take for thy lesson.	
75	Gabull of the Chancery begynyth "*Hew michi,*"[65]	
	That is his preve bande and detent of treson.	privy bound; encumbered
	"*Homo natus de muliere,*"[66] seyth the Master of Sent Laurence,[67]	
	"*Repletur multis miseriis,*"[68] and that shall he wayll,	wail
	Of Jake Napes sort that hath done gret offence,	
80	And never whill he lyvyd cheffe of his counceyll.	chafe

	"*Ne recorderys,*"⁶⁹ Stephen Shegge⁷⁰ shall synge.	
	"*Quis michi tribuat*⁷¹ for wichecraft," seyth Stace,	
	"*Domine, non secundum actum meum,*⁷² for then I shall hynge"	hang
	For Jake Napys sowle *placebo* and *dirige*.	
85	"*Expectans expectavi,*"⁷³ seyth Sir Thomas Hoo.⁷⁴	
	"*Complaceat tibi,*"⁷⁵ begynneth John Hampton.⁷⁶	
	"*Beatus qui intelligit*⁷⁷ and dredith also,"	dread
	Seyth John Fortescw,⁷⁸ "all this fals treson."	
	"*Sana Domine,*"⁷⁹ owre wittes with reson,"	our wits; reason
90	The Lorde Sudeley⁸⁰ devoutly prayth.	
	"*Quem admodum desiderat,*"⁸¹ the Lord Stowrton,⁸²	
	"*Sitivit anima mea,*"⁸³ for hym lyeth.	lies
	The Lord Ryvers⁸⁴ all onely seythe.	only
	"*Requiem eternam,*"⁸⁵ God grawnt us to se.	
95	A pater nostar⁸⁶ ther must be in feyth	faith/truth
	For Jake Napis sowle *placebo* and *dirige*."	
	"*Spiritus meus attenuabytur,*"⁸⁷ Blakney⁸⁸ shall begyn.	
	"*Pecantem me cotidie,*"⁸⁹ seyth Myners.⁹⁰	
	"*Pelle me consumptus carnibus*⁹¹ to the nynne,"	nine/extreme
100	Robert Horne,⁹² alderman, that shall be thy verse.	
	"*Requium eternam*"⁹³ for the respons.	
	Phylip Malpas⁹⁴ be thow redy to synge,	
	It wexeth derke, thow nedys a scons,	grows dark; need a candle
	Com forth, Jude,⁹⁵ for thow shalt in brynge.	bring
105	"*Quare de vulva eduxisti?*"⁹⁶	
	Ser Thomas Tudnam,⁹⁷ that rede ye.	read
	Abbot of Westmystar, com stond by	
	In thy myter and cope, and sey "*libera me.*"⁹⁸	miter and vestment
	Arys up, Thorp⁹⁹ and Cantelowe,¹⁰⁰ and stond ye togeder,	Arise
110	And sing, "*Dies illa, dies ire.*"¹⁰¹	
	Pulford¹⁰² and Hanley,¹⁰³ that drowned the Duke of Glocester,¹⁰⁴	
	As two traytors shall synge "*ordentes anime.*"¹⁰⁵	
	And all trew comyns ther to be bolde	true commons
	To sey "*Requiescant in pace.*"¹⁰⁶	
115	For all the fals traytors that Engelond hath sold,	
	And for Jake Napis sowlle *placebo* and *dirige*.—Finis.	
	Amen. Writn owt of David Norcyn¹⁰⁷ his booke by John Stowe.	Copied out

NOTES

1. *Nicholas of the Tower* is the name of the ship that stopped the Duke of Suffolk's ship in the sea.
2. "I will please," Psalms 114:9.
3. Richard Beauchamp.
4. "I loved," Psalms 114:1; used in many places in the Bible.
5. William Booth.
6. "Woe is me," Psalms 119:5.
7. William Ayscough, Bishop of Salisbury. He was also the clerk of the Council to Henry VI and was murdered on June 29, 1450, right after Suffolk was killed.
8. "To the Lord with trouble [I called out]," Psalms 119:1.
9. Reginald Boulers, Abbot of Saint Peters, also king's counselor and diplomat.
10. "The Lord guards," Psalms 120:5.
11. "I lifted my eyes," Psalms 120:1.
12. John Stanbury (d. 1474), the Bishop of Bangor in 1447, Bishop of Hereford in 1452.
13. "If iniquities [you will observe]," Psalms 129:3.
14. John Carpenter (d. 1476), Bishop of Worcester.
15. "from the depths I called out." Psalms 129:1.
16. "The works of your hands," Psalms 137:8.
17. John Kemp (1380–1454), Archbishop of York in 1426, Archbishop of Canterbury in 1452, Cardinal in 1439, and twice Chancellor of England (1426 and 1449).
18. "I will confess," Psalms 137:1.
19. "I heard a voice," response to Psalm 137 in Office for the Dead; Revelation 10:4.
20. "My soul praises the Lord." Luke 1:46.
21. Reginald Peacock, Bishop of Saint Asaph.
22. "My words with ears," Psalms 5:2.
23. John Thorne, Abbot of Reading.
24. "Turn, Lord," Psalms 6:5.
25. John Stoke, Abbot of Saint Albans.
26. "God not in furor." Psalms 6:2.
27. Walter Lyhert (or Liard), Bishop of Norwich.
28. "That not at any time." Psalms 7:3.
29. Abbess of Saint Aldeburgh, though Griffiths (662n208) argues convincingly that this is the Abbess of Saint Ethelburgha's, Barking, who took the 7 July 1450 general pardon. Another version of this poem in London, British Library MS Cotton Vespasian B.XVI has instead "The Abbot of Westmynstre," who would have been Edmund Kyrton.
30. "Lord, my God, in you I have trusted." Psalms 7:2.
31. "Eternal rest." In the Offices for the Dead, each Psalm ends with this phrase.
32. *Pater Noster*, "The Lord's Prayer"
33. John De le Bere, Bishop of Saint David's in Wales.
34. Adam Moleyns, Bishop of Chichester, Keeper of the Privy Seal.

35. William de la Pole, Duke of Suffolk.
36. Sir Robert Roos, one of Henry VI's carvers.
37. James Fiennes, Lord Saye and Sele, Esquire of the King's Body, Warden of the Cinque Ports, and Lord Treasurer of England.
38. "Spare me, Lord, / For my days are nothing," Job 7:16.
39. Marmaduke Lumley, Bishop of Carlisle.
40. "I believe that he lives," Psalm 26:13; "credo . . . vivit" ("I believe . . . he lives") can be found in the response to Job 7 in the Office for the Dead, but Psalm 26 is also included in the Office for the Dead, but it is out of sequence here.
41. "It tired my soul of my life," Job 10:1.
42. "Your hands [made me]," Job 10:8.
43. Thomas Daniel, Remembrancer of the Exchequer, Esquire of the King's Body.
44. "Who raised Lazarus," Response to Job 10 in Office for the Dead.
45. John Trevilian, Esquire of the King's Body.
46. Lord Robert Hungerford.
47. "your hands made me," Job 10:8.
48. "Where I will hide myself," Response to Job 10 in Office for the Dead.
49. An esquire in London and related to James Fiennes.
50. "The Lord rules me; / And nothing will be lacking from me," Psalms 22:1.
51. "To you Lord I lifted [my soul]," Psalms 24:1.
52. Edmund Beaufort, Duke of Somerset. He is blamed for the losses of Rouen and Caen; he dies on 1458 at the Battle of Saint Albans.
53. John Pennycook, Esquire of the King's Body.
54. "The sins of my youth," Psalms 24:7.
55. "Lord [my] light," Psalms 26.1.
56. Lord Saye and Sele.
57. "I believe that I see," Psalms 26:13.
58. Lord Thomas Stanley, Household Chamberlain of Henry VI.
59. "In eternal memory," Psalms 11:7; may also be used here in a more general fashion.
60. Thomas Kent, Keeper of the Privy Seal and council Clerk.
61. "Our father."
62. Sir Gervase Clifton, beheaded at the Battle of Tewkesbury in 1471.
63. John Bromley, Abbot of Bermondsey.
64. "I have how many iniquities," Job 13:23.
65. "Woe is me."
66. "Man born of woman," Job 14:1.
67. John Thurston, Master of the College of Saint Laurence Pountney.
68. "Is filled with many miseries," Job 14:1.
69. "May you not recall," response to Job 14 in Office for the Dead.
70. This is perhaps a man whose surname is "Slegge," who is listed as one of the extortionists from Kent in the rebels' complaints.
71. "Who may grant me," Job 19:23; also elsewhere in Bible.
72. "Lord, [judge me] not according to my deed," response to Job 19 in Office for the Dead.

73. "Waiting I waited," Psalms 39:2.
74. Thomas Hoo (1396–1455), Baron Hoo and Hastings, Keeper of the Privy Seals, Chancellor of France.
75. "May it please you," Psalms 39:14.
76. John Hampton, Usher of the Chamber of the King, Esquire of the King's Body, and one of henry VI's closest confidants.
77. "Blessed is he who understands," Psalms 40:2.
78. John Fortescue (1394–1479), Justice of the King's Bench, loyal to Henry VI, attainted of treason by Edward IV and lived in exile in France with Queen Margaret from 1463 to 1471.
79. "Heal Lord," Psalms 40:5.
80. Lord Ralph Botiller (Boteler) Sudley (ca. 1394–2 May 1473), Captain of Calais and Treasurer of England.
81. "Just as it desires," Psalms 41:2.
82. Lord John Stourton, (19 May 1400–25 November 1462), High Sheriff of Wiltshire, Somerset, Dorset, and Gloucestershire, Treasurer of the Household.
83. "My soul thirsts," Psalms 42:2
84. Lord Richard Woodville, Earl Rivers (1405–12 August 1469), served under Suffolk in France, Warden of the Cinque Ports, father of Elizabeth Woodville.
85. "Eternal rest."
86. "The Lord's Prayer," "our father."
87. "My spirit will be wasted," Job 17:1.
88. John Blakeney, household servant to Henry VI.
89. "Me sinning everyday," response to Job 17 in Office for the Dead.
90. William Mynors, King's Serjeant and Usher of the Chamber, also one of Suffolk's keepers.
91. "To my skin, with flesh consumed," Job 19:20.
92. Robert Horne, alderman of London.
93. "Eternal rest."
94. Philip Malpas, draper and alderman of London.
95. John Judde, London merchant and master of the King's Ordinances.
96. "Why out of the womb did you lead me forth?" Job 10:18.
97. Sir Thomas Tuddenham, Abbot of Westminster.
98. "Free me," response to Job 10 in Office for the Dead; also several other places in Job and Psalms.
99. Thomas Thorpe (d. 1461), senior official at the Office of the Exchequer and later Chancellor of the Exchequer, Speaker of the House of Commons, Keeper of the Privy Wardrobe in the Tower of London. A Lancastrian, he twice escaped prison but was captured by a mob and beheaded.
100. William Cantelow, London merchant and Victualler of Calais.
101. "That day, day of anger," response to Job 10 in Office for the Dead; also at Zephaniah 1:15.
102. Thomas Pulford, esquire to Henry VI.
103. Bartholomew Halley, esquire to Henry VI.

104. Humphrey of Lancaster, Duke of Gloucester (3 October 1390–23 February 1447), fourth son of Henry IV, Lord Protector to the young Henry VI, patron of the arts. He was married to Eleanor Cobham, who was convicted of witchcraft. He quarreled with Suffolk but was popular among the commons. He was arrested and to be indicted on charges of treason but became ill – more than likely from a stroke – and died before formal charges were presented. Many of the commons, and especially Cade's rebels, believed his death was murder, either by poisoning or, as this poem states, by drowning.

105. "Ardent souls," reading as "ardentes anime"; versicle following Job 10 in Office for the Dead. See Knud Ottoson, *The Responsories and Versicles of the Latin Office of the Dead* (Arhus, Denmark: Arhus University Press, 1993), p. 404.

106. "May they rest in peace."

107. David Norcyn was, like John Stow, an Elizabethan antiquary. See A. G. Watson, *The Library of Sir Simonds D'Ewes* (London: British Museum, 1966), 199.

Chapter 30

"On the Corruption of the Times I"

OVERVIEW

This poem, which Robbins titles "The Bisson Leads the Blind" (i.e., the blind leading the blind, or the dim-witted leading the blind) after the refrain, dates to 1456 based on internal evidence. The couplet in lines 41–42 ("He yslovyd thatwele can lye / Andthevystru men honge") corresponds to an event in 1465 that is recorded in that year in *Gregory's Chronicle*, in which Thomas Whytehorn is spared the gallows because he provided evidence to the king. Having been caught stealing, he accused others of treason; those men who could not pay for their freedom were hanged, while Whytehorn received a bounty for his service to the crown. As Wright's title makes known, the poem concerns the ills of the age and presents a litany of social and moral offenses. It is a poem that recognized the topsy-turvy nature of the mid-fifteenth century, where, among other offenses, the poor are now wealthy, robbers are now in positions of power, once lawful judges are now dispensing justice based on the amount of bribes received, and church official are profiting from the pardons being sold. The tone is one of apocalyptic dread, brought on by the sinful nature of the populace.

MANUSCRIPT

London, British Library MS Harley 5396

SOURCE FOR TRANSCRIPTION

Wright, 235–37.

NOTE ON TRANSCRIPTION

Middle English grapheme yogh has been silently regularized as "gh" and "y" in this transcription.

FURTHER READING

Robbins, xxiv–xxv; 127–30.
———. "On Dating a Middle English Moral Poem." *Modern Language Notes* 70, no. 7 (1955): 473–76.
Wright, lx.

TRANSCRIPTION

	Fulfyllyd ys the profesy for ay	*is; always*
	That Merlyn sayd, and many on mo,	*More*
	Wysdam ys wel ny away,	*wisdom; gone*
	No man knowe hys frend fro foo.	*from foe*
5	Now gyllorys don gode men gye;	*deceivers do; lead*
	Ryght gos redles all behynde;	*Uncounseled*
	Truthe ys turnyd to se trechery;	
	For now the bysom[1] ledys the blynde.	*blind lead*
	Now gloserys fulle gayly they go;	*Flatterers very*
10	Pore men be perus of this land!	*Poor; nobles*
	Sertes sum tyme hyt was not so,	*Certainly; it*
	But sekyr alle this ys synnes sonde.	*surely; sin's mission*
	Now mayntenerys be made justys,	*prosecutors; justices*
	And lewde men rewle the lawe of kynde;	*uneducated; rule; nature*
15	Nobulle men be holdyn wyse,	*Noble; are held wise*
	For now the bysom ledys the blynde.	
	Truthe is set at lytyl prys;	*little price*
	Worschyp fro us longe hath be slawe;	*Worship from; slain*
	Robberys now rewle ryghtwysenesse,	*Robbers; rule righteousness*
20	And wynnerys with her sothe sawe;	*profiteers; saw truth*
	Synne sothfestnesse has slawe;	*Since faithfulness has been*
	Myrth ys now out of mannys mynde;	*Mirth; man's mind*
	The drede of God ys al todrawe;	*torn to pieces*
	Ffor now the bysom ledys the b[l]ynde.	
25	Now brocage[2] ys made offycerys;	*brokerage; official*

"On the Corruption of the Times I"

	And baratur ys made bayly;	a contentious person; a superior
	Knyghtus be made custemerys,	Knights; customs collectors
	************3	
	Flatererys be made kyngus perys;	Flatterers; king's peers
30	Lordys be led alle out of kynde;4	
	Pore men ben knyghtus ferys;	are knights' companions
	For now the bysom ledys the blynde.	
	The constery5 ys combryd with coveytyse,	overwhelmed; covetousness
	For trouth his sonkyn undur the grounde;	is sunken
35	W[ith] offycyal nor den no favour ther ys,	offical; dean
	But if sir symony shewe them sylver rounde.	simony; shows; silver coins
	Ther among spiritualté it ys founde,	Spirituality
	For peté ys clene out of ther mynde.	mercy; free from; mind
	Lord, whan thy wylle is, al ys confounde;	for whom; confounded
40	For now the bysom ledys the blynde.	
	He ys lovyd that wele can lye;	loved; well; lie
	And thevys tru men honge;	thieves; hang
	To God I rede that we cry,	Counsel
	That this lyfe last not longe.	
45	This world is turnyd up-so-doune among;	world; upside-down
	For frerys ar confessourys, ageyn a kynde,	friars; confessors; unnatural
	To the chefe ladyes of this londe;	chief ladies
	Therfor the bysom ledys the blynde.	
	Lordys the lawe they lere,	Teach
50	**********6	
	Japerys syt lordys ful nere;	Jesterssit very near lords
	Now hath the devylle alle hys devys;	devil; devices
	Now growyth the gret flour-de-lys;7	grows; fleur-de-lis
	Wymmonis wyttes are fulle of wynd;	Women's wits; wind
55	Now ledres ladyn the leward at her debres;8	
	For caus the bysom ledys the blynde.	
	Now prelates don pardon selle,	do prelates sell pardons
	And holy chyrche ys chaffare,	church; merchandise
	Holynes comyth out of helle,	Holiness comes
60	For absoluciouns waxyn ware.	absolutions grow wares
	Gabberys gloson eny whare,	Deceivers flatter anywhere
	And gode feyth comys alle byhynde;	good faith comes all behind
	Ho shalle be levyd the sothe wylle spare?	Who; left; truth
	For now the bysom ledys the blynde.	
65	The grete wylle the sothe spare,	
	The comonys love not the grete;	commons
	Therfor every man may care,	
	Lest the wade growe over the whete.	weed
	Take hede how synne hath chastysyd Frauns,	heed; chastised France
70	Whan he was in hys fayrest kynde;	choicest manner
	How that Flaundrys hath myschannys;	Flanders; misfortune
	Ffor cause the bysom ledyth the blynde.	
	Therfor every lord odur avauns,	either advance
	And styfly stond yn ych a stoure;	stiffly standan inch in any kind of battle

75	Among you make no dystaunce,	*Dissention*
	But, lordys, buskys yon out of boure.	*haste yourselves out of your abode*
	For to hold up this londus honour,	*land's*
	With strenkyth our enmys for to bynde,	*strength; enemies; bind*
	That we may wynne the hevynly tour;	*win; heavenly tower*
80	For here the bysom ledys the blynde.	

NOTES

1. See *MED* "bĭsne," adj., 1. Having defective vision, dim-eyed, purblind; also (loosely), blind.

2. See *MED* "brōkāǧe," n., 1.(a) Transaction of business, esp. by an agent or intermediary; brokerage; (b) clandestine or dishonest mediation, as by bribery, shady dealing; bribery, a bribe; (c) the offering of a bribe (to an intermediary).

3. The manuscript is cut at the bottom, and a line is missing.

4. "Lords are led away from the natural order."

5. See *MED* "consistōrie," n., 1. (a) The court of a diocese for adjudication under canon law, bishop's court; also, a session of such a court.

6. The manuscript is cut at the bottom, and a line is missing.

7. The mention of the fleur-de-lis is more than likely a reference to Calais, then England's sole possession in France.

8. An awkward line to accurately convey in a translation. "Now, leaders load the ignorant until they break."

Chapter 31

"On the Corruptions of the Times II"

OVERVIEW

This poem (ca. 1456), much like the previous "On the Corruptions of the Times I," is one that identifies the root cause of misfortune in the world, that is sin, or, more specifically, the cardinal sins. In this poem, S. H. Rigby observes how "concepts of justice and gratitude thus allowed medieval social theory to combine an emphasis on the inevitability of social inequality with a belief in the fundamental harmony and reciprocity of interest between the different social orders" (504). The poem is a call to God for help, though the deity appears to be absent in these desperate times.

MANUSCRIPT

Cambridge, Cambridge University Library MS Ff.1.6

SOURCE FOR TRANSCRIPTION

Wright, 238–42.

NOTE ON TRANSCRIPTION

Middle English grapheme yogh has been silently regularized as "y" in this transcription.

FURTHER READING

Rigby, S. H. "England: Literature and Society." In *A Companion to Britain in the Later Middle Ages*, edited by S. H. Rigby, 497–520. London: Blackwell, 2003.

TRANSCRIPTION

How myschaunce regnythe in Ingelond   *misfortune reigns*

	Now God, that syttyst an hyghe in trone,	sits; on high; throne/ heaven
	Help thy peple in here greet nede,	their
	That trowthe and resoun regne may sone,	truth; reason; reign; soon
	For thanne schal they leve owt of drede.	then shall; omit dread
5	In that wyse conscience schal hem lede,	manner; lead them
	Hem to brynge onto good governaunce;	bring
	That yt may sone be doon in dede;	it; done
	Of alle oure synnys, God, make a delyveraunce.	sins; deliverance
	And men wolde, and take good hede,	would; heed
10	This lond ys now full of inyquyté;	land is; inequity
	And al that causyth the mayde Mede,[1]	causes; maid reward
	The wyche feer bannyd ys from felycyté	far; felicity
	There that sche regnyth ther ys no prosperyté,	
	To holy cherche sche doth greet grevaunce;	church; grievance
15	For of here apeyryd ys the hyghe dygnyté,	Because of her; damaged; dignity
	Of al oure synnys, God, make a delyveraunce.	
	Mede makyth fele men for to weepe,	many; weep
	Wyth here frendys sche wol abyde,	friends; will abide
	The wyche cunne here goodys wysely kepe,	can her; wisely
20	Be manye false weyes here wyttys gyde.	ways; wits guide
	Untrowthe regnyth in many a syde,	Untruth; on many sides
	For agayn here ys a greet distaunce,	dischord
	That knowen ys ful feer and wyde;	is known
	Of al oure synnys, Good, make a delyveraunce.	
25	Meed and falseheed assocyed are;	associated
	Trowthe bannyd ys, the blynde may not se;	cursed; blind; see
	Manye a man they make fulle bare,[2]	
	A strange compleynt ther ys of every degré	complaint; degree
	The way ys now past of tranquyllyté,	tranquility
30	The wyche causyth a full greet varyaunce;	variance
	Amange the comunys ther ys no game nor gle;	Among; commons; glee
	Of al oure synnys, God, make a delyveraunce.	
	And men myghte wel the hyghe wey fynde	higher path find
	Of trowthe and resoune, and where they dwelle;	

35	Meede wyth here help stand scholde behynde,	should behind
	In dyspyte of alle the develys of helle.	despite; devils
	Untrowthe wyt many oon scholde no more melle;	with man one; meddle
	Falsehed and sche byn bothe of oon substaunce,	falsehood; are; one substance
	Alle be they not worth an oyster-schelle;	oyster shell
40	Of alle oure synnys, God, make a delyveraunce.	
	Murdre medelythe ful ofte, as men say;	Murder very often intensifies
	Usure and rapyne stefly dothe stande,	Usury; robbery stiffly
	Here abydynge ys wythe her that goon ful gay;	go very
	For whanne they wele they have hem in hande.	riches
45	And thus they regne throughe thys lande;	
	Ful manye they brynge to myschaunce.	
	Wyse men, beholden, be wayr al afore hande;	beware; beforehand
	Of alle oure synnys, God, make a delyveraunce.	
	Idylnesse and thefte yet have they no care,	Idelness; theft
50	Thoughe that thys worlde thus endure ever more;	
	Oftyn tymes here wyde purse is full bare,	wide
	And other whyles here schoon be al totore;	other times; soon; torn to pieces
	The mete that thei ete ys alle forlore;	they eat; spoiled
	On the galwys they scholde anhaunse;	gallows; raise up
55	They greve the comunys, and that ryghte sore;	grieve
	Of alle oure synnys, God, make a delyveraunce.	
	Slowthe and neclygence ful sore empeche	Sloth; negligence; impede
	Justise, that scholde regne contenually;	Justice; continually
	Coveytyse causyth that, for he dothe teche	Covetous causes; teach
60	Of all astatis seme fulle besyly.	ranks; diligently
	The prosperity of thys land thus they gy	rule
	Forthewyth togedere al to the daunce;	together; dance
	A wronge way to werke alle they be redy;	
	Of alle oure synnys, God, make a delyveraunce.	
65	Wyght ys blak, as many men seye,	White; say
	And blak ys wyght, but summe men sey nay;	some
	Auctoryteys for hem they toleye;	Authorities; them; put forward
	Large conscience causyth they croked way.	crooked
	In thys reame they make a foul aray.	realm; state
70	Whanne the dyse renne, ther lakkythe a chaunce;	When; dice run; lack
	Clene conscien bakward goth alway;	Clean conscience; goes always
	Of al oure synnys, God, make a delyveraunce.	
	Myscheef mengid ys, and that in every syde;	Mischief mixed
	Dyscord medelytho ful fast amonge;	Discord blends
75	The gatis of glaterye standen up wyde,	gates; flattery; stand
	Hem semythe that al ys ryghte and no wronge.	It appears to them
	Thus endurid they have al to longe;	endured
	Crosse and pyle standen in balaunce;	Head and tails stand

	Trowthe and resoun be no thynge stronge;	
80	Of alle oure synnys, God, make a delyveraunce.	
	Rychesse renewyd causithe the perdicioun	renewed causes; destruction
	Of trowthe, that scholde stande in prosperyté;	
	Between here and hope ys mayd a devisioun,	division
	And that ys al for lak of charyté;	charity
85	Wherfore ther regnethe no tranquilly;	
	Thys mateer causithe the fool ignoraunce,	matter
	That the peple may not in eese be;	people; comfort
	Of alle oure synnys, God, make a delyveraunce.	
	He that hathe the word at hys owne wylle,	
90	Helthe, rychesse, and contynual tranquillyté,	
	Ech mannys hestes ys glad to fulfylle,	man's commandments
	He thenkyth upon noon deversité	thinks; not any diversity
	Ful unsewyr atte the laste may he be	Very insecure in the end
	To sette hys herte in swyche abundaunce;	heart; such abundance
95	Dampnacioun yt schewythe, as thenkythe me;	Damnation; shows; it occurs to me
	Of alle oure aennys, God, make a delyveraunoe.	
	Wyghte is wyghte, yf yt leyd to blake;³	
	And soote⁴ ys swettere aftur bytternesse;	Sweet is sweeter; bitterness
	And falsenesse ys evere drevene abake,	driven aback
100	Where tho throughte ys rootyd wytheowte dubbilnesse.⁵	
	Wytheowte preef may not be sykernesse;	Without proof; certainty
	Wherfore trowthe and resoun scholde hem avaunce,	advance to them
	For to take to hem stedefastnesse.	
	Of all oure synnys, God, make a delyveraunce.	
105	That unhappy insacyable simonia	insatiable simony
	Now regnethe in Ingeland, and that sore;	England; sorrow
	He sparithe not for closynge of alleluya;	refrains; ceasing of "Halleluiah"
	Woo worthe the tyme that evere was he bore!	Curse the time; born
	Unavysyd clerk soone may be forlore	Thoughtless; damned
110	Unto that theef to donne obeysaunce;	thief; to obey
	For as afore God they ben forswore;	before; have been forsworn
	Of alle oure synnys, God, make a delyveraunce.	
	Hatrede and praptyk of fals auctorité	Hatred; practice
	Al good consciencie they putten owte;	conscience; push out
115	Of trowthe and resoun lettynge the prosperyté;	impeding
	Wherfore concord ys put feer abowte.	harmony; far away
	And yf men wolde stonden owt of dowte	stand in in fear
	Drede of God, with a good atemperaunce	In dread; moderation
	From these synnys scholde make hem schowte,	shout/cry
120	And put hem alle to a pleyne delyveraunce.	
	Vengeaunce and wrathe in an hastyvyté,	Vengeance; rashness

	Wyth an unstedefast speryte of indyscrecioun,	*unsteadfast sprit; indiscretion*
	Been the cause that men may not yn eese be;	*Comfort*
	For here consentynge drawith to confusioun.	*consenting leads*
125	Al londys putten thys land in derisioun.	*lands put; derision*
	For thys usyd ys oonly of acustomaunce,	*used; habit*
	If that day may come of a good conclusioun,	
	Of alle oure synnys to make a delyveraunce.	
	Men of holy cherche, that been ful wyse,	*very wise*
130	Scholde meekly preye with good devosioun,	*pray; devotion*
	That trowthe and resoun myghte sone aryse,	*Arise*
	For to bryng away thys false tribulacioun;	*Tribulation*
	And that the heyere herd with good medytacioun	*higher; meditation*
	May the pore peple swych wyse avaunce,	*in such a manner advance*
135	In the drede of God to sette here ocupacyoun,	*their occupation*
	Of al here synnys to make a delyveraunce.	
	And men wolden weel hem self knowe,	*who control themselves well know*
	Grace for to aske in here greet nede,	*their; need*
	To God here hertis bowyng ful lowe,	*hearts bowing*
140	Almesse doynge weel to taken heede,	*Alms doing*
	Pylgremage goyng to gete hem mede,	*Pilgrimage going; get; reward*
	Prayeng and fastynge with good rememoraunce,	*Remembrance*
	Body and sowle so they may hem lede	
	Into blysse of eternalle purvyaunce.	*Knowledge*
145	Now, God, that art fill of al pletevousnesse,	*full; abundance*
	Of al vertuys grace and charyté,	*Virtuous*
	Putte from us al thys unsekyrnesse,	*Remove; uncertainty*
	That we stande ynne in grete necessyté,	*continue in great*
	That agayn trowthe no varyeng be,	*against; uncertainty*
150	Al tymes that art founteyne of al felycité,	*fountain*
	Of al oure synnys thou make a delyveraunce.	

NOTES

1. The personification of "Mede" as "mayde Mede" is likely an allusion to the allegorical figure of Lady Mede, first depicted as an aristocrat in Passus II of the C-text of William Langland's *Piers Plowman*. "Mede" can also be read as a bribe.
2. "Bare" here can have numerous meanings, including "naked," "empty," "poor," "deficient," and "impotent."
3. Proverbial: "White is white, if it is next to black."
4. "Soote" here can also be read, figuratively, as "good fortune."
5. "Where for them the situation is rooted without duplicity."

Chapter 32

Robin Hood and the Monk

OVERVIEW

The poem *Robin Hood and the Monk* is the earliest surviving work of Robin Hood literature. The manuscript that contains the text dates to ca. 1463. Thomas H. Ohlgren has identified the owner of the manuscript as Gilbert Pilkington, a priest from Lichfield, Staffordshire. Fittingly, the manuscript is a clerical miscellany: besides *Robin Hood and the Monk*, the other works are didactic, devotional, catechetic, as well as secular. Robin Hood and his men are outlaws, though the poem does not detail the offence that led to this declaration. Outlawry was in medieval England a legal procedure, and to be declared an outlaw by the courts meant that one was outside of the boundary and protection of the law. As such, outlaws could be hunted and killed with impunity. In the early medieval period in England, most individuals were outlawed for committing criminal acts, and by the later Middle Ages persons were outlawed in increasing numbers for civil offenses. Jack Cade was not an outlaw, though he was a criminal and one who rebelled in ways similar to Robin Hood. In *Robin Hood and the Monk* and the other early poems of the English outlaw, such as *Robin Hood and the Potter* and *A Lytell Geste of Robyn Hode*, Robin's enemies were the corrupt members of the church, unscrupulous bureaucrats, crooked judges, immoral lawmen, and unjust laws. Robin and his men, much like Cade, has faith in the king and wants to see him prosper and lead the people. Moreover, the Robin Hood of this poem is not the Robin Hood of the post-medieval literary and film tradition. He is not the Saxon Lord of Loxley, or the Earl of Huntington; instead, he is a yeoman. The yeoman class of individuals in the late Middle Ages was a sizable portion of the population. Yeomen were free born and could own land. Being designated a yeoman meant that a person could have any number of professions or trades, such as an attendant in a royal household; a subordinate military officer, perhaps serving in a noble or royal house; a seaman; or hired laborer. In terms of rank, a yeoman was always below that of a squire. In examining the names of those individuals listed on the General Pardon for the Cade rebellion, the designation of persons as being a "yeoman" is widespread. The stories of Robin Hood in the fifteenth century and beyond were and remain popular literature, works that appeal to a many but are especially of interest to those who are living outside of the norms of society or have an interest in transgressive actions and attitudes.

MANUSCRIPT

Cambridge, Cambridge University Library MS Ff5.48

SOURCE FOR TRANSLATION

Ohlgren, Thomas H., and Lister M. Matheson, ed. *Early Rhymes of Robyn Hood: An Edition of the Texts, ca. 1425 to ca. 1600*. Medieval and Renaissance Texts and Studies 428. Tempe: Arizona Center for Medieval and Renaissance Texts and Studies, 2013. Pp. 3–17.

FURTHER READING

Gray, Douglas. "The Robin Hood Ballads." *Poetica* 18 (1984): 1–39.
Kaufman, 175–94.
Keen, Maurice. *The Outlaws of Medieval Legend*. Rev. ed. London: Routledge, 2000.
Knight, Stephen. *Robin Hood: A Mythic Biography*. Ithaca, NY: Cornell University Press, 2003.
Ohlgren, Thomas H. *Robin Hood: The Early Poems, 1465–1560: Texts, Contexts, and Ideology*. Newark: University of Delaware Press, 2007.
Pearsall, Derek. "Little John and the Ballad of *Robin Hood and the Monk*." In *Robin Hood: Medieval and Post-Medieval*, edited by Helen Phillips, 42–50. Dublin: Four Courts Press, 2005.
Pollard, A. J. *Imagining Robin Hood: The Late-Medieval Stories in Historical Context*. London: Routledge, 2004.

TRANSLATION

      In early summer, when the woods are bright,
      And the leaves are large and long,
      It is very merry in the fair forest
      To hear the birds' song,
5   To see the deer draw to the dale,
      And then to the high hills flee,
      And shelter themselves in the green leaves,
      Under the greenwood tree.
      This all happened at Pentecost,
10   Early in a May morning.
      The fair sun did shine,
      And the merry birds did sing.
      "This is a merry morning," said Little John,
      "By Him who died on the tree;
15   A more merry man than I
      Lives not in all Christianity.
      "Pluck up your heart, my dear master,"
      Little John did say,
      "And think that it is a very fair time
20   In a morning of May."
      "Yet one thing grieves me," Robin said,
      "And does my heart much woe:
      That I may not on any solemn day
      To mass or matins go."
25   "It has been a fortnight and more," he said,
      "Since my Savior I did see.
      Today I will go to Nottingham," said Robin,
      "With the might of mild Mary."
      Then Much spoke (the miller's son),
30   May good things happen to him!
      "Take twelve of your strong yeomen,
      Well armed, by your side.
      He who wants to kill you,
      Those twelve he will not abide."
35   "Of all my merry men," said Robin,
      "By my faith I will have none,
      But Little John shall bear my bow
      Until the arrows run."
      "Master, you shall bear your own," said Little John,
40   "and I will bear mine, as you see,
      And we will shoot a penny," said Little John,
      "Under the greenwood tree."
      "In faith, Little John," said Robin Hood,
      "With you I will not shoot a penny.

	But for every one that you shoot,
45	In faith I'll raise it to three."
	At both bushes and shrubs these yeomen shot,
	And each hopes he will not lose,
	Until Little John won from his master
50	Five shillings for socks and shoes.
	Just then a great row fell between them,
	As they went along their way.
	Little John said he had won five shillings,
	And abruptly Robin Hood said "nay!"
55	With that Robin called Little John a liar,
	And struck him with his hand.
	Little John grew angry and annoyed,
	And with his drawn sword did stand.
	"If you were not my master," said Little John,
60	"For that you would sorely pay.
	Go find yourself another man —
	You have me no more today."
	Then Robin goes to Nottingham,
	He is grieving all alone,
65	And Little John's off to merry Sherwood,
	The paths he knows everyone.
	When Robin came to Nottingham,
	Certainly without a lie,
	He prayed to God and to mild Mary,
70	To make sure he would not die.
	He went inside to Saint Mary's church,
	And before the Cross did kneel.
	All those within the church's walls
	Knew of Robin a great deal.
75	Beside him stood a wide-hooded monk,
	I pray to God woe to him!
	At once he recognized the good outlaw,
	As soon as he saw proud Robin.
	Very quickly and at once,
80	Out of the door Robin ran.
	But the monk was also swift
	And barred the gates of Nottingham.
	"Rise up," he said, "you arrogant sheriff,[1]
	I have spied the felon of the crown.
85	Hurry now, and get yourself ready,
	For in truth he is in this town.
	"I have seen the false felon –
	He stands at his Mass.
	It will be your fault," said the monk,
90	"If from our hands he will pass.
	"This traitor's name is Robin Hood.
	He lives in the greenwood you will find.
	He robbed me once of a hundred pounds,
	And that is never far from my mind."

95	Up then rose this haughty sheriff,
	And he quickly made himself set.
	Many a man followed him,
	And the church is where they met.
	At the door they fiercely thrust,
100	Using staves they swiftly press on.
	"Alas, alas!" said Robin Hood,
	"Now I miss Little John."
	But Robin took out a two-handed sword
	That hanged down by his knee.
105	Where the sheriff and his men stood thickest,
	In that direction Robin did flee.
	He ran right at them three times,
	In truth this I say,
	And wounded many a mother's son,
110	And twelve he slew that day.
	He swung his sword at the sheriff's head,
	But it broke in two, just like a limb.
	"The smith who made you," said Robin,
	"I pray that God brings woe to him."
115	"Now I am weaponless," said Robin,
	"Alas! Again I'm in a quandary.
	Unless I can flee from these traitors,
	I know that they will kill me."
	Robin ran into the church,
120	And he threw out everyone.
	....[2]
	Some swooned as if they were dead,
	And lay still as a stone.
	None of them had kept their wits,
	Except only Little John.
125	"Stop your complaining," said Little John,
	"For His love that died on the tree.
	All of you should be brave men,
	And this is a great shame to see.
	"Our master has been badly beset,
130	And yet he escaped away.
	Pluck up your hearts, and leave this weeping,
	And listen to what I shall say.
	"He has served Our Lady many a day,
	And by Her words he always complies.
135	Therefore, I trust her especially,
	And from no wicked death shall he die.
	"Therefore, be glad," said Little John,
	"And let this mourning be.
	And I shall take care of this monk,
140	With the might of mild Mary.
	I will meet him," said Little John,
	"And it will just be him and me."
	"Be sure to look after our trysting tree,

```
         Under the small leaves in the dale.
145      And do not spare any of the deer
         That lives within this vale."
         Then these two yeomen went forth,
         Little John and Much united,
         And looked on at Much's uncle's house;
150      The highway was almost sighted.
         In the morn, Little John stood at a window,
         And gazed from an upper stage.
         He knew from whence the monk rode,
         And with him was a little page.
155      "By my faith," said Little John to Much,
         "I can tell you some good tidings.
         That wide hood I know quite well,
         And I see where the monk is riding."
         Both these yeomen went to the highway,
160      Like courteous and gracious men.
         The asked news from the monk,
         As if they had been his friend.
         "From whence did you come?" said Little John,
         "Tell us tidings, I pray.
165      Is there any news of a false outlaw
         Who was captured yesterday?
         "He robbed me and both my fellows
         Of twenty marks for certain.
         In truth we would be glad,
170      If that false outlaw is taken."
         "He did the same to me," said the monk,
         "Of a hundred pounds and more.
         I laid the first hand upon him,
         You may thank me, therefore."
175      "I pray to God, thank you," said Little John,
         "And we will again when we may.
         We will go with you, with your trust,
         And bring you on your way.
         "For Robin Hood had many a wild fellow,
180      And I'll tell you this in words plain:
         If they knew you rode this way,
         In truth you would be slain."
         As they went talking by the highway,
         The monk and Little John,
185      John took the monk's horse by the head,
         Very quickly and at once.
         John took the monk's horse by the head,
         The truth to you I say,
         And so did Much, the little page,
```

190	So he should not run away.
	By the gullet of the hood
	John pulled the monk down;
	John was not afraid of him,
	And he let him fall on his crown.
195	Angry and annoyed, Little John drew his sword –
	It flashed in the blink of an eye;
	The monk saw that death was to come soon,
	And "mercy" he began to cry.
	"He was my master," said Little John,
200	"That you have brought in misery.
	You shall never meet with our king,
	For to tell him your story."
	John struck off the monk's head,
	On this he would not dwell;
205	So did Much kill the little page,
	For fear that he would tell.
	There they buried both of them,
	In neither moss nor heather.
	John took the letters meant for our king,
210	And both rode off together.
	Little John came before the king,
	And he kneeled down upon his knee.
	"God save you, my liege lord,
	May Jesus watch over thee."
215	"God save you, my liege king!"
	To speak John was very bold.
	He gave him the letters that were in his hand,
	Which the king began to unfold.
	"So may I thrive," said the king,
220	As he read the letters immediately,
	"There was never a yeoman in merry England,
	I longed so much to see."
	"Where is the monk who should have brought these?"
	Our king started to say.
225	"By my honor," said Little John,
	"He died along the way."
	The king gave Much and Little John
	Twenty pounds for their deed.
	And he made them yeomen of his crown,
230	And said he had one more need.
	The king gave John the seal in his hand,
	The sheriff for to bring,
	And to carry Robin to him,
	And that no man cause him suffering.
235	Little John took leave of our king,
	The truth to you I say.
	He chose the shortest path to Nottingham,
	And then quickly he went on his way.

	When John arrived at Nottingham,
240	The gates were barred all the way.
	John called up to the porter,
	And he answered him right away.
	"What is the cause," said Little John,
	"For you to close the gates so fast?"
245	"Because of Robin Hood," said the porter,
	"In a deep prison he is cast."
	"John, and Much, and Will Scathelock,[3]
	Truly as I say,
	Slew our men upon our walls,
250	And they attack us everyday."
	Little John asked about the sheriff,
	And very soon he was found.
	He opened the king's privy seal,
	And gave it to him in his hand.
255	When the sheriff saw the king's seal,
	He took off his hood at once.
	"Where is the monk who carried the letters?"
	He said to Little John.
	"The king is so pleased with him," said Little John,
260	"Truly as I say,
	That he has made him abbot of Westminster,
	A lord of that abbey."
	The sheriff made sure John was happy,
	And he gave him wine that was the best.
265	By night they made their way to bed,
	And every man went to rest.
	When the sheriff was sound asleep,
	Drunk from wine and ale,
	Little John and Much, indeed,
270	Made their way to jail.
	Little John called up to the jailer,
	And told him to rise immediately.
	He said that Robin Hood had broken the prison,
	And out of it he did flee.
275	Indeed, the porter rose at once,
	As soon as he heard John call.
	Little John was ready with a sword,
	And he stabbed him through to the wall.
	"Now I will be the jailer," Little John said,
280	And he took the keys in his hand;
	He made his way to Robin Hood,
	And he freed the leader of his band.
	He gave him a good sword in his hand,
	But no protection for his crown.

285	And there where the walls were lowest,
	Quickly they leapt down.
	By then the cock began to crow,
	And the day began to spring.
	The sheriff found the jailer dead,
290	And the town bell he ordered to ring.
	He made a call throughout the town,
	Whether one was a yeoman or a knave:
	That whoever could bring to him Robin Hood,
	A reward he should have.
295	"For I dare not," said the sheriff,
	"Come before our king.
	For if I do, I know for certain,
	From the gallows I will swing."
	The sheriff went to search Nottingham,
300	Both the streets and the alleys.
	But Robin was in merry Sherwood,
	As merry as a leaf on a tree.
	Then spoke good Little John,
	And he turned to Robin to say,
305	"I have done for you a good deed for an ill,
	Repay me when you may.
	"For you I did a good turn," said Little John,
	"In truth to you I say.
	I have brought you under the greenwood tree.
310	Farewell, and have a good day."
	"No, by my honor," said Robin,
	"This shall never be.
	I make you the master,
	Of all my men and me."
315	"No, by my honor," said Little John,
	"To this I will not agree.
	But let me be a fellow,
	There is nothing else I want to be."
	Thus John broke Robyn out of prison,
320	Certainly without a lie.
	When his men saw him whole and safe,
	They let out a joyous cry.
	They drank some wine, which made them glad,
	Under leaves so small,
325	And then ate pasties of venison,
	Which were very good with ale.
	Then word came to our king
	How Robin Hood got away,
	And how the sheriff of Nottingham

330	Thus John broke Robyn out of prison,
	Certainly without a lie.
	When his men saw him whole and safe,
	They let out a joyous cry.
	They drank some wine, which made them glad,
335	Under leaves so small,
	And then ate pasties of venison,
	Which were very good with ale.
	Then word came to our king
	How Robin Hood got away,
340	And how the sheriff of Nottingham
	Robin's cell he never dared to survey.
	Then spoke our comely king,
	And in anger did decree:
	"Little John has beguiled the sheriff,
345	In faith so has he me.
	"Little John has beguiled us both,
	And that very well I see.
	Perhaps the sheriff of Nottingham
	High hanged should he be.
350	"I made them yeomen of the crown,
	And gave them money with my own hand.
	I gave them a pardon," said our king,
	"Throughout all of merry England.
	"I gave them protection," then said our king,
355	"Truly, such a yeoman as he,
	(And this I say, so I may prosper)
	In all of England are not three.
	"He is true to his master," said our king.
	"I say, by sweet Saint John;
360	He loves Robin Hood better
	Than he does everyone.
	"Robin is forever bound to him,
	Both in the street and in the stall.
	Speak no more of this matter," said our king,
365	"But John has beguiled us all."
	Thus ends the story of the monk and Robin Hood,
	But before we part, let us remember this:
	That God, who is forever a crowned king,
	Might bring us all to His bliss.

NOTES

1. The monk, in disclosing the whereabouts of Robin Hood within the church, violates the ancient privilege of sanctuary.

2. A single leaf of the manuscript is missing, and so part of the narrative is missing. More than likely, this part of the story would have entailed the outlaws learning that Robin was captured.

3. Will's name here is not Scarlet as in later poems but rather Scathelock, which suggests his skill is picking locks.

Bibliography

MANUSCRIPTS

Aberystwyth, National Library of Wales MS 21608
Cambridge, Cambridge University Library MS Ff.1.6
Cambridge, Cambridge University Library MS Ff5.48
Cambridge, Corpus Christy College Cambridge MS 417
Dublin, Trinity College MS 509
Dublin, Trinity College MS 516
Dublin, Trinity College MS 604
London, British Library MS Additional 10099
London, British Library MS Additional 43488
London, British Library MS Additional 43491
London, British Library MS Additional 48031A
London, British Library MS Additional 70520
London, British Library MS Cotton Nero C XI
London, British Library MS Cotton Roll II 23
London, British Library MS Cotton Vitellius A XVI
London, British Library MS Egerton 1995
London, British Library MS Harley 545
London, British Library MS Harley 5396
London, Lambeth Palace MS Lambeth 306
London, British Library MS Royal 18 C VIII/IX
London, Metropolitan Archives CLC/270/MS03313
Norfolk, Holkham Hall MS 671
Oxford, Bodleian Library MS Gough London 10
Vatican, BAV, MS Codices Urbinates Latini 497 and 498

PRINTED AND DIGITAL SOURCES

Barron, Caroline M. "The Government of London and Its Relations with the Crown, 1400–1450." Ph.D. Thesis, University of London, 1970.

Boffey, Julia. *Manuscript and Print in London c. 1475–1530*. London: The British Library, 2012.

———. "Robert Fabyan's Two Hats: Compiling *The Great Chronicle of London* and *The New Chronicles of England and France*." In *Editing and Interpretation of Middle English Texts: Essays in Honour of William Marx*, edited by Margaret Connolly and Raluca Radulescu, 171–88. Texts & Transitions 12. Turnhout: Brepols, 2018.

Bonha, Montgomery. "Armed Force and Civic Legitimacy in Jack Cade's Revolt, 1450." *English Historical Review* 118 (2003): 563–82.

Brie, Friedrich W. D., ed. *The Brut or The Chronicles of England*. Part II. EETS, os 136. London: Oxford University Press, 1908.

Broadie, Alexander. *The Circle of John Mair: Logic and Logicians in Pre-Reformation Scotland*. Oxford: Clarendon Press, 1985.

———. *A History of Scottish Philosophy*. Edinburgh: Edinburgh University Press, 2009.

———. "Mair [Major], John." In *Oxford Dictionary of National Biography*. Oxford University Press, 2019. https://www.oxforddnb.com/. Accessed 21 June 2019.

Bryan, Elizabeth. "Prose Brut, English." In *The Encyclopedia of the Medieval Chronicle*, edited by Graeme R. Dunphy, 2: 1239–40. Leiden and Boston: Brill, 2010.

Caldwell, Ellen C. "Jack Cade and Shakespeare's *Henry VI, Part 2*." *Studies in Philology* 92, no. 1 (1995): 18–79.

Calendar of Patent Rolls. Henry VI, Vol. V, 1446–1452. London: His Majesty's Stationary Office, 1909.

Connell, William J. "Vergil, Polydore [Polidoro Virgili]." In *Oxford Dictionary of National Biography*. Oxford University Press, 2019. https://www.oxforddnb.com/. Accessed 21 June 2019.

Carley, James P. "Polydore Vergil and John Leland on King Arthur: The Battle of the Books." *Interpretations* 15, no. 3 (1984): 86–100.

Clegg, Cyndia Susan. "Holinshed [Hollingshead], Raphael." In *Oxford Dictionary of National Biography*. Oxford University Press, 2019. https://www.oxforddnb.com/. Accessed 21 June 2019.

———. *Press Censorship in Elizabethan England*. Cambridge: Cambridge University Press, 1997.

Connor, Meriel. "Brotherhood and Confraternity at Canterbury Cathedral Priory in the Fifteenth Century: The Evidence of John Stone's Chronicle." *Archaeologia Cantiana* 128 (2008): 143–64.

———. "Fifteenth-Century Monastic Obituaries: The Evidence of Christ Church Priory, Canterbury." In *Memory and Commemoration in Medieval England: Proceedings of the 2008 Harlaxton Symposium*, edited by Caroline M. Barron and Clive Burgess, 143–58. Harlaxton Medieval Studies 20. Donington: Shaun Tyas, 2010.

———. "The Political Allegiances of Christ Church Priory 1400–1472: The Evidence of John Stone's Chronicle." *Archaelogia Cantiana* 127 (2007): 393–406.

Conrad, Robert T. *Alymere, or The Bondman of Kent; and Other Stories*. Philadelphia: E. H. Butler, 1852.

Currency Converter: 1270–2017. The National Archives. http://www.nationalarchives.gov.uk/currency-converter/. Accessed 6 August 2018.

Davis, Norman, ed. *Paston Letters and Papers of the Fifteenth Century, Part II*. EETS, ss 21. Oxford: Oxford University Press, 2004.

Djordjevic, Igor. *Holinshed's Nation: Ideals, Memory and Practical Polity in the Chronicles*. Farnham: Ashgate, 2010.

Edwards, J. G. "The 'Second' Continuation of the Crowland Chronicle: Was It Written in 'in ten days'?" *Bulletin of the Institute of Historical Research* XXXIX (1966): 117–29.

Eklund, Hillary. "Revolting Diets: Jack Cade's 'Sallet' and the Politics of Hunger in *2 Henry VI*." *Shakespeare Studies* 42 (2014): 51–62.

Ellis, Henry, ed. *Three Books of Polydore Vergil's English History Comprising the Reigns of Henry VI, Edward IV, and Richard III*. Camden Society, os 29. London: J. B. Nichols and Sons, 1844.

Fabyan, Robert. *The New Chronicles of England and France, in Two Parts*. Edited by Henry Ellis. London: F. C. and J. Rivington, et al., 1811.

Fitter, Chris. "'Your Captain is Brave and Vows Reformation': Jack Cade, the Hacket Rising, and Shakespeare's Vision of Popular Rebellion in *2 Henry VI*." *Shakespeare Studies* 32 (2004): 173–219.

Flenley, Ralph, ed. *Six Town Chronicles of England*. Oxford: Clarendon Press, 1911.

Freeman, Thomas S. "From Catiline to Richard III: The Influence of Classical Histories on Polydore Vergil's *Anglica Historia*." In *Reconsidering the Renaissance: Papers from the Twenty-First Annual Conference*, edited by Mario A. Di Cesare, 191–214. Medieval and Renaissance Texts and Studies 93. Binghamton: Medieval and Renaissance Texts and Studies, 1992.

Furnivall, Frederick J., ed. *Political, Religious, and Love Poems*. EETS, os 15. London: Trübner & Co., 1866.

Gairdner, James, ed. *The Historical Collections of A London Citizen of the Fifteenth Century*. Camden Society, ns 17. Westminster: Nichols and Sons, 1876.

———. *Three Fifteenth-Century English Chronicles*. Camden Society, ns 28. Westminster: Camden Society, 1880.

Gies, Joseph and Frances Gies. *A Medieval Family: The Pastons of Fifteenth-Century England*. New York: Harper Perennial, 1999.

Given-Wilson, Chris, gen. ed. *The Parliament Rolls of Medieval England, 1275–1504*. Vol. 12. Henry VI, 1447–1460. London: The Boydell Press and The National Archives, 2005.

Gransden, Antonia. *Historical Writing in England II: c. 1307 to the Early Sixteenth Century*. Ithaca, NY: Cornell University Press, 1982.

Gray, Douglas. "The Robin Hood Ballads." *Poetica* 18 (1984): 1–39.

Griffiths, R. A. *The Reign of King Henry VI*. Phoenix Mill: Sutton, 1998.

Grummitt, David. "Deconstructing Cade's Rebellion: Discourse and Politics in the Mid Fifteenth Century." In *The Fifteenth Century VI: Identity and Insurgency in the Late Middle Ages*, edited by Linda Clark, 107–22. Woodbridge: Boydell Press, 2006.

———. *Henry VI*. London and New York: Routledge: 2015.

Hall, Edward. *Hall's Chronicle*. Edited by Henry Ellis. London: J. Johnson, et al., 1809.

Hanham, Alison, trans. *John Benet's Chronicle, 1399–1462: An English Translation with New Introduction*. New York: Palgrave Macmillan, 2016.

Harris, G. L. "Benet, John." In *Oxford Dictionary of National Biography*. Oxford University Press, 2019. https://www.oxforddnb.com/. Accessed 21 June 2019.

Harriss, G. L., and M. A. Harris, ed. *John Benet's Chronicle for the Years 1400–1462*. In *Camden Miscellany*, Vol. XXIX, 151–233. Camden Fourth Series, Vol. 9. London: Royal Historical Society, 1972.

Harvey, I. M. W. *Jack Cade's Rebellion of 1450*. Oxford: Clarendon Press, 1991.

———. "Poaching and Sedition in Fifteenth-Century England." In *Lordship and Learning: Studies in Memory of Trevor Aston*, edited by Ralph Evans, 169–82. Woodbridge: Boydell Press, 2004.

Hay, Denys. *Polydore Vergil: Renaissance Historian and Man of Letters*. Oxford: Clarendon Press, 1952.

Herman, Peter C. "Hall, Edward." In *Oxford Dictionary of National Biography*. Oxford University Press, 2019. https://www.oxforddnb.com/. Accessed 21 June 2019.

Holinshed, Raphael. *Holinshed's Chronicles of England, Scotland, and Ireland*. 6 vols. London: J. Johnson, et al., 1807–1808.

The Holinshed Project. http://www.cems.ox.ac.uk/holinshed/. 2008–2013. Accessed 20 November 2018.

Ingulph's Chronicle of the Abbey of Croyland. Translated by Henry T. Riley. London: Henry G. Bohn, 1854.

John Stone's Chronicle: Christ Church Priory, Canterbury, 1417–1472. Selected, Translated, and Introduced by Meriel Connor. TEAMS Documents of Practice Series. Kalamazoo, MI: Medieval Institute Publications, 2010.

Kaufman, Alexander L. *The Historical Literature of the Jack Cade Rebellion*. Farnham: Ashgate, 2009.

———. "John Mair's Historiographical Humanism: Portraits of Outlaws, Robbers, and Rebels in His *Historia Maioris Britanniae tam Angliae quam Scotiae* (*History of Greater Britain*)." *Enarratio* 19 (2015): 104–18.

———. "Stone, John (John of Canterbury)." In *The Encyclopedia of the Medieval Chronicle*, edited by Graeme R. Dunphy, 2: 1393. Leiden: Brill, 2010.

Keen, Maurice. The Outlaws of Medieval Legend. Rev. ed. London: Routledge, 2000.

Kekewich, Margaret Lucille, et al., ed. *The Politics of Fifteenth-Century England: John Vale's Book*. Phoenix Mill: Alan Sutton for Richard III and Yorkist Historical Trust, 1995.

Kennedy, Edward Donald. "Chronicles and Other Historical Writing." *A Manual of the Writings in Middle English, 1050–1500*, edited by Albert E. Hartung. Vol. 8. Hamden, CT: Archon Books for the Connecticut Academy of Arts and Sciences, 1989.

Kennedy, Ross. "North, George." In *Oxford Dictionary of National Biography*. Oxford University Press, 2019. https://www.oxforddnb.com/. Accessed 21 June 2019.

Kewes, Paulina, Ian Archer, and Felicity Heal, ed. *The Oxford Handbook of Holinshed's Chronicles*. London: Oxford University Press. 2013.

Kingsford, Charles Lethbridge, ed. *Chronicles of London*. Oxford: Clarendon Press, 1905.

———. *English Historical Literature in the Fifteenth Century*. Oxford: Clarendon Press, 1913.

Kippola, Karl. "'The Battle-Shout of Free Men.' Edwin Forrest's Passive Patriotism and Robert T. Conrad's *Jack Cade*." *Journal of American Drama and Theater* 13, no. 3 (2001): 37–86.

Kleineke, Hannes. "*Robert Bale's Chronicle* and the Second Battle of St. Albans." *Historical Research* 87, no. 238 (2014): 744–50.

Knight, Stephen. *Robin Hood: A Mythic Biography*. Ithaca, NY: Cornell University Press, 2003.

Lin, Chiu-Yen. "Innocent and Simple: The Making of Henry VI's Kingship in Fifteenth-Century England." In *Perceiving Power in Early Modern Europe*, edited by Francis K. H. So, 103–20. New York: Palgrave Macmillan, 2017.

Major, John. *A History of Greater Britain As Well England and Scotland*. Translated and edited by Archibald Constable. Scottish History Society. Vol. 10. Edinburgh: Edinburgh University Press, 1892.

Marshall, John. "'Fortune in Worldys Worschyppe': The Satirising of the Suffolks in *Wisdom*." *Medieval English Theatre* 14 (1992): 37–66.

Martyn, William. *The Historie, and Lives, of the Kings of England*. London: W. Stansby for Henrie Fetherstone, 1615. STC 17526.

Marx, William, ed. *An English Chronicle, 1377–1461: A New Edition*. Medieval Chronicles 3. Woodbridge: The Boydell Press, 2003.

———. "Middle English Manuscripts of the Brut in the National Library of Wales." *Cylchgrawn Llyfrgell Genedlaethol Cymru / The National Library of Wales Journal* 27 (1991–1992): 361–82.

———. "Reception and Revision in the Middle English Prose *Brut*." In *Readers and Writers of the Prose Brut*, edited by William Marx and Radluca Radulescu, special issue, *Trivium* 36 (2006): 53–69.

Mason, Roger A. "From Chronicle to History: Recovering the Past in Renaissance Scotland." In *Building the Past/ Konstruktion der eigenen Vergangenheit*, edited by Rudolf Suntrup and Jan R. Veenstra, 53–66. Medieval to Early Modern Culture/ Kultureller Wandel vom Mittelalter zur Frühen Neuzeit 7. Frankfurt am Main: Peter Lang, 2006.

———. *Kingship and the Commonweal: Political Thought in Renaissance and Reformation Scotland*. East Lothian: Tuckwell Press, 1998.

Matheson, Lister M. "Printer and Scribe: Caxton, the *Polychronicon*, and the *Brut*." *Speculum* 60 (1985): 593–614.

———. *The Prose Brut: The Development of a Middle English Chronicle*. Medieval and Renaissance Texts and Studies 180. Tempe, AZ: Medieval and Renaissance Texts and Studies, 1998.

McCarthy, Dennis, and June Schlueter. *"A Brief Discourse of Rebellion and Rebels" By George North: A Newly Uncovered Manuscript Source for Shakespeare's Plays*. Cambridge: D. S. Brewer in association with the British Library, 2018.

McKisack, May. *Medieval History in the Tudor Age*. Oxford: Clarendon Press, 1971.

McLaren, Mary-Rose. "Fabyan, Robert." In *Oxford Dictionary of National Biography*. Oxford University Press, 2019. https://www.oxforddnb.com/. Accessed 21 June 2019.

———. *The London Chronicles of the Fifteenth Century: A Revolution in English Writing*. Cambridge: D. S. Brewer, 2002.

Middle English Dictionary. Ed. Robert E. Lewis, et al. Ann Arbor: University of Michigan Press, 1952–2001. Online edition in Middle English Compendium. Ed. Frances McSparran, et al. Ann Arbor: University of Michigan Library, 2000–2018. http://quod.lib.umich.edu/m/middle-english-dictionary/. Accessed 21 June 2019.

Neumaier, Marco. "Fabyan, Robert." In *The Encyclopedia of the Medieval Chronicle*, edited by Graeme R. Dunphy, *EMC* 1: 604–5. Leiden: Brill. 2010.

———. "Vergil, Polydore [Virgilio, Polidoro]." In *The Encyclopedia of the Medieval Chronicle*, edited by Graeme R. Dunphy, 2: 1427. Leiden: Brill. 2010.

Ohlgren, Thomas H. *Robin Hood: The Early Poems, 1465–1560: Texts, Contexts, and Ideology*. Newark: University of Delaware Press, 2007.

Ohlgren, Thomas H., and Lister M. Matheson, ed. *Early Rymes of Robyn Hood: An Edition of the Texts, ca. 1425 to ca. 1600*. Medieval and Renaissance Texts and Studies 428. Tempe: Arizona Center for Medieval and Renaissance Texts and Studies, 2013.

Ottoson, Knud. *The Responsories and Versicles of the Latin Office of the Dead*. Arhus, Denmark: Arhus University Press, 1993.

Palgrave, Francis, ed. *The Antient Kalendars and Inventories of the Treasury of His Majesty's Exchequer*. Vol. 2. London: Eyre and Spottiswoode, 1836.

Patterson, Annabel. *Reading Holinshed's Chronicles*. Chicago: University of Chicago Press, 1994.

Pearsall, Derek. "Little John and the Ballad of Robin Hood and the Monk." In *Robin Hood: Medieval and Post-Medieval*, edited by Helen Phillips, 42–50. Dublin: Four Courts Press, 2005.

Peverley, Sarah L. "Vale, John." In *The Encyclopedia of the Medieval Chronicle*, edited by Graeme R. Dunphy, 2: 1466. Leiden: Brill, 2010.

Pollard, A. F. "Edward Hall's Will and Chronicle." *Bulletin of the Institute of Historical Research* IX (1932): 171–77.

Pollard, A. J. *Imagining Robin Hood: The Late-Medieval Stories in Historical Context*. London: Routledge, 2004.

Pollard, A. W., and G. R. Redgrave. *A Short-Title Catalogue of Books Printed in England, Scotland, and Ireland and of English Books Printed Abroad, 1475–1640*. 2nd ed., rev. and enlarged by W. A. Jackson, F. S. Ferguson, and K. F. Pantzer. London: Bibliographical Society, 1976–1991.

Pronay, Nicholas, and John Cox, ed. *The Crowland Chronicle Continuations: 1459–1486*. London: Richard III and Yorkist History Trust, 1986.
Radulescu, Raluca. "London Chronicles." In *The Encyclopedia of the Medieval Chronicle*, edited by Graeme R. Dunphy, 2: 1042–43. Leiden: Brill, 2010.
Rajsic, Jaclyn, Erik Kooper, and Dominique Hoche, ed. *The Prose Brut and Other Late Medieval Chronicles: Books Have Their Histories: Essays in Honour of Lister M. Matheson*. Manuscript Culture in the British Isles 8. Woodbridge: York Medieval Press, 2018.
Richmond, Colin. *The Paston Family in the Fifteenth Century: Endings*. Manchester: Manchester University Press, 2000.
———. *The Paston Family in the Fifteenth Century: Fastolf's Will*. Cambridge: Cambridge University Press, 1996.
———. *The Paston Family in the Fifteenth Century: The First Phase*. Cambridge: Cambridge University Press, 1990.
Rigby, S. H. "England: Literature and Society." In *A Companion to Britain in the Later Middle Ages*, edited by S. H. Rigby, 497–520. London: Blackwell, 2003.
Rissanen, Matti. *Studies in the Style and Narrative technique of Edward Hall's Chronicle*. Mémoires de la Société néophilologique de Helsinki 40. Helsinki: Société Neophilologique, 1973.
Robbins, Rossell Hope, ed. *Historical Poems of the XIVth and XVth Centuries*. New York: Columbia University Press, 1959.
———. "On Dating a Middle English Moral Poem." *Modern Language Notes* 70, no. 7 (1955): 473–76.
Robertson, Kellie. "The Rebel Kiss: Jack Cade, Shakespeare, and the Chroniclers." In *Renaissance Retrospections: Tudor Views of the Middle Ages*, edited by Sarah A. Kelen, 127–40. Studies in Medieval Culture LII. Kalamazoo, MI: Medieval Institute Publications, 2013.
Scattergood, Vincent John. *Politics and Poetry in the Fifteenth Century*. London: Blandford Press, 1971.
Siddons, Michael Powell. *Heraldic Badges in England and Wales. Volume II, Part 2: Non-Royal Badges*. Woodbridge: Boydell Press, 2009.
Sutton, Anne F. "Robert Bale, Scrivener and Chronicler of London." In *Regional Manuscripts, 1200–1700*, edited by A. S. G. Edwards, 180–206. English Manuscript Studies, 1100–1400 14. London: British Library, 2008.
Sutton, Dana F. Polydore Vergil, *Anglica Historia* (1555 version). http://www.philological.bham.ac.uk/polverg/. Last modified 25 May 2010. Accessed 27 February 2018.
Thomas, A. H., and I. D. Thornley, ed. *The Great Chronicle of London*. London: The Sign of the Dolphin, 1939; repr. Gloucester: Alan Sutton, 1983.
Tomlins, T. E., and Thomas Colpitts Granger. *The Law Dictionary*. 3 vols. Philadelphia: R. H. Small, 1836.
Virgoe, Roger. "Some Ancient Indictments in the King's Bench Referring to Kent, 1450–1452." In *Documents Illustrative of Medieval Kentish Society*, edited by F. R. H. Du Boulay, 214–65. Kent Archaeological Society 18. Ashford: Headly Brother, 1964.

Watson, A. G. *The Library of Sir Simonds D'Ewes*. London: British Museum, 1966.

Watts, John. *Henry VI and the Politics of Kingship*. Cambridge: Cambridge University Press, 1996.

Woolf, Daniel R. *The Idea of History in Early Stuart England: Erudition, Ideology and 'The Light of Truth' from the Accession of James I to the Civil War*. Toronto: University of Toronto Press, 1990.

———. "Martyn, William." In *Oxford Dictionary of National Biography*. Oxford University Press, 2019. https://www.oxforddnb.com/. Accessed 21 June 2019.

———. *Reading History in Early Modern England*. Cambridge Studies in Early Modern British History. Cambridge: Cambridge University Press, 2000.

Wright, Thomas, ed. *Political Poems and Songs Relating to English History, Composed During the Period from the Accession of Edward III to that of Richard III*. Vol. 2. Rolls Series 14. London: Longman, et al., 1861.

Yamamoto, Dorothy. *The Boundaries of the Human in Medieval English Literature*. Oxford: Oxford University Press, 2000.

Index

Note: This index includes mostly the names of individuals who played a major role in the Cade Rebellion. As both Jack Cade and Henry VI occur in most chapters, they have not been included.

Arden, Peter, Chief Baron of the Exchequer, 21

Bailey, William (John?), 14, 237, 44–45, 62, 69, 74
Barron, Caroline M., 3
Beaumont, John, Lord, Constable of England, 3, 13, 203–4
Boffey, Julia, 65, 71
Burgundy, Philip, Duke of, 2
Butler, James, Earl of Wiltshire, 24

Chalton, Thomas, mayor, 3, 15, 21, 34–35, 39–40, 55–56, 61–62, 68–70, 73–75, 79, 84–85, 91, 103
Chamberlain, Sir Roger, 4
Cheyne, Thomas (aka "Bluebeard"), 19–20, 60, 66
Cook, Sir Thomas, 3, 105n2, 123–25, 127–29
Courtenay, Thomas de, Earl of Devon, 23–24
Crowmer, William, sheriff of Kent, 2, 4, 14, 21, 30, 35, 39, 44–45, 51, 55, 62, 69, 74–75, 85, 103, 120, 213

Daniel, Thomas, 3, 13, 21, 24, 34, 55, 61, 67, 207–8

Est, Robert, 120, 159

Fabyan, Robert, 71–76
Fastolf, Sir John, 3, 190, 193–94, 196–98
Fiennes, James, Lord Saye and Sele, treasurer of England, 3–4, 13–15, 19, 21–22, 24, 30–31, 34–35, 39–40, 44, 51, 55, 61–62, 67, 69, 73–75, 78–79, 84–85, 91, 102–3, 207–8, 216
Fitzalan, William, Earl of Arundel, 24

Gest, John, 14, 40, 62, 69, 75
Given-Wilson, Chris, 185–86
Golightly, Evan, 123–25
Gough, Matthew, 4, 15, 22, 31, 35, 40, 44, 51, 52n6, 56, 62, 70, 73, 75, 85–86, 91–93, 103–4, 196
Grafton, William, 81
Gransden, Antonia, 81
Griffiths, R. A., 3, 113, 131, 213
Grey, Edmund, Lord, of Ruthin, 13

254   *Index*

Grummitt, David, 1, 3–4, 113, 127

Hall, Edward, 81–88
Harvey, I. M. W., 6, 113, 131, 213
Hawarden, 22, 44
Henry VII, 89
Heysant, Roger, 56, 62, 70, 75, 86
Holand, Henry, Duke of Exeter, 12, 21, 24, 39, 119, 196
Holinshed, Raphael, 99–106
Horne, Robert, alderman, 14, 39, 44, 61, 69, 73, 85, 103, 127, 217
Humphrey, Duke of Gloucester, 29, 34, 42, 44, 60, 78, 108, 117, 119, 121, 203–4, 205n6, 221n104

Iden, Alexander, sheriff of Kent, 4, 35, 40, 56, 62, 70, 76, 87, 93, 96, 105
Isle, William, 120, 213

Kekewich, Margaret Lucille, 113, 127
Kemp, John, Archbishop of York and Canterbury, chancellor, 3, 12, 19, 23, 31
Kennedy, Edward Donald, 71
Kingsford, Charles Lethbridge, 59, 65

Lomnor, William, 193–96

Mair, John, 77–80
Malpas, Philip, alderman, 3–4, 14, 21, 35, 39, 43, 55, 61–62, 69, 75, 85, 103, 127, 181–82, 217
Margaret of Anjou, Queen of England, 4, 24, 51n1, 73, 83, 101–2, 108–9, 138, 198
Martin, Molly A., 17–25, 213–23
Martyn, William, 107–9
Marx, William, 27
Matheson, Lister M., 27, 53
Mayn, Thomas, 15, 22, 25n18, 44
McCarthy, Dennis, 93
McLaren, Mary-Rose, 11, 33, 37, 41, 59, 65

Moleyns, Adam, Bishop of Chichester, keeper of privy seal, 2, 19, 28, 42, 216
Mowbray, John, Duke of Norfolk, 18, 24, 119

Neville, Richard, Earl of Salisbury, 18, 24, 204
North, George, 93–98

Ohlgren, Thomas H., 233
Oldhall, Sir William, 185, 188–92

Parys, [John?], 3, 68, 73, 76n2
Paston, John I, 193–99
Payn, John, 3, 194, 196–99
Percy, Henry, 2nd Earl of Northumberland, 12–13
Pole, de la, William, Earl, Marquis, and Duke of Suffolk, 1–2, 17–20, 23, 34, 38, 42, 50, 51n2, 60, 66, 78, 82, 90, 108, 114, 119, 193, 195, 203–7, 209, 211–14, 216
Poynings, Robert, 3, 186, 190–91, 197

Richard, Duke of York, 2, 4, 18, 23–24, 27, 54, 60, 63, 68, 72, 82–83, 86, 91, 100, 102, 108, 117n4, 119, 123, 186
Robbins, Rossell Hope, 213
Roos, Sir Robert, king's carver, 24

Scales, Thomas, Lord, 12–13, 22, 31, 35, 40, 44–45, 56, 62, 69–70, 73, 75, 79, 84–85, 103
Schlueter, June, 93
Slegge, Stephen, 120, 217, 219n70
Stafford, Humphrey, 1st Duke of Buckingham, 3, 12–13, 18, 20, 23–24, 38, 55, 61, 68, 73, 84, 102, 109, 127
Stafford, Sir Humphrey, 3, 13, 21, 30, 34, 38, 43, 55, 60–61, 67, 72–73, 83–84, 91, 95, 102, 109

Stafford, John, Archbishop of Canterbury, chancellor, treasurer of England, 3, 12, 18, 20, 31, 40, 55, 68, 73, 76, 84, 86, 102, 104, 109, 127
Stafford, William, 3, 13, 21, 30, 34, 38, 43, 55, 60–61, 67, 72–73, 83–84, 95, 102, 109
Stanley, Sir Thomas, Lord Stanley, 3, 13, 216
Stow, John, 65, 99, 101, 116, 123, 127, 217
Sutton, Anne F., 11, 127
Sutton, Dana F., 89
Sutton, John, alderman and goldsmith, 15, 22, 31, 40, 44, 56, 62, 70, 75, 86, 104
Sutton, John, Lord Dudley, 3, 21, 23–24, 34, 55, 79

Talbot, John, Lord Lisle, 12, 24, 203–4
Tiptoft, John, Earl of Worcester, 24
Trevilian, John, esquire of the body, 24, 55, 61, 67, 216

Vale, John, 113, 123, 127–28
Vere, John de, Earl of Oxford, 24
Vergil, Polydore, 89–92

Watts, John, 1, 123
Wayneflete, William, Bishop of Winchester, chancellor, 3, 13, 18, 45, 86, 104, 109, 119
Wydeville, Sir Richard, Lord Rivers, 3, 12–13

About the Editor

Alexander L. Kaufman is Reed D. Voran Distinguished Professor of Humanities and professor of English at Ball State University where he teaches in the Honors College. He is the author of *The Historical Literature of the Jack Cade Rebellion* (2009; repr. 2016), coeditor of *Food and Feast in Modern Outlaw Tales* (2019), *Telling Tales and Crafting Books: Essays in Honor of Thomas H. Ohlgren* (2016), and *Robin Hood and the Outlaw/ed Literary Canon* (2019), and editor of *British Outlaws of Literature and History: Essays on Medieval and Early Modern Figures from Robin Hood to Twm Shon Catty* (2011). He cofounded the journal *The Bulletin of the International Association for Robin Hood Studies* and also serves as co-administrator for the scholarly blog Robin Hood Scholars: IARHS on the Web. He is also a general editor of the series *Outlaws in Literature, History, and Culture*. His research and teaching interests include outlaws from the medieval period to the present day, the Robin Hood tradition, historical writing and medieval chronicles, Chaucer, Arthuriana, and medievalisms.

www.ingramcontent.com/pod-product-compliance
Ingram Content Group UK Ltd.
Pitfield, Milton Keynes, MK11 3LW, UK
UKHW042005230426
12048UKWH00009B/565